Prayer to St. Aloysius Gonzaga.

O holy Aloysius, beautiful for thy angelic virtues, I, thy most unworthy client, recommend to thee, in a particular manner, the purity of my soul and body. I beseech thee, by thy angelic chastity, to recommend me to the Immaculate Lamb, Christ Jesus, and to His Most Holy Mother, the Virgin of Virgins, and to preserve me from all sin. Never permit me to be defiled by any stain of impurity, but when thou seest me exposed to temptation and the danger of sin, remove far from my heart all impure thoughts and affections, and, renewing in me the remembrance of eternity, and of Jesus crucified, imprint deeply in my soul the fear of God, and enkindle within me the fire of divine love, that, imitating thee on earth, I may be worthy to have God for my possession with thee in Heaven. *Amen.*

To the above prayer is attached an indulgence of 100 days, to be gained once a day, applicable to the dead.

PICTURES

OF

Christian Heroism.

JOHN DE BRITTO
In the costume
of an Indian Missionary.

PICTURES

OF

CHRISTIAN HEROISM.

With Preface

BY THE

REV. HENRY EDWARD MANNING, D.D.

NEW YORK:

D & J. SADLIER & Co, 31 BARCLAY-STREET.

NOVICES' LIBRARY

MONTREAL, C. E.

CORNER OF NOTRE-DAME AND FRANCIS XAVIER STREETS.

The Author reserves to himself the right of Translation.

CONTENTS.

～��～

CONTENTS.

Preface.

OUR Divine Lord forewarned us that His service should be a warfare: "Do not think that I am come to send peace upon earth: I came not to send peace, but a sword." These seem strange words from the lips of the Prince of Peace. His kingdom had been foretold as a reign of peace: "Behold a King shall reign in justice: and Princes shall rule in judgment." "The work of justice shall be peace, and the service of justice quietness and security for ever; and my people shall sit in the beauty of peace, and in the tabernacles of confidence, and in wealthy rest." "He shall come down like rain upon the fleece, and as showers falling gently upon the earth." "In His days shall justice spring up, and abundance of peace till the moon be taken away." "The government shall be upon His shoulder, and His Name shall be called Wonderful, Counsellor, God the Mighty, the Father of the world to come, the Prince of Peace. His empire shall be multiplied, and there shall be no end of peace." We should have looked for a reign of tranquillity, with the even sway of royal mercy, just laws, glad obedience, and universal calm upon the earth.

But He, by His own words, broke this illusion, and prepared us for suffering and for conflict: " I came not to send pea:e, but a sword." The course of my kingdom shall be marked by division, strife, sorrow, and death. If, indeed, the kingdom of Jesus Christ were only a philosophy or an opinion, it might pass through this world with the security which is the privilege of impotence ; but being a law demanding submission of mankind, a cause in which the honour of God is at stake, a claim of Divine authority upon a revolted world, and a supernatural sovereignty establishing itself upon the earth, it is therefore an universal invasion, and an endless warfare against the usurpation of the human will.

And it may be truly said that this sword which our Divine Lord has sent on earth is " a flaming sword turning every way;" for there is no path in the life of faith in which its keenness is not to be felt.

First comes the sword of separation from kindred ، " I am come to set a man at variance against his father, and the daughter against her mother, and the daughter-in-law against her mother-in-law. And a man's ene mies shall be they of his own household." " If any man come to Me, and hate not his father and mother, and wife and children, and brethren and sisters, yea, and his own life also, he cannot be My disciple." To one who said unto Him, "I will follow Thee, Lord; but let me first take my leave of them that are at my house," Jesus answered, " No man putting his hand to the plough and looking back, is fit for the kingdom of God." To another He said : " Follow me. And ne said : Lord, suffer me first to go and to bury my

father. And Jesus said to him : Let the dead bury their
dead; but go thou and preach the kingdom of God."
So it was from the beginning, in Galilee and Judæa, in
Nazareth, Bethania, and Jerusalem. Out of every city,
out of every synagogue, out of every household, out of
every home, first one, then another, brother or sister,
son or daughter, wife or husband, was called. The
call was Divine, and the obedience inevitable. Forth
they went, counted evil, apostate, beside themselves,
forsakers of the faith and church of their fathers, not
only by Priest and Scribe and Pharisee, but by the
dearest and the nearest of heart, by friend and brother,
by father and mother, by wife and child. And so it was
in all the world. In the refined and cultivated society
of Athens, in the stern and stately life of Rome, as the
light of Faith descended on the heart, each one had to
come forth lonely and unarmed to this single combat
against the world. It is perhaps impossible for us at
this day to realise what was the trial of faith, constancy,
and courage through which they had to pass who
confessed the Name of Jesus in Rome, at the seat of
empire, under the throne of the Cæsars, in opposition
to the majesty of laws both public and domestic, which
with grave and austere sway, bore down the will of
races and of nations. We can little understand what
was the terror inspired by the stern anger of a father,
and the wounded pride of a mother, when their children
were discovered worshipping among the slaves, paupers,
and foreigners who lurked in the catacombs; or what
was the haughty indignation and terrible wrath of the
senator and patrician who traced his blood from the
Fabii or the Clodii, when his first-born, the heir of his

name, proclaimed himself before the public opinion of the empire to be a brother of the scorned and the hated, of the bondsman and the captive, whose blood made sport in the Flavian amphitheatre.

But it was not only worldly anger, or national hereditary, or personal pride which sharpened the sword of separation. It had a far keener edge, which divided those whose love was strong as death, less strong only than the love of Jesus. The Searcher of hearts alone knew what anguish and wounds were there. The most precious affections bore the deepest wounds and the sharpest sorrows. The love, confidence, and mutual trust of long friendships, interwoven with all that knits hearts together, was to be cut asunder. The inward, personal griefs of private homes offered to God when the Kingdom of the Cross first entered into the world were akin to the sacred sorrow in the prophecy of Simeon: "And thy own soul a sword shall pierce."

Again, there is another sword which the Son of God has sent on earth in the perpetual conflict between His Church and the ·ivil powers of the world.

Of a sudden the empire found itself encompassed by an empire mightier than itself. A power arose in all its cities, and spread into all its provinces, setting up its throne in the presence of the sovereign magistrates, and concentrating itself in imperial Rome. Of a sudden the rulers of the world found themselves within the grasp of a dominion "here, but not from hence"—of a kingdom "not of this world;" one organised, universal, which arose, with irresistible expansion, as an exhalation from the earth, or descended in silence as a flood

of light from heaven. The first instincts of human
authority in the presence of a superior were fear and
hatred. As Herod's first impulse was to slay the Child
who was born King of the Jews, so the empire of the
world precipitated itself with all its weight upon the
kingdom of God. It could not endure the sovereignty
of God upon His own earth. It arrayed its powers
against Him in all its outskirts, and an universal warfare broke out, to be carried on through ten relentless
persecutions. Conflict is the inevitable state of the
Church on earth; for the world is in revolt against
God; it is the rival of His sovereignty, and the usurper
of His dominion. The Church, therefore, is an expulsion
of usurping powers, and a restoration of the rightful
Prince. It is universally opposed to the world in every
point where the laws of God are violated. It is by its
very nature aggressive. What was the apostolic mission, which descended from Jerusalem into all the earth,
conquering and to conquer, but an aggression upon
apostate Judaism, and upon the world-wide Paganism
of the whole earth? What has been the office of the
Church and the sway of its Pontiffs in the long course
of 1800 years, but one unsleeping, unresting aggression
upon all that refuses to own the sovereignty of God?
What were the missions of Palladius and Patrick, and
Augustine and Boniface, but open and formal inva-
sions, launched and directed by the Church against the
powers of spiritual evil which rule the nations of the
world?

From the beginning, the annals of the Church are
but one long history of warfare, ever renewing, ever ad-
vancing,—chronicles not of "peace, but a sword." And

so it must be to the end: for the Catholic Church is the sovereignty of Jesus Christ, who reigns personally through His Vicar upon earth, and the hierarchy of pastors deriving their jurisdiction from him, over the mystical body of the Son of God.

And once more; though the Church has borne no weapons but the Cross and the Pastoral Staff, this conflict has not been without blood. In the hand of the world has been ever unsheathed the sword of martyrdom. The history of the Body is as the history of its Head, the King of Martyrs. The sacrifice of Himself on Calvary was not only the atonement for the sin of the world; it was also a Divine martyrdom. It was the great witness in attestation of the truth: "For this was I born, and for this cause came I into the world, that I should give testimony unto the truth." St. Paul charges Timothy to be faithful for the truth's sake, after the example of the Great Confessor, Jesus Christ: "I charge thee before God, who quickeneth all things, and before Jesus Christ, who gave testimony under Pontius Pilate, a good confession, that thou keep the commandment without spot, blameless, unto the coming of our Lord Jesus Christ." Martyrdom is the closest conformity to our Divine Master; and to be like Him in life and death has ever been the thirst of His servants. What is the history of the Church but the prolonging and filling up of the history of His Passion? "always bearing about in our body the mortification of Jesus." The whole band of the apostles and their successors have presented to the world the image of their suffering Lord: each one, in turn, aspiring with all his strength, as St. Paul, to "know Him, and the power of His resurrection, and the fellowship of His sufferings, being made conformable to His death:" and longing "to fill up those things which are wanting of the sufferings of Christ" in the flesh, "for His body, which is the Church." Such was the long line of the Pontiffs who ruled for the first two centuries from the Chair of Peter: and such also were the tens of thousands of bishops, pastors, and faithful of every condition — patricians and people, soldiers and artisans, women of every age and state, widows, mothers, virgins, little children, in all the provinces of the Roman Empire, in Asia, Africa, and Europe, in Lyons and Vienne, in Antioch and Alexandria, in Milan and Syracuse. Martyrdom was counted as the highest gift of grace. It was coveted and prayed for with tears of desire. To be permitted to sacrifice all things for Jesus was joy; to be called to sacrifice self for Him was greater joy than all. It was happiness to live for Him; but to be permitted also to die for His sake was the crown of all desires.

And such has been the inextinguishable longing of the true Church of Jesus Christ. In every age, and in every land, this ardent love of martyrdom has burned, and the martyr's crown has been perpetually won. Men are wont to speak of martyrs as they do of the apostles, as of a race long since passed away, — glorious, but extinct; seen through the long, dim haze of history; to be admired, but not followed. It sounds far-fetched and unreal to speak of martyrdom as among things possible in these days, and of a martyr's spirit as among the graces we ought to seek and to cherish. It is indeed too true, that the present days are soft, and that

the spirit of endurance is low among us. Men have
been unnerved by tranquillity, and by a dangerous love
of peace. Home affections, and the softness of a happy
life, the fair and smooth things of the world, its honours,
gifts, and comforts, have brought upon us a sickly and
feeble tone, which makes men stand in awe of the
world's opinion, displeasure, and contempt. There is
not a little of spiritual cowardice among us; and many
are ready to compromise even principle to unite with
those who contradict the faith;—to make separate peace
for themselves with the adversaries of the Church;—to
be silent when they should speak out;—to suffer our
Divine Lord to be betrayed, and Truth to hang upon
the Cross between contradictions, rather than to be un-
popular, despised, shunned, disliked, or even ridiculed.

In such a time as this, then, it is most opportune to
be reminded, that the age of martyrs is not over yet;
that it is continual; that the conflict is endless; that
not peace, but a sword, is the perpetual portion of the
Church. And for this the following pages will bear
witness. The sixteenth, seventeenth, eighteenth, and
nineteenth centuries have their martyrs as great and
as glorious as the first, the second, and the third.
Not Asia and Africa alone, but Europe; not remote
lands only, but France and England have been steeped
with blood sacred to Jesus. In these modern days
of the nineteenth century, which seem so unheroic
and so commonplace, while we have been treading
the every-day path of life, martyrs have been continually ascending to their crown. Hardly a year has
passed but in China some servant of our Lord has been
conformed to his Master's Passion. It is well that we

should bear this in mind, and make it familiar to our
thoughts.　For it is most certain that, if we would be
faithful, we must learn to be ready for the sword.　In
some form it will come to us.　If we would be crowned
with Him, we must also suffer with Him; and though
not martyrs in deed, we must bear a martyr's will; for
if we be not martyrs, at least in will, we should not be
even confessors in the hour of trial; and if not confessors,
how Christians?　It would be a fearful scrutiny into
our life if we were now to be asked, 'what have you
ever suffered, what have you ever risked for the truth,
and for our Lord's sake?'

It is good, then, to have the realities of martyrdom
brought home to us in our own land and day, and to
see how it looks in the context of modern society, and
to put it to ourselves how we should endure in such
an hour.

In the following histories will be found all the sharpness of the sword and all the circumstances of suffering;
and these so brought near to us in these later days, as
to show us that we are never to believe, that our turn
may not yet come.

In these few prefatory words, it is not intended to
write a review of the martyrdoms here recorded; but
one or two may be specially pointed out, as coming home
with a peculiar closeness to our own times and trials.

And first in significance is the martyrdom of Margaret Clitherow.　She suffered since the Protestant
Reformation in modern England, in York Castle, by a
hideous torture, for the Christian deed of sheltering
the priests of God from those who sought their lives.

And next, in the life-time of living men, a persecu-

tion worthy of Rome drunk with the blood of saints,
was directed against hundreds of helpless and innocent
men, laymen, priests, and bishops, in the gay and refined city of Paris.   The scene of this glorious confession was the quiet garden and silent sanctuary of the
Carmelite Convent in the Rue Vaugirard.   When we
now walk through these sacred precincts, it is difficult
to realise to ourselves, that the marks we see upon the
passage-wall are the bloody fingers of a martyr in his
agony; that the deep saturating stain on the bench of
the garden-house is the impression of a bleeding head;
and the gore which reddens its pavement is the life-
blood of an army of martyrs, who won their crowns
while our fathers were yet in the midst of life, as we
are now.   In the tranquil vaulted church, where the
lamp now hangs bright and still before the Divine Presence, after hours of heroic anguish, the servants of
Jesus were derided with the mockeries of trial, and hurried away one by one to the slaughter.   As we now
kneel on that silent pavement, we can hardly believe
that men among whom we live can remember that
day.

Lastly, the book before us closes with the record of
one who "resisted unto blood" for "the faith and patience
of Jesus" on July 3d, in the year 1853.   It was on a
Monday;—we know not, perhaps, where we were, or
what we were doing, or whether it was a morning fair
or foul; we were full of our every-day thoughts, im-
mersed in this modern world, in which the martyrdoms
of saints read as tales of dim antiquity rather than as
trials which may come on ourselves;—on that day and
hour Father Philip, a native priest in Cochin-China, was

kneeling before the executioner. A supernatural awe, as of old, came over the very heathen who stood by; and as the martyr fell upon the earth, they cried out, "The holy priest has ascended to heaven."

A slight observation of the signs which are upon the face of modern society is enough to teach us that, while the Catholic Church is extending its circuit every year into new regions of the earth, the powers of evil are becoming more intense in the older races of Christendom. Nations still professedly Christian and Catholic contain within them elements of hostility both against the Catholic Church and against Christianity itself, which are kept under by the feeble pressure of authority. The great outbreak of license called the Reformation really began a divorce between the spiritual and civil powers; that is, between mere natural civilisation and Christianity: the result of which is becoming more apparent in every successive generation. What begun in separation is ending in conflict. Nations are striving to gain supremacy over the Church; and failing, they oppose and denounce it as an usurper and invader. Meanwhile, the Church, as a pure spiritual kingdom, grows every year more wide-spread and conscious of its unity. But its very successes and advances are a provocation and a challenge. Unless the Divine Head of the Church avert it, an outbreak of this Antichristian spirit might come in any country of Europe at any moment. We saw in the year 1848 what elements lie seething and boiling under the thin surface of the deep upon which society is resting. The last times foretold by the Apostle are already upon us, and the persecutions of the latter days, for which the

Church has been preparing from the beginning, are yet to come. The professed indifference to all religious which for a time reigns among the adversaries of the Church, is but the prelude of assault: it is the lull before the storm. Let us not be deceived by thinking that the world will persecute no more. It is still the world; changed outwardly, by refinement of social customs, by the visible garb of Christianity, and by a smooth homage to truth, which it secretly disbelieves; but it is as averse as ever from the sovereignty of Christ, wielded by Him through the jurisdiction of His Church, one and undivided, Catholic and Roman. If the present bonds of society were broken, and its balance overturned, there is no kind of persecution which might not follow. Whether it come by laws or against laws, or by civil rulers or by the populace, would depend on the peculiarities of place and nation. It might differ in form and mode in different countries; but in all it would be real and unrelenting, demanding once more of those in whose days it shall befal the fidelity of confessors and the will of martyrs.

H. E. M.

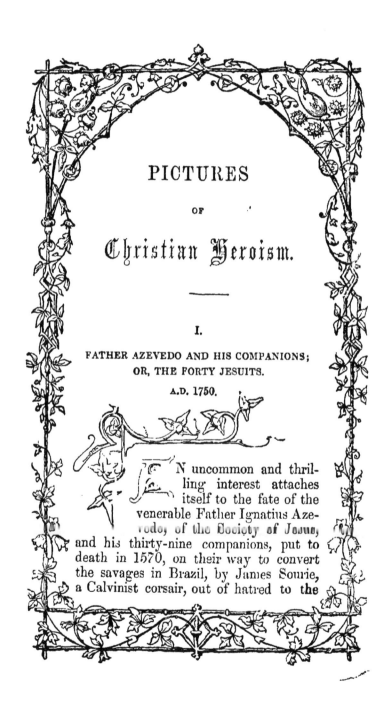

PICTURES

OF

Christian Heroism.

I.

FATHER AZEVEDO AND HIS COMPANIONS;
OR, THE FORTY JESUITS.

A.D. 1750.

AN uncommon and thrilling interest attaches itself to the fate of the venerable Father Ignatius Azevedo, of the Society of Jesus, and his thirty-nine companions, put to death in 1570, on their way to convert the savages in Brazil, by James Sourie, a Calvinist corsair, out of hatred to the holy faith which they professed, and particularly to the religious order to which they belonged.

Born in 1527, of one of the most illustrious families in Portugal, the young Ignatius at eighteen years of age desired to become a religious, and was advised by a friend, Henri Govea, to make a retreat, which decided his vocation. Father Azevedo had not completed his forty-third year at the time of his martyrdom; but notwithstanding the lengthened period of study and preparation generally required of all who enter the society, his talents and piety were of so exalted a character, that, being promoted to the priesthood before the usual age, he was appointed rector of a college in his twenty-sixth year by St. Ignatius himself, who was then living, and was temporary Provincial of Portugal even before he had finished his theological studies. His conduct as rector commanded the admiration of all who knew him. Having renounced in his twentieth year all the wealth and consideration which was due to him as the eldest son of a noble family, he continued during the remainder of his life to show the most marked contempt for the honours and riches of the world. His clothes, always poor, were frequently shared, to his own great inconvenience, with any shivering beggar; he chose by preference the meanest employments in the house, and devoted himself not only to the students under his care, but to all the children of want and misery that were within his reach, with a tenderness and unwearied solicitude that left no room for selfishness or sloth. He generally slept in his clothes on the ground, ate only dry bread, moistened with the juice of oranges, and took from the time he should have given to repose the four hours he daily spent in prayer. It was, however, only in his own humble heart that Father Azevedo took so low a place. His learning and wisdom had early won for him the most universal respect, whilst his devout life, and the almost miraculous success which attended his labours as a priest, caused him to be regarded already as a saint

In 1565 the General of the Order dying, the congregation was convoked at Rome by St. Francis Borgia for the appointment of a successor. Father Azevedo was, by the general consent of the order in Portugal, sent as their representative to Rome, under the title of Procurator-General of the Indies and Brazil, that he might treat with the Sovereign Pontiff and the new general on the subject of missions to these idolatrous countries. Although the dignity of this appointment was contrary to Father Azevedo's humility, yet he willingly accepted it, having long cherished in secret an earnest desire to consecrate his life to the conversion of the heathen.

St. Francis Borgia being elected general, Father Azevedo, who had been very intimate with him in Portugal, made use of this friendship to solicit for himself a mission to the Indies. The new general promised to send him to Brazil, and ordered him to return home and prepare for his departure. So fervent, however, were the protestations raised by all the Jesuit fathers of Portugal against the removal of one whom they so justly valued, that it was finally resolved that Father Azevedo should only go in the character of visitor, not of missionary, and that he should return to Europe, and give an account of the state of religion, and the Society of Jesus in particular, as he should find it in Brazil. This arranged, Father Azevedo departed, invested with the quality of Superior.

A few words may here be necessary as to the nature of the country to which he went. Although discovered and conquered by the Portuguese from the beginning of the sixteenth century, it was not until 1549 that the faith of Christ had been preached there, by six Jesuits. They found this immense country peopled by the most inhuman savages, who lived like wild beasts, devoured human flesh, even that of their dead parents and children, and who were divided into so many tribes, each speaking different languages, that the heroic courage which nerved these six fathers to go amongst them and attempt their conversion has in it something incredible to the mere human understanding. Where man is willing, however, to do much, God is ever ready to do more; and so, in spite of all infirmities and difficulties, though the first Bishop of Brazil, with more than a hundred of his followers, was put to death and devoured by these terrible savages four years after his arrival amongst them, yet at the time of Father Azevedo's visit, when the Church had been planted there about sixteen years, he found more than sixteen thousand Christians and as many catechumens. The different houses of the company in Brazil were numerous and widely separated; yet the indefatigable visitor went to every one. A knapsack on his shoulders containing his instruments of penance, which were his daily and inseparable companions, and the tools necessary for the different mechanical arts which, in the earlier years of his study, he had made a point of acquiring, as much by humility as for his greater usefulness in the sacred ministry,—this was his whole equipment, as on foot and unattended he journeyed from one colony of Christians to another, weeping with a holy envy as he embraced the devoted fathers of his order whom he found scattered amongst them; whilst they, on their part, looked on him as a consoling angel sent to cheer them in their superhuman labours. After a fatiguing sojourn of more than three years, Father Azevedo, thinking he had sufficiently examined into the state of the Church in Brazil, prepared for his return to Europe, where he was anxiously expected; but before he left America an incident took place, which, as it was supposed at the time to draw all its interest from the influence of his sanctity, is worth recording in this place. On his way to visit the College of Rio de Janeiro with the bishop and other fathers, Father Azevedo begged permission, whilst the vessel was becalmed, to go on shore in a boat and say Mass. All at once the fathers, when at some little distance from the ship, saw a monstrous whale, which had been wounded by the fishermen, coming down upon their little boat. Two fountains of water poured from its nostrils, and with its tail raised for the fatal blow, it threatened to en gulf the little company in the ocean. The bishop and all who were in the ship gave themselves up for lost, when Father Azevedo, already bathed in the waters which the whale had dashed over the boat, raised his eyes to heaven, and made the sign of the Holy Cross before the frantic creature. Instantly the whale became perfectly quiet, and sinking beneath the surface, showed itself no more.

On his return to Europe, Father Azevedo repaired to Lisbon, in order to give an account to the young and zealous king of the great benefits his royal bounty was assisting to spread in Brazil. He also communicated with several young Jesuits whom he was anxious to enlist in the good work he meditated, and then set off to Rome to confer with the general. St. Francis Borgia, delighted to welcome back his beloved friend, received him with tears of joy, took the warmest interest in all the details of his visit, and lamented that it was not possible for him to go himself amongst the heathen, and join his labours to chose of the pious missionaries already there. Father Azevedo gave a glowing account of the wonders that had been effected; but impressed deeply upon the saintly general the necessity of sending a numerous supply of fresh labourers into such a fruitful vineyard. Many as were the priests, they were yet grievously inadequate to the demands made upon them, and on every side the petitions for additional assistance had touched him to the heart. St. Francis warmly responded to the wishes of Father Azevedo; he gave him permission to seek throughout Spain and Portugal for young men fitted to this arduous and yet glorious work; and when the humble Father, with downcast eyes, and the profoundest expression of self-abasement, added, "And if the excess of my unworthiness does not render me quite unfit for so exalted a favour, I would solicit the same at your generous hand, asking but to be the last and least of those whom you deign to honour with so happy a destination," St. Francis could not refuse to grant his request instantly. Being appointed superior

of all the missions to Brazil, Father Azevedo was empowered to go through Spain and Portugal gathering
fit elements for the work, not only from amongst priests,
but students, novices, and lay brothers, that he might
train them each according to their rank and talents to
be useful in converting the heathen.   Before leaving
Rome, Father Azevedo received the special blessing of
the Pope St. Pius V., and having signified to St. Francis Borgia his desire to have an image of the Blessed
Virgin, whom he had chosen as the patroness of his
missions, copied on the model of that said to have been
painted by St. Luke, which is reverenced in the Church
of St. Mary Major, although this favour had never
yet been accorded to any one, the Pope gave instant
permission for as many copies to be taken as Father
Azevedo wished.   Paintings and images were immediately multiplied for the use of the father and his companions, and we shall have occasion hereafter to refer to
one of these images which was in the hand of the martyr
at the time of his death.

Father Azevedo, on leaving Rome, went to Spain,
where he travelled from college to college in quest of
candidates for the mission.   Every where, filled with a
holy zeal, they thronged around him, having but one
fear, that they should be found unworthy of the favour
they craved.   Amongst others, a young relative of St.
Teresa, named Godoy, had the happiness of being chosen.
Proceeding thence to Portugal, he waited on the king,
having written to the different superiors mentioning the
young men he had formerly selected, who were then
despatched to join him at Lisbon, whither he journeyed
with his companions as soon as his audience with the
king at Eoven was concluded.   These holy missionaries
travelled on foot, lengthening out each day's march to
the utmost limits of their powers, in order to bring
themselves as near as possible to the day of departure
for Brazil.   They begged their daily food as they went
along; and being joined at the entrance of Lisbon by the
Portuguese detachment, found their numbers to amount

in all to sixty-nine. Lisbon being at that time scarcely free from an epidemic disease which had been scourging the inhabitants for many months, it was not thought safe to trust the precious lives of so many young men within the walls of the city, and therefore Father Azevedo took refuge with his children in a country-house belonging to the college. Here he remained for five months, training them for the important work to which they were called; and nothing could be more edifying than the conduct of the saintly master and his faithful pupils during this time. As for the former, he taught them daily with the authority of a master, yet with the gentleness of a saint; and at the same time he was always first in the performance of any servile labour that the necessities of the house required: and as for the rest, they were said to be more like angels than men. Those amongst them who were priests anxiously laid aside all superiority, and requested their common father to make no distinction between them and the youngest lay brother; whilst the most delicately nurtured youths vied with each other in fasts, mortifications, and the most severe austerities, never sleeping in a bed, feeding only on dry bread and vegetables, which they begged as an alms, and devoting many hours in each day to visiting the sick and teaching the catechism to the poorest people in the neighbouring villages. Daily they walked in procession to a cross erected by their father on a distant hill; there, in a long station, they poured out their devoted hearts in all the fulness of the love and zeal of martyrs,—for such already by anticipation they were, feeling, as if by intuition, that they were to glorify God by a speedy death rather than by tedious labours in a distant land. A marble cross has since been put up in the place of that planted by F. Azevedo, and it now bears the title of the Cross of Martyrs.

So beautiful was the life they led in this Valley of Rosal, as it was called, that even Father Azevedo himself seemed to forget his impatience to be gone; and writing to a friend, he declared that "he found the

Valley of Rosal a foretaste of the happiness of heaven, and that he had never enjoyed a purer felicity, or a more delicious peace." The time was, however, now come for the offering up of these holy souls, already salted for the sacrifice; and having arranged with the captain of a merchant-ship, the *Saint James*, for half of his vessel, Father Azevedo, with thirty-nine of his companions, went on board June 5th, 1570, taking nothing with them but objects of devotion or instruments of penance. For the remaining number of his children, thirty in all, Father Azevedo was obliged to accept the offer of Don Louis de Vasconcellos, the new governor of Brazil, to accommodate them in the different vessels of his squadron. The ships were, however, to sail in company, both in order that Father Azevedo might remain as near as possible to all his beloved flock, and also for the sake of the protection which the governor's six ships of war would afford in the voyage. He took care to reserve the younger missionaries for his own companions, with that tender watchfulness which leads the shepherd to keep under his own eye the weakest lambs of the flock. He also caused a perfect division to be made by boards between his portion of the vessel and that destined to the captain and crew. Each Jesuit had a separate cell, and little altar; a bell called them to all religious exercises, to table, or to work, as if they had been still in college; and they were only permitted to leave the enclosure he had made for them to perform some act of corporal or spiritual mercy for the crew or passengers. They undertook the cooking on board, and served each person in due order. They also taught the catechism and nursed the sick; and wonderful were the results which followed their holy teaching, and, perhaps still more certainly, their holy example. Lives of saints or works of piety were scattered as if by chance about the most frequented parts of the vessel; an idle sailor was lured into a profitable conversation, and at night, when dancing or drinking might otherwise have beguiled the tediousness of

the voyage, the men were hushed into reverent silence
on hearing the young voices of those amongst the Jesuits
who had any talent for music breaking forth in holy
concert to chant the Litanies of the Virgin or the Saints,
or some other canticle of prayer or praise. The consequence was, that bad books, cards, and dice were
banished from the ship; many came to beg for books of
devotion or sacred images; words of blasphemy and sin
were no longer heard to pollute the deck, and a spirit of
gentleness, modesty, and devotion gradually spread
itself over all on board.

The seven ships arrived safely at Madeira, where the
Jesuits spent a short time; and then Father Azevedo
and the thirty-nine companions returned to the *St.
James.*

Vasconcellos, being strongly advised to defer his
voyage for a time for various prudential reasons, determined to remain at Madeira awhile; but nothing that
could be urged would induce the captain of the *St.
James* to delay. He was anxious to proceed immediately to the Isle of Palma, for which much of his
merchandise was destined; and being seconded by most
of the passengers in this wish, there was nothing to
keep him but the uncertainty which Father Azevedo
felt for a time as to the prudence of departing,—for
there was at this time a famous corsair, named James
Sourie, who infested these seas with five ships. He
was a Calvinist; and, to the bitter hatred of his sect
against the Holy Church, he added a yet deeper fury
against Jesuits in particular, persuaded, as he said, that
their object was to do battle every where with the reform of Calvin, and to raise upon its ruins the authority
of the Romish Church. Having heard, then, that the
new governor of Brazil had many missionary Jesuits
on board his squadron, he came hastily across those
parts of the sea which he thought they must pass, and
ravaging the coasts of the Canaries in his blind rage,
avowed his determination to destroy the whole of this
saintly company. Vasconcellos, who was aware of this,

in vain represented to the captain of the *St. James* the unprotected situation of his passengers if they should fall in with the corsair; he was resolute in leaving for Palma. Of course, Father Azevedo was not ignorant of the dreaded danger, and ready for martyrdom as he was, could not for some time determine what to do for the best; but having recourse to his usual refuge in difficulty, prayer, he at last resolved to embark. It seemed as if his impending fate, and that of his companions, was revealed to him from above; for after celebrating Mass and giving holy communion to all his flock, he suddenly began a long and fervent discourse to them on the excellence of martyrdom. Afterwards, assembling them all in the college, he spoke more plainly of their probable danger, desiring all who were ready to die for Jesus to follow him, and those who did not feel called upon to make so great a sacrifice, to stay behind and join the other missionaries in the squadron. All, except four, with a burning zeal, accepted, as the most exalted favour, the hope of martyrdom; and these four timid souls were soon replaced by others; for no sooner was the news made known amongst the Jesuits than such numbers came crowding to Father Azevedo, emulous with a holy jealousy of being chosen first, that he had the greatest difficulty in selecting some lest he should seem unjust to the others. He then made every preparation as for a certain and immediate death. He named another father, who was to remain at Madeira, as vice-provincial, giving up to him all the papers concerning the mission to Brazil,—that mission which he felt he never should himself fulfil; and causing all who were going with him to approach the tribunal of penance, he said Mass and administered communion to them; then taking a touching farewell of those who were to remain behind, and who lamented with tears that they also might not go and share his glorious fate, Father Azevedo and his young companions hurried on board, as if every moment that kept them from the crown they coveted were an intolerable loss.

Some most interesting particulars of the last days of this holy band have been recorded by Brother John Sanchez, himself the only member of it who unwillingly escaped death. He declared that, animating themselves with the examples of some amongst the noble army of martyrs, they waited even with impatience for the appearance of the corsair's hostile flag, whilst in the space of six days he heard more than fifty times from the lips of Father Azevedo such short and earnest prayers as these: "My God, is it true that I shall have the happiness of dying for Thee? What a glorious fate! Oh, happy death, why dost thou delay to open the portals of my true existence? Where are these enemies of Jesus and His Church? Alas, that my bliss is so long delayed!" But, externally, all went as calmly as before, and the little company of expectant martyrs pursued their former orderly and regular life in the ship, which arrived safely within sight of the Isle of Palma. But when making its way to the usual port, a sudden wind arose, and turning it out of its course, the crew, after many fruitless efforts to regain their destination, were obliged to land in another part of the island. Here, most unexpectedly, Father Azevedo was recognised by an old friend, an officer, who, delighted to meet with him and his companions, insisted that all the Jesuits should come and stay at his house. They did so for five days very agreeably; but at the end of that time, the captain was anxious to proceed to the usual port, as he could not dispose of his merchandise where he was. Father Azevedo also was anxious to go, that he might await in the appointed haven the arrival of Vasconcellos and his other companions. The friendly officer had, however, many misgivings, and earnestly besought the missionaries to cross the island instead of trusting themselves again upon the sea, then terrible from the reports continually coming in of the corsair's violence. He offered horses and all needful assistance; but the martyrs were not thus to be cheated of their crown. It is true, Father

Azevedo again found himself at first unwilling to de-
cline his friend's offer; and requesting all his companions to join him in asking light from above, he spent
one night in prayer, and then went with them in procession to a neighbouring church, where, after celebrating Mass and giving communion to his companions,
he was again, as before, supernaturally enlightened as
to the course he was to pursue; and addressing the
young men, said to them: "My brethren, let us be
careful not to be guided in this matter by motives of
human prudence: it is God who has hitherto led us on:
His designs are above all the foresight of men. It is
His will that we should again embark on the sea, it
will speedily carry· us to the port of eternal bliss."
These words were received as a revelation to Father
Azevedo by his obedient children; and with alacrity
they prepared to follow him. Indeed, a particular
manifestation of the approaching martyrdom had been
given to several amongst them, so that their hearts
were fully prepared for all that might be required.
Excusing himself, therefore, to his hospitable friend, on
the ground that it would be scarcely gracious to the
rest of the passengers on board the *St. James* if he
were to secure his party from all risk, by going across
the island, whilst they were exposed to the corsair,
he ordered his little baggage to be carried to the ship;
whilst this was being done, his companions seeing along
the shore some solitary cells, begged leave to retire to
them and pass the few last moments in prayer. "My
brethren," he answered, with an angelic smile, "God
has reserved for us far purer meditations, and a place
far worthier, where we may praise Him and enjoy His
wonderful majesty. Courage, my dear children, the
servants of the Lord have nothing to fear. If the
heretics encounter us, we shall soon be citizens of
heaven."

Meanwhile, Vasconcellos having learnt that Sourie
was within a few miles of him, made ready his ships to
go and capture the corsair and his pirate crew; but

Sourie, unwilling to risk the unequal combat, retired in haste towards the Isle of Palma, thus, in a remarkable manner, preparing the way for all that was to befal the holy Jesuits. On the 13th of July, 1570, the *St. James* left the harbour where it had been at anchor, and, two days after, Sourie came within reach of Palma. Contrary winds impeded the *St. James,* and the captain could make no way; it was necessary also to stand out far at sea, in order to avoid the dangers of the coast; but at length they seemed to have surmounted all difficulties, and were within three leagues of port, when suddenly the wind dropped, and they were compelled to cast anchor and remain there all night. At break of day the sentinel gave notice of a distant vessel coming at full sail, and hopes were entertained that it was one of Vasconcellos' ships, especially when four others were observed taking the same direction. The anchor was therefore weighed to join them, when the arms of the hostile Queen of Navarre on the approaching vessels betrayed to the *St. James* her fatal mistake.

The captain immediately took counsel with the rest, and found both soldiers and sailors ready to die in defence of the ship; but as it was only a merchant vessel, and had but fifty soldiers on board, they could hope to offer but a feeble resistance. Every preparation was, however, made for a gallant defence; and to procure greater freedom of action for the men, the division which separated the Jesuits from the crew and passengers was removed. And now Father Azevedo was seen, his face radiant with a supernatural brightness, and holding one of the cherished images of our Lady in his hand which had been copied for him at Rome. Words of confidence and joy flowed from his lips, as he stood before his young companions and congratulated them that their hour was come. " Now is the happy moment to show our love for God, our zeal for the faith. We must shed our blood this day to bear this twofold witness. Fear nothing from those who can

but destroy our bodies. Let all our thoughts be in
heaven. Let us remember who we are, and how
ardently we have hitherto longed for this. Our sufferings can last but a few moments; our reward will be
eternal." Then holding on high the sacred image in
his hand, he began to recite the Litany of the Blessed
Virgin. Every voice responded clear and loud, un-
troubled by a single tremour of fear. The *Confiteor*
followed, after which the father, having bade them
prepare themselves by a sincere contrition, bestowed a
general absolution. Their innocent lives and recent
confessions rendered more than this unnecessary, even
had time permitted it.

The captain, astonished at the self-possession and
calmness of so many young men, all unaccustomed as
they were to scenes of bloodshed, was instantly anxious
to secure their services in defending the vessel, declaring they were better fit than all the rest to handle arms;
but to this Father Azevedo would not consent. He
offered his own services, and those of his companions, for
every other ministration of which they were capable,
promising to watch over the wounded and dying, and
do all that could be done to comfort both their souls
and bodies. For this purpose he chose eleven of the
oldest and most experienced of his companions, and
placed them in different parts of the vessel, and bade
the younger ones go below and await in prayer the moment of their death. For himself, still holding the cherished image in his hand, he took his post at the foot of
the mainmast, from whence he could have a full view
of all that went on.

Meanwhile Sourie, in his largest vessel, had approached within musket-shot, and called upon the Portuguese to surrender. Their only reply was a broadside
from their guns, which swept his deck of the chief part
of its forces. Sourie enraged, made desperate efforts to
board the *St. James;* and already three Calvinists, one
his own near relative, had reached the deck, when they
were instantly beheaded and thrown into the sea. Find-

ing himself unable, after repeated efforts, to succeed, he made signs to his other ships to come to his assistance, and the gallant crew of the *St. James* was at once surrounded on all sides. Grappling-irons were thrown out, and fifty men, with Sourie at their head, sprung upon her deck. Resistance, hopeless as it now was, was nevertheless maintained with all the energy of despair for a time; and in the midst of all the noise and confusion the voice of Father Azevedo was heard from the foot of the mainmast, "There is but one only true religion, and it is that of the Holy Roman Church; and happy is he who shall lay down his life rather than lose his faith."

Meanwhile the eleven missionaries, disposed about the deck, lent all possible assistance to the wounded and dying, binding up their wounds, and exhorting them with the tenderest words of encouragement and consolation. Two of these zealous men were at length themselves wounded, and obliged to join their companions below. The Calvinists, fully occupied in defending themselves at first, cast nevertheless most bitter looks of hatred at the Jesuits on the deck, especially at Father Azevedo, to whose noble presence and animating words they justly ascribed much of the heroic resistance of the Portuguese, and several times they endeavoured to get near enough to stab him; but he was too jealously guarded for this to be possible, though he was slightly hurt by an arquebus aimed from a distance. The generous defenders of the *St. James* could not long maintain this unequal warfare; and when their captain was struck down, the few still able to bear arms surrendered at discretion. The victorious Calvinists immediately took possession of the ship; and their first impulse was to destroy the Jesuits, especially Father Azevedo. But Sourie gave orders that no one should be put to death without his particular command; for he wished few but Jesuits to die, and was anxious first to ascertain the amount of plunder he had secured. In searching the vessel, the twenty-eight young mis-

sionaries and their two wounded companions were discovered, to the great triumph of the Calvinists.   Father Azevedo and his nine friends still remained on the
upper deck, ministering as calmly to the dying men as
if they had not known that their own last moment was
immediately at hand.   The captain expired in the good
father's arms, after having received all the assistance
such a holy priest could render at the hour of death.
Meanwhile an account was brought to Sourie of all who
were still alive, soldiers, sailors, passengers, and Jesuits.
With the coolest deliberation he gave his orders; first,
that those who had killed his own three men on attempting to board the *St. James* should be instantly
put to death.   There was little difficulty in finding
them and carrying this sentence into execution.   To the
other soldiers, sailors, and passengers, he granted their
lives; and then raising his voice, he cried, "As for the
Jesuits, kill them without mercy.   Murder those ras-
cally Papists, who are only going to Brazil that they
may spread abroad their false doctrines."   The furious
troop who surrounded him, like wolves hungry for their
prey, had only waited for these words to let loose upon
the unresisting missionaries all the violence of their
hatred.   They rushed with one accord to the spot where
Father Azevedo and his nine companions still consoled
the dying Portuguese.   Raising his eyes at the sound
of their approach, the father calmly said, "Courage,
brethren, let us give our lives generously for Jesus
Christ, who has first shed His blood for us!" and stepping forward in advance of the others, he confronted
the heretics, who instantly recognised him as the leader
of that saintly band, and resolved that he should be the
first victim, little conscious that he desired no greater
favour at their hands.   One of the soldiers with a sword
then struck him so fiercely on the head that he fell to
the ground bathed in torrents of blood, with his skull
fractured.   Four others, of whom it was afterwards reported by eye-witnesses that total blindness succeeded
their impious act, then drew near and pierced him with

their lances. But in spite of these mortal blows, the undaunted soldier of Christ rallied his strength with one last effort to exclaim, "I call angels and men to witness that I die in the Holy Roman Catholic Church, and that I die with all my heart in defence of her dogmas and her practices." Then turning his dying eyes to his beloved companions, who stood motionless with grief at the sight of their expiring father, he added in a faint voice, "My dear children, rejoice with me at my happy fate; hope confidently the same for yourselves. I am going but a few moments before you; to-day, if it please God, we shall all meet again in heaven." Even his barbarous executioners were silent one instant, as if spell-bound by the angelic demeanour and unflinching courage of the dying martyr; but the evil spirit within them was not to be chained long, and with still greater fury, like beasts that grow fiercer after tasting blood, they turned their rage against the image of the Blessed Virgin, which they perceived clasped in his hand. But no effort they could make sufficed to tear it from his grasp, and at length they were content to cast it, with his still living body, into the sea. That very night, when all was silent in the ship, the corpse of Father Azevedo, which all day long had floated near the ship, its arms extended in the form of a cross, and the precious image raised by the right hand above the surface of the water, as if for public veneration, came so near the side that the image struck several times against it. One of the Portuguese, who looked on this as rather the will of Providence than as a matter of chance, put out his hand and took the image from the relaxing fingers, which yielded up the treasure without difficulty to a worthy disciple of the faith. He contrived to conceal it from the Calvinists, and afterwards presented it to the Jesuits of Madeira, who sent it to their college in the Bay of All Saints at Brazil, where it is revered in one of the chapels with singular devotion, and is said to be still stained with the martyr's blood.

The next victim was Jacques Andrada, who having
seen his superior fall, had rushed to give him a last absolution.   Incensed at seeing him perform this priestly
function beneath their very eyes, they pierced him in a
dozen places at once, and threw him also into the sea.
Benoit de Castro seeing this, and that it was the profession of the faith that drew down the vengeance of
the Calvinists, held up his crucifix, crying with a loud
voice, " I am a Catholic—I am a Catholic."   Three
muskets were fired upon him at once, and he fell, struggling however to rise again, and still repeating, " I am
a Catholic," till they stabbed him with their swords,
and threw him overboard.   Blaire Ribera, and Pierre
Santoura, two lay-brothers, who were kneeling before a
crucifix nailed to one of the masts, were next attacked
for this idolatry ; and after being loaded with insults,
the skull of the one, and the jaw of the other, were
fractured by repeated blows with a musket, and they
were drowned.   Jacques Perès, a young man, whose
gentle and amiable manners had made him the delight
of all his companions, then stood modestly before the
executioners, whose hands were wet with blood, and
said quietly, " I also profess the Catholic faith ; it is
the only faith that ought to be maintained, for without
it there is no salvation."   Transported with rage at
this calm declaration, one of the men thrust his pike
with such violence through the breast of the speaker
that it pierced him through and through ; and his last
words and his innocent soul went forth at the same
moment.

The four other Jesuits on deck, each holding his
crucifix in his hand, came forward to the persecutors,
entreating that they might not be spared any more
than their companions.   They were thrown alive into
the sea.   And now the thirty young men who had remained below were called for.   They had not seen the
dreadful fate of their ten brethren ; and when they
stepped upon the deck, in the very flower of their age,
with no crime but that of professing the Catholic faith,

their youth, modesty, and gentle demeanour might have disarmed any hearts less savage than those of Sourie and his heretical band. They had in no way assisted or encouraged those on board, but had remained till now silently praying in the cabin; when, however, they came on deck, and saw it flowing with the blood of their murdered companions, one amongst them, who had long since known by a special revelation the very manner of his death on this day, Emmanuel Alvarès, transported with a holy anger against these impious executioners, cried out, "Do you think to frighten us by the sight of the tortures you are preparing for us? Barbarians, you deceive yourselves; we shall die without forfeiting our constancy, happy and content to give our lives for Jesus Christ, who deigned Himself to die the first for us. We are ready to die, and our death will be nothing but a passage from this frail and transitory life to one which is immortal; but you, unhappy creatures, may expect the vengeance of God upon your obstinacy and cruelty." Enraged at this, the Calvinists threw themselves upon him, trod him under their feet, and broke all his limbs by repeated blows, leaving him still alive that they might prolong his torture; but he, radiant with a martyr's triumph in the midst of his excessive agony, cheered on his companions to partake his happiness, and blessed God aloud for vouchsafing him the unutterable bliss of martyrdom. At this the Calvinists threw him into the water, together with the bodies of two whom they had slain with daggers, and to whom, thinking they were priests, from their being older than the others, they said, with insolent jests, "Go to the bottom of the sea, and there say your Popish mass, and hear confession." It would be too painful to go on relating one by one the different sufferings by which these holy martyrs glorified God; nor indeed were those eye-witnesses who stood near at this awful hour able distinctly to recal every circumstance. By twos and threes the remaining victims were dragged to the ship's side, and there strangled or

pierced with daggers, and thrown, yet living, overboard
It is recorded that the water all around the vessel was
filled with floating bodies, and that they were heard
repeating incessantly the name of their Redeemer, until
the waves swallowed them up. Full of horror, and yet
how deeply touching must have been the sight! Some
already dead, some still full of life, but all pierced with
wounds and covered with blood, these bodies were
dashed against each other by the waves, and then, one
by one, buried beneath their depths; whilst a concert of
dying voices breathed above their murmurs, "Jesus,
Jesus," with the tenderest expressions of confidence and
love. The Portuguese could not restrain their tears,
remembering the saintly lives of the departed, and the
benefits one and all had received at their hands, to see
them butchered in so execrable a manner. These
wretches did indeed deserve the name of worse than
butchers; they even made sport of the sufferings of at
least one of their victims. Fastening him to the mouth
of one of their cannons, they blew his body in fragments into the air. Meanwhile, not one tear, not one
groan, was forced from the martyrs, even in the extremity of their torments; weakness itself, in such a
cause, became strength. Two of them who had been
keeping their beds from illness, hearing of what was
going on, had risen hastily and dressed themselves, to
mingle with their companions, lest they should lose the
crown of martyrdom. Another, Simon de Castex, a
young man of only eighteen years of age, whose refined
manner and peaceful bearing inspired the Calvinists
with the belief that he was of high family, and might
be worth a considerable ransom, was brought before
Sourie, that his fate might be decided on. The corsair, with an insidious tone, inquiring who he was, the
young man nobly replied, "I am a Catholic, and I am
of the Society of Jesus." He aspired to no higher title,
he acknowledged no other family. Thinking himself
insulted by this reply, Sourie ordered him instantly to
be throttled and flung into the sea.

Thus perished thirty-nine of the Jesuits, and one only was left to record the sacrifice, Jean Sanchez, a lay brother, who had acted as cook on the voyage, and was spared by the Calvinists on the score of his employment, which would not, they thought, be very injurious to their heresy in Brazil. In vain he assured them he was a Catholic and a Jesuit; they made little account of it, not seeing him clad in the obnoxious garments, and they made him cook in one of their own ships. Thus was a credible eye-witness of these wonderful events preserved, one whose testimony of what happened, both before and at the time of the martyrdom, could not be questioned; but the number of the forty martyrs was not to be left unfulfilled, and this was the way in which it was accomplished.

There was a young man on board the *St. James*, a nephew of the captain, named Saint John, of excellent character and most edifying piety; his heart had been completely won by the conduct of the young religious since they embarked from Lisbon, so that he had appealed very earnestly to Father Azevedo that he might be admitted amongst his novices. Father Azevedo promised that this favour should be granted him on reaching Brazil, provided his behaviour during the voyage should correspond. Nothing could exceed the zeal of Saint John; he frequented the spiritual exercises of the young Jesuits, so far as was permitted him, looked upon them already as his brothers, and gave himself up to all the austerities and mortifications which they practised. Renewing from time to time his supplications to Father Azevedo, he at length obtained the happiness he craved, and was admitted as a novice; although his being invested with the habit was still delayed, because the poor equipment of the missionaries included but the barest necessaries for their own number. When this young candidate for the religious life saw those with whom he already reckoned himself one falling side by side, victims for their holy profession, a burning desire to share their death and glorious

crown carried him beyond all earthly considerations,
and, rushing amongst the Calvinists, he cried, "I too
have been received into the Society of Jesus, and I am
on my way to Brazil to preach the holy Catholic
faith." Seeing that they hesitated to believe him, because he was dressed in secular habits, he went away
towards the place where one or two young missionaries
were already stripped of their upper garments ready
for death, and clothing himself in the habit of one of
them, re-appeared on the upper deck, and mingling
amongst those who were actually being strangled, received the grace for which he thirsted, and was cast
with the others into the ocean.

It was on Saturday, July 15th, 1570, that these
forty martyrs entered into rest. That very day, St.
Teresa, in her monastery at Avila, being at meditation,
was suddenly rapt in an ecstasy, and beheld the
heavens opened, and forty of those who had shed their
blood for Jesus raised up to enjoy His presence, their
countenances dazzling with a celestial light, crowns
upon their heads, and palms in their hands. Seized
with a profound sensation of delight, she remained absorbed for a long time in the contemplation of their
glory, especially when she perceived by their habits
that they were of the Society of Jesus, and that her
own near relation, François Perès Godoy, was amongst
their number. She confided this vision to her confessor, Father Balthaser Alvarès, by whom it was made
known before the tidings had reached Spain, and veri-
fied it in every detail.

Father Azevedo appeared also on the very day and
hour of his death to his brother Jerome, then with the
Portuguese army in the East Indies; his face serene,
his voice full of a tranquil joy, declaring that he had
that moment died by the hands of heretics, and was
entering into the glories of heaven. Jerome recovering
at these words from the trance into which the sudden
apparition had cast him, exclaimed, "My brother, my
dear brother!" but Father Azevedo had already van-

ished. From this moment, through all the great military honours he obtained, and the harassing disappointments which afterwards befel him, Jerome had but one real object in life, to work out his salvation and become worthy of his near relationship to the glorious martyr. He chose him for his special protector; and causing a painting to be made which represented him as he appeared at that moment, it was hung up in his oratory, and became the object of his tenderest devotion. No one could doubt, from the effect on the after-life of Jerome, that he had really beheld what he said.

Amongst the martyrs nine only were Spaniards, the rest were Portuguese; two only were priests, twenty-two were intended for the priesthood, but had not yet completed their studies, the other sixteen were lay-brothers, who performed domestic functions, and were also employed when necessary as catechists.

The Calvinists did not long hesitate, when they had despatched their victims, to lay their sacrilegious hands upon whatever they could find that had belonged to them. They expected, no doubt, to discover hoards of valuable treasure; but altar-furniture, church-ornaments, chalices, missals, reliquaries, spiritual books, rosaries, images, and medals,—all presents to Father Azevedo from the Pope and different prelates at Rome, for the mission in Brazil,—these were all they could find. Disappointed in their covetous search, they wreaked the most wanton outrages on the simple but sacred objects of devotion. They even cut with their knives the adorable image of their crucified God, and crushed beneath their feet medals, rosaries, and Agnus Deis. They dressed themselves in the sacerdotal vestments, with shouts of derision and contempt. One of them having discovered, by its superscription, a piece of the true cross, called one of the Portuguese, who was looking on in horror and indignation, and exclaimed, as he cast it into the fire, " Come, superstitious men, and see if this wood will not burn as well as any other." The silver chalices and ciboriums were profaned at

their Bacchanalian feasts; and every outrage in fact
that impiety could suggest was heaped upon all that
bore witness of the Holy Faith. A few of the garments of the missionaries were preserved, and afterwards bought at a high price by the governor of
Gomera, one of the Canary Islands.

On returning to France, these pirates boasted greatly
of having killed forty Jesuits. The low mob of their
sect made it a subject of great triumph, but those of
more enlightened sentiments felt ashamed of the blot
thus cast on the honour of their nation. Nay, they
went further, and condemned the barbarity with which
men who offered no resistance, and whose only crime
was their faith, had been slaughtered in cold blood.
The Queen of Navarre ordered that the prisoners should
be instantly released; and they returned to Portugal
to carry the mournful tidings of the fate of Father
Azevedo and his companions. As to the other missionaries, who had been left behind at Madeira, they learnt
the news at first with the profoundest and bitterest
grief; but there was so much of consolation in the
nature of their brethren's death, that by degrees they
felt only sorrow that they had lost the same glorious
privilege. Especially Father Pierre Diaz, to whom
Father Azevedo had committed his authority before
his departure, regretted unceasingly that he had lost
the opportunity of sealing with his blood the holy
truths of Catholic doctrine. But for him the crown
was only suspended a little longer,—his glory was but
deferred. The very next year, when continuing his
voyage to Brazil with Vasconcellos' squadron, he fell
into the hands of the same heretics, and, with eleven
of his companions, went to receive the same crowns
and palms as Father Azevedo and his sainted band of
martyrs. But before leaving Madeira this father
sent full tidings of what he had heard to St. Francis
Borgia, General of the Society; and his letter was
translated from Portuguese into Italian, and circulated
widely through Rome. Engravings of the forty mar-

tyrs were made, and cherished with veneration; the Pope, Pius V., expressed his conviction that they were already beyond all need of prayers; St. Francis ordered thanksgiving to be made for their happy death; and many bishops permitted them to receive the public worship given to martyrs. Gregory XV. had even allowed this in Rome, when a decree of Urban VIII. forbade any honour of this kind to be paid, in any case, until it had been pronounced upon authoritatively by the Apostolic See. On this the Jesuits universally interdicted public homage to the forty martyrs; but the process of their canonization was soon after commenced, and necessary informations were taken in Portugal, Brazil, and Rome. Many causes contributed to delay the affair; and it was not until Benedict XIV. was Pope, in September 1742, that the decree so long desired was published, and all necessary formalities for the beatification proceeded with. No sooner was the decree promulgated, than devotion to these holy martyrs spread with wonderful vitality; and within the same month many singular graces were obtained through their intercession.

II.

SISTER HONORIA MAGAEN

AND HER COMPANIONS.

IRELAND, 1656.

HEN the accession of Elizabeth put the final stroke to the destruction of the Church in England, and all the religious institutions, which had been partially restored during Mary's life, were again swept away,—it was not found possible to proceed with the same severity in Ireland, where the old faith was too firmly fixed in the hearts of the people to place it in the power of their rulers to root it out of the land as ruthlessly as they had been able to do in England. Many religious houses even still survived during the reigns of James and Charles, and were not finally suppressed until the bloody persecution of Cromwell; and it was under the shadow of one of these houses that the three heroic women of whom we are about to speak lived during many years, although they were not actually members of the religious community.

Honoria Burke was the daughter of Richard Burke, an Irish gentleman of noble birth; and was brought up in the strictest attachment to the ancient faith during the troublous times succeeding the English Reformation. At fourteen, she consecrated herself to God by vow, and received the habit of the third order of St. Dominic from the hands of Father Thaddeus O'Dowd, the Provincial of the order. She had a friend, who also wore the Dominican habit, named Honoria Magaen; and together they arranged a plan for retiring, with one servant, to a little cottage attached to the Dominican convent, which was at that time fixed at Burrishool, County Mayo. Accordingly they all three took up their abode in the cottage, where they continued to live for many years in the undisturbed exercise of devotion and works of charity. They seem to have attempted a close imitation of their great patroness and mother, St. Catherine of Sienna; and it was probably with the idea of following her footsteps the more perfectly that they chose a life which left them at greater liberty to exercise their charity towards others, in preference to enclosing themselves in the convent under whose protection they lived. Of Honoria Burke it is said, that the purity of her life was such, that her confessors bore testimony to her never having committed mortal sin. They all undertook the most heroic labours of charity, and specially during a famine which desolated Ireland during the latter end of Elizabeth's reign, when crowds of miserable beings assembled at their cottage-door, and were kept alive by their means alone for many weeks. Poor themselves, they had but little to give, but their charity never failed; and it is said their Divine Spouse sent an angel to them, under the form of a pilgrim, who brought them the food which they distributed to the starving people. This might have been but the popular way of explaining the abundance of a charity which seemed to have something marvellous, coming as it did from the hands of those whose own life was one of the strictest poverty; yet we are assured that many supernatural graces were shown them, and that they were ordinarily looked on as special objects of the Divine love and favour. Thus they continued to live until that persecution under the usurper Cromwell, which is probably hardly equalled in cruelty and atrocity by any to be found in the pages of history.

The Convent of Burrishool did not escape in the general attack made on the Irish Catholics. The nuns were some of them put to death, and the rest were driven out of their house, and the two Honorias and their faithful servant fled for refuge to a little uninhabited island in a neighbouring lake, which bore the name of the Isle of Saints. Here they concealed themselves in the thick woods for some days; but their reputation was too widely extended for them to be overlooked by the persecutors. Diligent search was made for them until the place of their retreat was discovered, and all three were seized. They were instantly stripped, bound to a tree, and cruelly scourged. Sister Honoria Magaen, the youngest of the three, fearing lest some worse insults might follow, prayed her Divine Spouse to protect her in this extremity, even at the cost of her life: and her prayer was heard; for in some extraordinary way she was enabled to escape from the hands of the soldiers, and again took refuge in the wood, where she concealed herself in the hollow of a tree. It was the month of February, and intensely cold; she was covered with wounds from the stripes she had received, and without a particle of clothing, and very soon hunger and exhaustion, combined with the loss of blood, put an end to her life.

Sister Honoria Burke, however, remained in the hands of the soldiers, who, after inflicting unheard-of tortures on her, threw her into the boat in which they had crossed the lake, as if she had been a bundle of sticks, and this so violently that three of her ribs were broken with the fall. They then pushed off from the island, and rowed over with her to the opposite shore; but when they had landed, and were about to lift her out after them, they found her half dead from the injuries she had received; and not thinking it worth while to trouble themselves with her any further, they again threw her on the bank, and left her there to perish. The servant, who saw that life was not extinct, sat down by her side, and tried to staunch her wounds and restore her to consciousness; and when Honoria came to herself, and found the soldiers were gone away, she begged her companion to try if she could not manage to carry her to the convent church, which was not far from the spot where they were. The servant, in spite of her own wounds, summoned strength enough to do as she wished, and laid her before the altar of our Lady, to whom she had been always particularly devout; then she left her in order to go and search for Sister Honoria Magaen, in hopes she might still find her alive.. After some time she did indeed find her hidden in the hollow tree, but she was quite dead. So she took the body on her shoulders and carried it to the church; and there she found that in her absence Sister Honoria Burke had also expired. She was in a kneeling posture, her head and body quite erect, and her hands folded in the attitude of prayer; and if we consider her exhausted state from loss of blood, and the agony of her broken bones, there was certainly something more than natural in the manner and posture in which she had supported her body in the hour of death. The faithful servant, whose name has not been preserved in the account left us of these circumstances, took both bodies, and buried them with her own hands in one grave. Their death took place in the year 1653; and the events are recorded in the acts of the general chapter held at Rome in 1656.

III.

THE BLESSED ANDREW BOBOLA, S.J.

OLAND, in the beginning of the seventeenth century, was in a most disturbed and critical condition. The great lords of the country, infected by the rebellious spirit which had gone abroad during the preceding age, had abandoned the Catholic religion; and profligacy and vice of every kind had followed, as usual, in the train of heresy. By these manifold abuses, and the maladministration of every department of government, the Cossacks were roused to rebellion, so that the throne of Poland was placed in very considerable jeopardy. Ladislas IV. was king, and to the line of conduct which he pursued may be traced all the disasters which afterwards befel his Church and nation. He was a politician of the new school, and thought to advance his own interests by the sacrifice of the cause of God. Instead of repressing the license of his nobility, and relieving the Cossacks of the burdens of which they had just cause to complain, he tried to conciliate them by abandoning to their religious animosity the monasteries and cathedrals which belonged to the United Greeks. This concession failed of its object; it whetted rather than quenched their avarice. They then demanded nothing short of the entire dissolution of the union, and the confiscation of all Catholic churches, especially those belonging to the Jesuits. And the Muscovites, ever hostile to Poland, fomented the disaffection of the Cossacks, and stirred up the flame which was shortly to set the whole country in a blaze.

At this critical moment Ladislas died, and his brother, John Casimir, succeeded to the throne. He was
a man of a very different stamp. He had been a
Jesuit, and was a cardinal when the Pope sent him to
wield his brother's sceptre, and to retrieve the fortunes
of the Church in Poland. Under the government of
Casimir all might have been well; but at the same time
rose up one Bogdau Khmielnicki, to be, under God, a
scourge to the profligate nobles, and a means of trying the
faith of the United Church. This man, though bred in
Polish castles and trained in Polish camps, nevertheless
joined with the Tartars in a war of extermination
against all Catholics, priests and laymen, men and
women. Upon this enterprise he entered with so much
energy and skill, that the schismatics regarded him as
the hero of another Crusade; the monks of Mount
Athos descended to preach the holy war; the patriarch
of Constantinople sent him a blessed sword, and the
patriarch of Jerusalem proclaimed him prince of Russia. The struggle on which Bogdau had entered with
Casimir excited intense interest in every quarter. Mahometans, schismatics, and Protestants, viewed him as
the arm of God for the extirpation of their common
enemy, the Catholic faith. Cromwell of England
wrote to him as the "Column of the Eastern Church,
the scourge of the Popes, the extirpation of the errors
of Popery." Many sovereigns offered him assistance,
and to them he promised a share of Poland when it
should be conquered.

After two undecisive engagements, Casimir, trusting
in God and the Blessed Virgin, completely routed the
hero of the Cossacks with the flower of their army in a
pitched battle at Berestesko, in 1653; and then turning
his attention towards Sweden, formed the gigantic pro-
ject of reconquering that country, and restoring it to
her faith. But a sovereign of no ordinary ability sat
upon the Swedish throne, and Bogdau, though defeated,
was not destroyed. Soon Berestesko was only a glorious vision. Charles Gustavus marched on Casimir to

punish his pretensions upon Sweden; and Bogdau, backed up by the patriarch of Moscow and the Grand Duke of Muscovy, invaded Poland in three places. This was in 1655. The Poles were beaten at all points: the Catholics were massacred; Casimir fled into Silesia, and Charles Gustavus marched in triumph into Warsaw.

The cause of religion and liberty seemed lost, when the Jesuits, issuing from their colleges, traversed the country, and roused the sinking patriotism of the people. Soon Casimir saw himself at the head of another army, and Poland escaped from the grasp of the Swedish monarch. From that time forward the hatred of the Cossacks was tenfold more bitter against the Company of Jesus, which had thus foiled their projects of extermination. It was a terrible mission to which the fathers of the company were called during this distracted period. They had not only to encourage the just and convert sinners; their confessional was often the battle-field; their hearers dying soldiers; their flock raging blasphemers and bigoted schismatics; their only shield, amid the dangers with which they were beset, an invincible confidence in God. They were the very vanguard of the Polish army, sent on in advance before the main body by John Casimir and the Bishop of Lithuania.

A most distinguished officer, so to call him, of this vanguard was the Blessed ANDRÉ BOBOLA, the subject of our present narrative. Born of a noble Polish family, in the year 1591, he entered the Jesuit novitiate at Vilna on the 13th of July, 1611, and twelve years later commenced his ministerial labours in the Church of St. Casimir in the same town. His function as a preacher, his deep spiritual wisdom as a director, and his indefatigable zeal in every department of sacerdotal duty, caused his name to be widely spread among his fellow-countrymen, an object of veneration to the faithful, and of mingled fear and hatred to the heretics. At the age of forty he was admitted to make the solemn vows in his society, and immediately afterwards was appointed rector of one of their colleges; an office, however, which he resigned at the end of five years, choosing rather the more painful and laborious life of a missionary. In this new sphere of duty, he at once adopted the method of the Saints. He set out on his missions fasting, lived on a little dry bread, slept constantly in the open air, and always travelled on foot; in a word, he considered himself bound to exhibit in his own person a picture of the sufferings of Jesus, to a people scandalised by the sight of luxurious and wicked *popes*, as the schismatic priests are called. He never lost an occasion of doing good : he would enter into conversation with the wayside traveller; would seek out the sick and console them, and the dying that he might administer the last Sacraments; or children, that he might instruct them. The hearts of all men burned within them at the very sound of his voice.

Nor was this all. He engaged in controversy also. The schismatic priests advanced to encounter this formidable enemy; but the learned Father added to his zeal an intimate acquaintance with the Greek language and the Greek Fathers, and exposed the misquotations of the priests, to their own confusion, and the conversion of the people who marked their defeat. Yet he argued with so much sweetness as to convince even his opponents themselves. To controversial disputations he added frequent preaching; and upon these labours Almighty God poured down such plentiful benedictions, that whole dioceses, with their bishops, were rescued from the schism.

All this was not achieved without the exasperation of the Cossacks and their allies the "popes." They watched with intense chagrin the progress of the Catholic faith. Scarcely in a single province of Poland, except Polesia, was their religion dominant; but in the fastnesses of that marshy and woody country they found a secure retreat. Their occupation gone in many districts which they had called their own, the schismatic clergy congregated here to devise fresh schemes of vengeance against the Jesuit missionaries. In the heart of Polesia

D

is situated the town of Pinsk; and this town, notwithstanding the residence of many staunch Catholics, they
were accustomed to consider their head-quarters.   But
the property in the neighbourhood belonged to one
of these zealous Catholics (Father André was accustomed to call them men of *gold*), and the Chancellor
Adelbert and he determined to strike a vigorous blow
for the Church.   He built and endowed with royal
generosity a college for the Jesuits in the town, as a
fortress under cover of which the faith might flourish.

Just about this time the arms of John Casimir had
suffered reverses from Charles Gustavus and Bogdau
Khmielnicki.   In this emergency a general council of
the company was assembled at Warsaw, and the Fathers
were distributed all over the country to rouse the Catholics of Poland.   Father André was appointed to Polesia,
and appeared at Pinsk at the very moment when a
Rector was wanted for the new college.   He was made
Superior, and undertook at once the duties of the college in conjunction with his missionary work.   The
consternation of the "popes" at the invasion of their
stronghold may easily be conceived; and the event very
shortly justified their worst fears.   The success which
had attended Father André's labours in Lithuania followed his steps here.   Converts poured in; the nobility
and their serfs alike returned to the bosom of the Church;
and the Chancellor saw in a very short time the blessed
effects of his noble foundation.   The schismatics vowed
to be revenged, and at once set about the destruction of
their foe.

They durst not lay violent hands on him themselves,
for fear of the Chancellor's displeasure; yet they did
what they could.   They spread on foot calumnies,—
which, however, were not credited; wretches were paid to
waylay him and abuse him: he escaped their hands;
they encumbered him in argument, and were signally
defeated.   Next, they hit upon a mode of persecution
to wound him in his natural love for children.   They
assembled a troop of the most wicked boys at the

gate of the college, to assail him with insults and mockery as he came out : " Dog of a Papist—Catholic Priest—Dutzochwat (which means robber of souls)— Dog of a Papist !" they shouted after him. But all this he bore with angelic patience ; and truly his mission was to rob Satan of the souls that were his prey, and these children did but bear testimony to his success.

These trifling persecutions could not satisfy a malice that thirsted for blood. While he lived there was danger, and they were determined he should die. On a certain day the Cossacks made a descent on Pinsk, to take him prisoner in his own college. He was not there, and they wreaked their vengeance on Father Maffon and some other Fathers; Father André was at Jans, for he did not confine his labours to the narrow limits of a single town. He was missionary in Polesia as well as Rector of Pinsk; and his life was one continual travel from place to place. He ranged the whole country round. He would leave Pinsk early in the morning with a single companion to serve Mass for him wherever he was going to labour for the day,—often in some remote village. Then he would preach, hear confessions, and administer the last Sacraments to the dying. Every where appeared the fruits of these abundant labours, and specially at Jansff, a town at twelve miles distance. The work that was going on here under his superintendence, and with the assistance of Zaleski, the Greek-unial priest, was well known to the Cossacks, and the name of the place only whetted their thirst for blood.

It was on Wednesday, the 16th of May, the eve of the Octave of the Ascension, in the year 1657, when the Cossacks rode into Jansff, and inquired for André Bobola. Already disappointed at not finding him in his college at Pinsk, their rage exceeds all bounds when they discover that he is not at Jansff either. They cast themselves on the Jews and Catholics, and so gave vent for a moment to their fury; but very soon returned to the pursuit of the special object of their hate, and were quickly on his track again.

He had gone to the little village of Poredilno, at some miles' distance. He had said Mass there that morning after preaching and hearing confessions, and was making his thanksgiving, when suddenly the terrified Catholics burst into the church, and told him that the Cossacks were coming. They had run from Jansff to warn him to escape, but at first he would not consent; but his children in Christ entreated him to save himself for their sake. Their charity conquered even his burning desire to die for Jesus Christ. A carriage was waiting outside with a guide. Not a moment was to be lost. André got in with his faithful companion John Domanowski. They took the Jansff road, hoping to reach in time another road which would favour their flight; but it was too late. Almighty God had heard the wishes of his heart, and was conducting him to martyrdom. The Cossacks had learned from the schismatics that he was at Poredilno, and were on the road to that place. The fugitive and his pursuers came face to face with each other by the farm of Mohilno. Terrified when he saw the Cossacks, the driver threw down the reins, and running into an adjoining wood left André to his fate; but the holy man felt no fear. Calm, and even happy, he alighted from the carriage, and kneeling down on the road, raising his eyes and his hands towards heaven, he cried, offering himself up as a sacrifice, "Thy will be done, O my God!" repeating several times those words of our Saviour before His own most sorrowful Passion. The passion of André was to have yet stronger points of resemblance to that of his divine Master.

The Cossacks rushed up to him at full gallop, screaming with savage joy at having found him at last. They leapt from their horses, and urged him vainly to embrace the schism, heaping upon him threats, insults, and blasphemies. When they found him immovable in his faith, they drew their sabres and gave him two frightful wounds on the shoulders, so that the blood burst forth in streams. The Cossacks were eager to complete his death; but they would first subject him to torture. After violently raising the Father from his knees, they pulled off part of his clothes and dragged him to a wood close by, where they tied him to a tree and cruelly scourged him. The labourers in the fields fled at the spectacle; but the Cossacks knew no pity, and vied with each other in tearing his flesh; yet he remained unmoved, calmly invoking the name of Jesus. At last they became weary of striking him; and while resting a little from their exertions, they began to make a crown in imitation of the Jews, and for the more perfect resemblance between the Master and the servant. They had no thorns, but this did not hinder their malicious intention. They cut young shoots from the trees, and steeping them in a brook to make them flexible, tied them so as to form a crown for the forehead of their victim. With this they squeezed his head as in a vice; and the twigs gradually contracting as they grew dry, cut through the skin more and more, while they themselves pulled them tighter to increase his agony. However, they took care not to fracture his skull; not out of any *humanity*, but in order to prolong his sufferings, and to receive the applause of their comrades. Their comrades were still at Jansff, so they hurried him away, bound with garlands, as a victim to the altar.

They now fastened a cord round his neck, and attaching the ends of the saddles of two horsemen, who set off at a rapid pace, he was violently dragged between them. A Cossack followed behind, armed with an axe, with which he struck him between the shoulders, sometimes even with the edge, whenever he appeared to flag. As they got nearer Jansff, they redoubled their blows with shouts of blasphemy, and urged on the horses faster. The Cossacks entered the town in triumph. "The robber of souls!" they cried, showing their prize. "Bobola! Bobola! the robber of souls!" and soon all their comrades rushed to the place. They had been amusing themselves till their comrades returned with Zaleski, the Greek-unial curé of Jansff, who had been seized and tied to a tree, and was already wounded with a sabre.

But the savages now cared nothing for him, and they took no notice when one of the inhabitants went to set him free; they were taken up with Bobola, the robber of souls. "I saw him," said one eye-witness, "when the Cossacks brought him to Jansff, his head cut with the twigs with which it was crowned." "From head to foot," said another, "he was nearly stripped of his garments, and covered with the blood that streamed from his wounds."   .

"Who art thou?" cried Assavonla, the Cossack chief, casting a terrible glance at his prisoner; "and what hast thou come hither to do? Art thou a Latin priest?"

"I am a Latin priest," replied the father, without blushing. "I have come hither to preserve the Catholic faith in this country; to reclaim to the true Church those who have abandoned her."

"Dog of a Papist!" answered the savage captain; "I know how to wrench the Catholic faith from your heart, or else I will wrench out your heart with it."

"My faith," exclaimed André, "is the true faith, it is the right faith : it is the faith that leads to heaven. I was born in that faith, and in that faith I will die. I will never renounce my faith. But you—convert yourselves, do penance, for you will never be saved in your errors. Abandon your schism, embrace the faith which I profess, and you will save your souls."

At these words, Assavonla was transported with rage : he brandished his sabre, and was just joing to cut off his head, when, by an instinctive movement, André put up his arms to ward off the blow. His head escaped; but the hand was nearly separated from the arm, and hung down by the skin. Assavonla struck a second time, but André tottered and fell, and the sabre descending made a great gash on his foot. There he lay, patient and meek, at the feet of his inhuman murderers; but when the Cossacks saw that he raised his eyes towards heaven, one of them, fearing that that under glance would bring down vengeance upon them from above, with the point of his sabre pushed out one of his eyes. At this he implored, not vengeance on his torturers, but pardon for their sin; and he implored for himself the grace of final perseverance, that he might remain firm in the midst of such fearful sufferings.

But all that we have hitherto seen was but the prelude, a sort of introductory child's play, to the scenes we have yet to describe. Admire as we must the heroism of the martyr, there is something in that long catalogue of atrocities to wound and tear the soul that does but listen to its rehearsal. Nevertheless, we shall conceal nothing; on the contrary, we would record all the sufferings of the martyr with the same pious care with which we would gather up every drop of his blood.

"Never, perhaps," says the Sacred Congregation of Rites, "was such a cruel martyrdom submitted to the judgment of this congregation." Let us not fear, then, to look down on the arena in which the gladiator of Christ exposes himself to fight with wild beasts; let us not turn away without counting his wounds. It will give us strength and perseverance in the struggles which in his militant life the faith of every Christian will inevitably have to sustain.

The victim, weltering in his blood, lay prostrate at the feet of his murderers. All at once, the sight of one of the adjoining houses suggested a diabolical idea to their minds. They seized André by one leg, and dragged him along the road up to that ill-omened house. It was a butcher's slaughter-house, provided with all sorts of instruments for their purpose! There they first strip off the rest of his garments, and then hold a consultation. "This cursed Jesuit, did he not richly deserve all the punishments? This robber of souls, was he not an unclean animal? He ought to be treated, then, as an unclean animal." The first thing to do was to purify him with fire; so they lighted torches of resinous wood, and set about burning the breast and sides of the malefactor.

" Give up your faith," they cried, putting the fire close to his body. " Give up the Catholic faith, or you shall suffer far more than this."

" You may," he replied with an intrepid humility, " you may put my courage to the proof; but if you do, you shall see what God can do in me. I believe and I confess, that as there is but one only true God, so there is but one only true Church, and that is the Catholic Church of Rome : one only faith, the Catholic faith, which Jesus Christ has revealed, and the apostles preached. I die gladly for that faith, as the apostles and so many martyrs have died before me."

Their rage redoubled at these words. They stabbed him, mutilated his limbs, and beat him with blows on the mouth; still he persisted in his faith. Then they applied the flames, and the flesh of the martyr fell off in drops. They hung his head downwards for some time; and when they saw his convulsions in this miserable position : " Look," they cried, with savage and brutal laughter; " look how well he dances."

Soon their cruelty suggested still more horrible devices.* " What a small tonsure you have !" said one of the Cossacks; " I will give you a larger one ;"—these impious railleries showing the hatred these wretches bore to the Catholic priesthood, for the schismatic priests do not wear the tonsure. One of them took a knife, and drawing with its point a large circle on his head, he gave him a new and bloody tonsure, by tearing off the scalp, like an Indian savage. Others, taking the hint, seized the hands of André, and scraped them down to the bones, to take away the unction of the holy oil with which they had been consecrated; thereby only adding to the original anointing with the further

---

* Some lads, horror-stricken at the sight, had hidden themselves behind the wall of the shambles, and remembered afterwards every word of the martyr and his murderers ; and one man climbed up into a tree, and saw and heard every thing that passed ; so that we give the evidence of eye-witnesses to all these details.

unction of his own blood, and so making it yet more
precious and holy. "We'll show you," they went on,
"how you do in the Romish Church. With those
hands you turn over the leaves of the Missal at the
altar; so we will turn over their skin." And immediately they flayed his hands; after which they tear
away the muscles, and cut off the joints. "Now, then,
what have you got to say for your Pope? What do
you think of your Romans? Will you not yield now?
Give up the Catholic faith, unless you wish to endure
greater torments yet."

But the priestly spirit, the spirit of faith, the spirit
of zeal, burned but with renewed ardour in the breast
of André, in the midst of all the agony of that sacrilegious consecration. "My dear children," he said, with
an intrepid sweetness, "my dear children, convert yourselves quickly, renounce your schism, If you persist
in your errors, you will lose your souls." Thus consecrated anew in his own blood, he sought still to gain
his very murderers, and offer them up to God as the
first-fruits of a new apostolate.

But the ceremony was not over yet. "Now that
he is a priest," said the Cossacks, with a ferocious ex-
ultation,—"now that he is a priest, we must give him a
chasuble." Then they seize him, cast him on a bench,
lay him on his face, and little by little pull the skin off
the whole of his back. Then they spread a quantity of
chopped straw over that large wound, and turning his
body over, press it against the bench, so that the bits of
straw caught up by the blood, and sticking into the
raw flesh, cause him the most excruciating agony.
"In church," said they again, "you wear a chasuble;
but we have given you a far more becoming orna-
ment."

These murderers seemed to consider it a fête. The
bleeding and mutilated body, its bruised, swollen, hideous appearance, provoked their mirth,—they regarded
it with laughter. But they still thought it retained
too much of the semblance of humanity. The saying

of Scripture was to be fulfilled in him as in Jesus Christ Himself: " From the sole of the foot to the top of the head there is no soundness in Him" (Is. i. 6). And again, "There was no sightliness in Him that we should be desirous of Him" (Is. iv. 2). The murderers cut off his nose and his lips: then he was no longer a man. " It is a monster;" and the Cossacks themselves began to be scared at last. "It is a monster; only he has no claws: let us give him some claws." And cutting up some splinters of pine-wood, they drove them in under the nails of his hands and feet.

But he had still enough strength left to raise his arms in charity towards heaven. His torments were to be yet more cruel, his prayers yet more fervent. "It is a battle," said St. Bernard, relating the sufferings of our Lord,—" a battle whether suffering shall be more bloody or charity more burning." Like the charity of Jesus, the charity of André prevailed; not a complaint, not a murmur, escaped from his heart. He made constantly acts of faith and hope and love. "Jesus! Mary!" he repeated incessantly; " Jesus and Mary, help me!" He invoked also St. Joseph. "Lord, Thy will be done! I commend my soul into Thy hands. Lord, enlighten these poor blind-people with Thy light; turn them from their errors. My dear children," he said again, "what are you doing? The Lord our God be with you, and make you repent. Do penance, and God will forgive you your sin."

Then the martyr struggled with his gentle voice against the impious rage of his murderers. Vainly they strove to stop the voice which troubled their conscience,—to smother it with blasphemies against the holy Church. That voice still raised itself always with the same triumphant song: "Jesus and Mary, help me: my dear children, repent." But they knew well how at length to impose silence upon it. They seized hold of the tongue which had so long caused schism and trouble; the tongue which had robbed souls. But for this new exploit some further consultation was necessary. How could they tear it up by its roots; that cursed tongue, which would go on blessing them to their shame and confusion? The most cruel mode that can be conceived was the mode best suited to their malice. They cast themselves once more on their victim; and behind the neck they cut a large opening, through which they thrust in their hands, and seizing the apostle's tongue, wrenched it out with violence. They held it up with shouts as a trophy, and hurled it down upon the ground. Even in the midst of this horrible torture, he makes a last effort to invoke the sacred names of Jesus and Mary, and faints in the attempt. His murderers, thinking him dead, take up the body, and cast it on a dunghill hard by. "I saw him," said one who approached to look at him in that state; "the blood was gushing from his head, his hands, his feet, from his whole body, as from an ox or a wild boar which had just been killed." However, they observed that their victim still breathed. It seemed as though that heroic soul, stronger than death itself, would not die, that it might be able to offer yet greater sacrifices to God. The chief of the Cossacks now drew near, and himself pierced his side with a sabre. Then all was over, the sacrifice was complete; after several hours the martyrdom was at length accomplished; and at the same moment a bright light gleamed from the sky, as if heaven, in opening its portals to receive the soul of the blessed martyr, had given earth a glimpse of its glory. The Cossacks fled in consternation; and the Catholics, timidly coming forth from their hiding-places, carried off the mangled body of their apostle, as a most dear and precious relic.

IV.

THE BLESSED JOHN DE BRITTO, S.J.

———

CHAPTER I.

FROM THE BIRTH OF THE BLESSED JOHN DE BRITTO TILL HIS ARRIVAL IN INDIA.

OHN DE BRITTO was born at Lisbon, March 1st, 1647; he was the son of Don Salvador de Britto Peregra and Beatrix his wife, both of whom were of noble birth. His father dying when he was only four years of age, he was committed by his mother to the care of the Jesuits; and under them he grew up full of the grace of God from his childhood.

At the age of nine years he was sent to court in the capacity of page to Don Pedro, the youngest son of the king, and probable heir to the throne of Portugal. During the six years which he passed in his new sphere, he persevered in the same devout habit which he had formed under his mother's roof; frequently retiring for prayer and study, attending Mass daily in the chapel-royal, and devoting himself to other pious exer-

cises. By this exemplary course of life he drew down
upon himself the admiration of the whole court; but he
incurred also the hatred of his fellow pages : for his rigid
and holy rule of life was a continual check upon their
profligacy ; and the open reproofs which he did not hesitate to give when any sinful action occurred beneath his
own eye, excited their strongest indignation. They
ridiculed his piety, and heaped upon him persecution,
not only by words, but also by blows. He bore their
ill-treatment with great patience; but it produced an illness which brought him into hourly danger of death.
At the very moment of his agony his dear patron St. Francis Xavier, at the earnest prayer of his mother, restored
his health. She had from his birth dedicated her son
to the apostle of India, and she now vowed that if her
child should recover, he should wear for the whole year
the Jesuit habit in honour of his deliverer. When,
therefore, he appeared at court again after his recovery,
it was in a little black robe, with a chaplet of the Blessed
Virgin hanging by his side ; and in this garb he served
the Prince, and attended the Jesuit college of St. An-
tony of Padua. The people stopped in the streets to
see him pass ; not on account of the strangeness of
such a dress on a child, but to mark his holy and edifying demeanour. When the term of his vow had expired, he put off the dress, but with the intention to as-
sume it one day for ever. Notwithstanding his infirm
health, he had long resolved to leave the world and
lead an apostolic life as a Jesuit, and at the age of
fifteen he carried this resolution into effect. He applied
for admission into the society to the father-provincial,
Michael Tinsco, by whom he was named into the novitiate at Lisbon. The Prince Don Pedro opposed his
resolution, but the mother rejoiced that her son should
possess a vocation for the Company of Jesus.

It was on the 17th of December, 1662, that John
de Britto entered the novitiate at Lisbon. A novena
had just commenced in preparation for Christmas. At
its close they each had to present the Infant Jesus with

a petition, according to their several wants. De Britto wrote his petition with the others, and when he assumed the habit after his retreat he offered it to Jesus. It was that he might be sent as a missionary to Japan, there to live and labour, and at length obtain the crown of martyrdom. After two years he took the three vows of poverty, chastity, and obedience, having passed through the novitiate a very model of holiness. He went among the novices by the name of the panegyrist of the wonders of the Holy Eucharist, on account of his insight into spiritual things after Communion. At this time, by visitation of the hospitals and submission to the convent offices, he laid the foundations of that habit of self-renunciation which, after a life of missionary labour, resulted at length in martyrdom.

On leaving the novitiate at Lisbon, he went to Evora for two years, and thence to Coimbra, to study literature and philosophy. He then removed to Lisbon to teach grammar; and while thus employed, his thirst to go out as a missionary received an additional impulse from the visit of Father Balthazar da Costa, who had just returned from Madeira to find recruits. To him he stated the wish of his heart, and he promised to plead his cause at Rome; the consequence of which was, that a few months afterwards orders were received by the father-provincial to despatch John de Britto, along with several other young missionaries, in the first ship which should sail for Madeira.

John returned hearty thanks to God for the favour, but his mother was distracted at the thought of losing her child. She appealed to the provincial, to her son himself, to the papal nuncio, and to the king, but without effect; and at length, fearing to offend God by persisting in her opposition, she offered him up as the dearest sacrifice she could render. His departure was fixed for the 25th of March, 1674. The night before he paid a visit to his mother; but to save her the pang of parting, he forbore to tell her that it was the last. He carefully avoided any thing which might interfere with his object; and therefore, instead of joining the other missionaries, when with a great crowd of people they attended church on the banks of the Tagus, he embarked secretly, and only appeared when all danger of being delayed was over.   He was ordained priest just before leaving.

During the voyage he won the favour of the captain, and took advantage of it to exercise his ministry with the utmost freedom.   He had to preach every Sunday, taught the catechism to the ignorant and the children on board, and continually engaged the passengers and sailors in exercises of devotion.   Near the line they were surprised by a calm, and placed in great straits.   Their biscuit became mouldy and their water tainted, and the greater part of the passengers fell ill,—among the number some of the missionaries.   Father de Britto, however, remained perfectly well, and occupied himself night and day in conveying corporal and spiritual relief to the sick.   One day he administered Extreme Unction to thirty persons.   They were relieved at night by St. Francis Xavier, in whose honour the whole crew of the ship, at the pious missionary's advice, had offered a novena.   Scarcely, however, were they delivered from this danger, when they were threatened by another.   A violent storm arose, and for several days they were in the greatest peril.   But by a second novena they were again saved, and at length they anchored happily in the harbour at Goa.

Scarcely had the father set foot on shore than he ran to embrace the brethren of the college.   Having then paid a visit to the Blessed Sacrament, he prostrated himself at the tomb of St. Francis Xavier, and venerated his uncorrupted body,—thus gathering fresh ardour for his apostolic course.   Here he resumed the studies which he had discontinued at Lisbon, and after five months' incessant application he pronounced himself ready to undergo an examination on the *Summa* of St. Thomas. He passed, to the admiration of the professors, and was excused from proceeding farther with his course of theology. At Goa he commenced the austere life of the Madura missionaries,—which consists in neither eating flesh-meat nor fish, in sleeping on the ground, and walking bare-foot,—that he might be ready for his apostolate when his summons should arrive. He also learned to defy human respect by reproving the licentiousness of the great men of the palace. The fathers of Goa were loath that so holy a man and so learned a scholar should be lost to the college; but they could not persuade him to give up his missionary aspirations, and in April 1674 orders arrived from the father-provincial that he should set sail from the harbour of Goa for Malabar, with Father Emmanuel Rodriguez and some other companions.

* * *

CHAPTER II.

THE INDIAN MISSION.

THE mission of Madura, to which Father de Britto was called, was not confined to the single limits of the town and kingdom bearing that name. It comprised the kingdoms of Gingi, Vetour, Golconda, and the principalities of Trichirapoli and Marava, a tract of country two hundred leagues long by eighty broad. It presents the most arduous field of labour for the missionary, on account of its extent, the denseness of the population, the climate and nature of the country, and the dangerous beasts with which it is infested. The heat is excessive, and almost fatal to those who have not passed through some years of seasoning. Towns and villages abound every where.

The inhabitants generally are very intelligent; they have made great progress in many sciences, and their Brahmins are perfectly able to sustain an argument in defence of their false religion. In this respect India differs entirely from other parts of the heathen world, which lie in stupid ignorance and intellectual blindness

To holiness, devotion, energy, and courage, the essential qualities of an apostle, the India missionary must add the advantages of a logical mind and a ready wit. The mental enlightenment of the Brahmins, if the term may be used of idolatrous error, forms one of the greatest hindrances to the propagation of the faith in that country.

But perhaps it is less to be feared by the missionary than the popular veneration for caste. Caste consists in an alleged descent from the God Brahma. This divinity boasts of three distinct lines of descendants: the Brahmins, who proceeded from his brain, and are noblest of all; the Rajahs, whose origin was the shoulder, and are the aristocracy of India; and the Shusters, who issued from the foot, in which class are to be found artisans, tradesmen, and mechanics. There exists besides a large part of the population who have no claim to divine extraction at all, who are called pariahs; and these are the object of the most profound contempt. All foreigners rank as pariahs, not being in any way connected with Brahma.

The first missionaries in India not possessing caste, found it impossible to obtain a hearing. With all their holiness, earnestness, and zeal, no one would listen to a pariah. It was reserved for Father Robert de Nobili to surmount, or at least show how to surmount, this obstacle. He was a Roman Jesuit, nephew of Cardinal Bellarmine, and grand-nephew of Pope Marcellus III. After carefully studying the peculiarities of the Brahmins, their laws, traditions, customs, and tenets, he saw the rock on which his predecessors had split. He determined to lay aside whatever should denote his European extraction, and adopt the dress and mode of life of some class of the natives possessing caste. First he appeared as a rajah, then as a secular Brahmin, with a long flowing robe and a silk shoulder-knot; but without success. He then discovered that, over and above caste, a mortified exterior is required to influence the Indians. He appeared, therefore, partly in the dress of the Sa

E

masks, or Brahmins of Penance; and in this he was completely successful. This class is in the highest repute
among the natives; they are regarded as the masters
of the law, and their word is final. They are distinguished by their ascetic life and their renunciation
of the pleasures of the world. They live on a little
boiled rice, which they receive only once a day, at sun-
set. In this character Father de Nobili converted a
vast number of Brahmins.

Father de Britto approved the principle of his great
predecessor, but somewhat varied his practice. He
adopted the dress of the Pandarists, a sect in very great
estimation on account of their asceticism; they are not
held in equal honour with the Samasks, but they mix
more with the various sects, and their garb therefore
affords greater opportunities of intercourse with the
natives. The reader then must imagine our blessed
martyr for the future not in his own black habit, but in
the long yellow wrapping of the Pandarist.

The Pandarists wear no other garment than a piece
of yellow cloth enveloping the whole figure. This dress
guards them from the dangerous rays of the tropical
sun, to which they are exposed the whole day. They
sometimes wear a cap, an addition absolutely necessary
to the European who would avoid a stroke of the sun;
but they walk barefoot, except on occasions of ceremony, and in crossing the burning sands of the country, when they adopt a sandal of a peculiar construction. It is not fastened by a strap, but attached to
the foot by means of a wooden peg between two toes.
This clog is of little value for purposes of travelling, as
it produces violent swellings of the legs and feet; but it
is useful in crossing the deserts. The Pandarists allow
the beard to grow, which is a mark of distinction in
India, and carry a staff as a symbol of authority.
Their diet is of the plainest kind, and entirely vege-
table; animal life being held too sacred among them
for the purposes of food, and therefore of course interdicted to all who would adopt their mode of life.

This rigorous rule might have discouraged souls less ardent than John de Britto; but to him no sacrifice, no painfulness, seemed too great in his Master's service; and he cheerfully entered upon it, in spite of his feeble health and European constitution, for the love he bore Jesus Christ, and his yearning for the salvation of the idolaters.

CHAPTER III.

FATHER DE BRITTO BEGINS HIS MISSIONARY LABOURS.

FATHER DE BRITTO set sail from Goa for the coast of Malabar, and landed at Ingapatam; then through Tanjore, where he was detained nearly a year by illness, he passed on to Ambalagata, to wait further orders and prepare for the four solemn vows. This district had originally been converted by St. Thomas the Apostle, but was afterwards infected with the Greek schism, till Alexius, primate of India, reconciled it to the Holy See, and established a Jesuit college for the superintendence of the mission, the education of native priests, and the instruction of European missionaries in the Oriental tongues. In this college Father de Britto, after a retreat of a month, took his monastic vows, and received his appointment to the Madura mission described in the last chapter.

He set out immediately with one other missionary and a few neophytes for Colli. They suffered excessive hardships on the route: they had to climb steep and rugged mountains,—to pass through forests dense with briers and brushwood, and swarming with reptiles,—to cross swollen rivers and pathless deserts; but at length they reached Colli, on the day of the festival of St. Ignatius.

There he found the plague raging, and he made it

the means of converting very many to the faith by his intrepidity in relieving the sufferers. After the pestilence had ceased, the conversions increased so rapidly, that it became necessary to divide the northern and southern district of the mission, and the latter was committed to Father de Britto.

His plan was to send on before him two or more catechists to get the work ready; so that when he arrived himself, he might proceed without loss of time. On arriving he assembled the Christians and catechumens, and preached a sermon; then he visited the sick and dying, and baptised the infants of Christian parents; after which he entered the tribunal of penance, in which he sat often for twelve consecutive hours, for the whole neighbourhood flocked and made their confessions to him. He preached on all Sundays and holidays, catechised the children, and passed from house to house to warn bad Christians, or to resolve the doubts of inquiring idolaters. In the evenings he assembled the whole congregation to recite the rosary of the Blessed Virgin, and in this way he made a vast number of converts; and when he had stayed long enough in one place for the requirements of the people, he passed on to some other station.

In his dress of a Pandarist, De Britto always obtained a ready hearing, and hence perhaps the great success of his preaching. But in all these labours he was obliged, by the universal prejudice against the pariahs, to direct his endeavours mainly towards the conversion of the upper classes. To his great sorrow, he found that even as a Pandarist he could not openly make proselytes among that sect without exposing his religion to universal contempt. He therefore was compelled to recognise their distinctions in society for the present, in order to establish Christianity on the broader basis ultimately. But, notwithstanding, he took care to advance the cause of the pariahs by showing to the converts the universality of the Gospel of Christ; and secretly he effected many conversions among the pa-

rials themselves.   But the prejudices of the natives
were so strong, that he found it impossible to overcome
them ; and he did not consider them incompatible with
the most sincere acceptance of Christianity.   As the
Apostles had for a time consented to circumcision, the
more effectually to recommend the new faith; and as
the early Christians had tolerated a certain admixture
of philosophy with the maxims of the Church,—so
the Indian missionaries judged it right to waive for
awhile, in the infant state of Christianity in India, their
objection to the social distinctions between man and
man.

When, however, heathen customs or prejudices in-
volved sin, no considerations of prospective advantage
to the Church could induce De Britto to make the
smallest concession.   The practice of polygamy is
universal among the native idolaters, and has always
proved an immense hindrance to the conversion of the
natives.   If our father had acted in regard to plurality
of wives as he acted with reference to caste, he might
have conciliated many powerful rajahs, who admired
the Gospel, but loved their wives better.   But on all
such points he was rigid and explicit; and rather than
yield one particle of the truth, either in morals or in
faith, he would see a whole province cut itself off from
Christianity.   And it was by this stern adhesion to
duty that he gained eventually his martyr's crown.

An amusing incident occurred at Travancore, which
will illustrate the feeling with which the pariahs are
regarded.   The Brahmins, in order to gain the king's
condemnation of Christianity, had to make him a present, as is usual in the administration of justice among
half-civilised people.   Costly gifts were accordingly
provided, and pariahs hired to carry the burden.   But
no sooner did they set foot within the royal precincts,
than the cry was raised, "The pariahs in the palace!
the pariahs in the palace!"   Forthwith the guard
rushed on the unhappy pariahs, who took refuge in
flight; and leaving their goods behind, the king had no

objection to receive the gifts, which, after due purifica-
tion, were stowed away in the treasury; but he was so
indignant at the mode in which they were sent, that he
forgot to inquire for what object they were offered.
Thus the conspirators were disappointed, and the Christians escaped.

CHAPTER IV.

THE FLOOD OF THE COROLAM—DE BRITTO'S SUC-
CESSES, MIRACLES, AND LABOURS.

In addition to the natural obstacle from caste, and the
talent of the Brahmins, which the Indian missionary
has to encounter, our blessed father had to labour at a
time when the whole country was convulsed with civil
war.   In all ill-organised states of society the breaking
out of war is the signal for every other disorder; and
Madura soon became the scene of frightful outrage.
Native banditti and hordes of savage Indians from the
interior traversed the country; fire and the sword destroyed whole villages; and the inhabitants being unable to take vengeance on the real aggressors, the tide
of popular fury set in against the Christians.   Thus it
was that in many cases prosperous missions had to be
given up, and the trembling Christians fled to celebrate
the rites of religion in secret places.   Solitary chapels
rose up in the depths of the forest, or by the lone river-
side, and thither the faithful repaired with their beloved
pastor.   But here they were exposed to a danger from
which they had been free in the cities.   The fury of
the inundations rendered their retreats exceedingly perilous.   An instance of this occurred near the river
Coralam, where the Christians, who had been driven
from Ginghi, erected a chapel.   De Britto was praying in the chapel with sixteen of his flock, when the cry
was raised that the building was surrounded with
water.   They tried to dam the water out, but unsuc-

cessfully; and were compelled to construct a raft out of the beams of the roof, and upon that they floated to a wood at a little distance, situated on an eminence. There they intended to remain till the flood subsided; but they had no food; and even their place of security threatened to fail them, for the waters run with terrible rapidity, and almost covered the hill; so one of the Christians, at the risk of his life, swam back to the chapel, and succeeded in obtaining a little rice; this, along with some bitter herbs, which they procured with difficulty, was all their sustenance during the three days they were encompassed by the floods. But this was not all; they were attacked by an immense number of serpents, which, driven out of their holes by the water, sought the same place of safety as the Christians. But throughout his missionary career our blessed martyr enjoyed that power over venomous beasts which our Saviour promised among other miraculous gifts to His followers, and the serpents were unable to hurt them. Power over serpents gives its possessor an unbounded influence with the Indians; and this terrible situation of the little band of Christians, being perfectly well understood by the idolaters, procured for De Britto a wonderful reputation. When the waters subsided, the Christians returned to their chapel, and found it almost swept away; but the foundations remained, and they set to work with such vigour, that in a short time the walls were raised again, and the chapel was ready for the Christmas solemnity. Fath r de Britto, with streaming eyes, thanked God for their escape, and besought Him to look down with pity upon the struggling society, and prosper the career of Christ in his lands.

Amid all the trials he had to endure, he enjoyed also great consolations in the constancy of his flock. A poor boy fell ill after baptism: the parents attributed his sickness to some poison in the water, or some magic in the form of words, and besought him to conciliate the gods by his return to their worship. The heroic had refused; and by the invocation of St. Francis Xavier, his holy father patron, he obtained a sudden and complete cure, to the utter astonishment of his friends.

On another occasion, a dying idolater became a Christian. When he died, an idolatrous priest in the house exclaimed that he saw the convert's soul ascending to heaven in glory. Thirty of the idolaters were instantly converted, and the Christians confirmed by this involuntary homage of a bitter adversary.

The miracles which the blessed father wrought were very numerous. He cast out many devils; he freed the fields from ravaging insects; averted hurricanes; made barren lands fertile; stopped the overflowing of rivers; and, more miraculous still, converted in a few months an immense number of idolaters.

In consequence of his wonderful success, his superiors would have made him rector of Ambalacata. This preferment he evaded; but he accepted the post of superior of both districts of the mission, as involving not more honour, but increased labour. His journeys now became longer and more arduous, and under infinite danger from soldiers and robbers. He walked on foot, and was detained neither by the heat of the sun nor the floods of the rainy season. Rocky mountains, sandy plains, dense forests, broad and rapid rivers, these were the obstacles he had to surmount. He wore a hair-shirt, he walked barefoot, and slept on the ground. But God sometimes miraculously assisted him. Once having to cross a river, he was ferried over by an angel. But he endured terrible hardships: for twenty-five days death stared him in the face; he was thrice shipwrecked; and he was exposed to great dangers from the idolaters. At Madura, as he was preparing for baptism 200 catechumens, a band of armed men rushed upon him and took him prisoner. They struck him with their fists and with sticks, and kicked him, and threw him into a dungeon with his hands tied behind his back. But God suffered them not to hurt him; and after trying to terrify him with threats of death, they at length let him go. The risk he ran from the heathen in no way checked his zeal; every fresh imprisonment raised his courage, as showing that God was mightier than his enemies, and could deliver him. He therefore ventured even into Tanjore, where the persecution was raging more violently than any where else; and that in spite of the tears and entreaties of the Christians, who protested he was only going to certain death. Martyrdom had been from his earliest noviciate his dearest wish, so that representations of danger only fired his apostolic ardour. But at Tanjore, where he had been threatened with death, he succeeded in putting a stop to the persecution altogether.

CHAPTER V.

FATHER DE BRITTO'S SUFFERINGS AT MANGALAM, AND RETURN TO PORTUGAL.

JOURNEYING northward, he made a stay at Marava of three months, in the year 1686, during which he baptised more than 2000 idolaters; but notwithstanding his success he was anxious to get on, in consequence of the accounts which reached him of the ripeness of the natives for Christianity still farther north. This anxiety was the cause of a long and painful imprisonment.

At Mangalam the idolaters laid wait for the missionary, and seized him as he was entering the gates of the city. They bound him hand and foot with iron chains, and conducted him immediately to the presence of General Conmara, the first minister of state of the King of Marava. This man had an implacable hatred of the Gospel of Jesus Christ, and an especial spite against the now celebrated servant of God; and when he beheld him, he grinned with a savage joy at the opportunity which he had at length obtained of satiating his cruelty. The father was first accused of being a magician—this was on account of his wonderful miracles; but he meekly answered that he was under no guidance of the spirit of darkness, but that he preached the law of the true God, the Maker of heaven and earth. The judge then addressed the two catechists and other churchmen who were taken with him :

"And you," he said, " what do you say?"

"We say the same," they replied.

For which answer they were all condemned to be scourged, unless they would acknowledge Sheeva. And so cruelly were they scourged, that some of them died from its effects. The tyrant then ordered them to be confined in dungeons, and loaded with irons. Afterwards he tried to shake the constancy of de Britto, believing that if he could gain over the leader the rest would follow. After heaping upon him insults and reproaches, he desired him to sprinkle his forehead with ashes consecrated to the idols, as that would have been tantamount to an acknowledgment of their divinity; the saint of course refused, and the judge in a fury exclaimed that he would have him torn limb from limb.

"Oh," cried the father, " when shall I enjoy so great a happiness?"

He was then beaten again, and taken back to his dungeon, from which lest he should escape by magic, he was laden with irons and tied to a pillar.

On the fourth day, the persecutors tried a new kind of torture, common enough in that country. The sufferer is taken to the bank of a river, and a cord is fastened to his feet; his hands are tied behind his back, and he is then allowed to fall into the water; then an executioner jumps upon his back, and with his whole weight presses the poor victim to the bottom, where he is kept till he is almost dead; then he is dragged out gasping for breath, and before he has recovered is cast in again; and so on, at the pleasure of his executioners, always being dragged out before life is extinct. It is horrible torture, and enough to overcome the staunchest courage. Up to this moment all the companions of the blessed father had remained stedfast; but now one of them, unhappily, entreated the executioners to let him loose. The unhappy man saved his life at the expense of his faith; and this defection of a Christian caused the father more real pain than all the bodily torture which he himself had to endure. He exhorted the others to remain stedfast, and none of them fell away. One of them, Valentine, a catechist, signalised himself by the most heroic fortitude.

After enduring farther hardships for some days, the father and his fellow-sufferers were brought into the judgment-hall, where all sorts of instruments had been laid out to terrify their minds,—axes, scourges, torches, pincers, knives, and all the horrible apparatus of torture. The sight of these things, however, inspired them with fresh courage, and a more vehement desire for martyrdom; and as the spectacle had only been produced to impress their minds, they were led back again, the better rather than the worse for what they had seen. But the next day an order came for the execution; and they were taken to Paganari to be tortured and put to death, unless they would offer worship to Sheevah. The executioners began with Valentine; and after they had cruelly used the heroic catechist, they led him, full of wounds and with one of his eyes forced out, to Father de Britto, and taunted the father with being the cause of the poor man's torments.

"He is a happy man," said Father de Britto; "when will you do the like for me?"

Amazed at fortitude such as this, the executioners perceived that while the father lived they could effect nothing by tormenting the disciples; and leaving Valentine alone, they cast themselves upon Father de Britto. Valentine's sufferings had been very great, but they had reserved a special and more cruel torture for the blessed father. Hard by was a flag of pumice-stone, which the sun had heated up to blister-heat; after beating the missionary violently, they stripped off his clothes and laid him down upon this burning stone; eight of the executioners then jumped upon his body, so as to press the sharp and heated points into his back, already raw with the scourges; and then they took him by the feet and shoulders, and rubbed him up and down till his back was entirely excoriated. In this miserable plight he was left to scorch in the sun, to die the death of a dog; but a charitable idolater, at the risk of his own life, at length dragged him into the shade; and a storm coming on, his murder was deferred till the following day, and he was thrown back into his dungeon more dead than alive. Valentine's eye was miraculously cured by the blessed father.

The most ignominious death which a criminal can die in that country is by impalement; and the idolaters determined to stamp Christianity in India with infamy by subjecting its ministers to this punishment. The next morning Father de Britto and his companions were marshalled for the execution: in front marched a detachment of armed men; then followed the man of God in irons, with his eyes raised to heaven and his face beaming with joy; last came the executioners and an immense crowd of people. But Almighty God had yet work for him to do, and suspended the blow as it was about to fall. A messenger arrived from court, bearing an order to General Conmara to come immediately to the capital with all his forces, as an insurrection had broken out against the government. At this news confusion and disorder spread every where; the crowd dispersed, the soldiers made ready to march, and the officers of justice retraced their steps with their prisoner. But they revenged themselves upon him for their disappointment by ill-usage of every kind. At last, after three weeks, he was ordered up to Kamanadabouram, the capital, to see the prince.

On his arrival, he was to his astonishment received with favour by Prince Ranganadademen. He made the missionary sit by his side, and explain the principal doctrines and practices of the Christian religion. The holy man recited the Decalogue, and showed from it the wisdom of the law of God with so much grace and power, that the prince exclaimed that no man ought to be injured for teaching such doctrines. The law of the Christian was a good law; it ordained what was virtuous—it condemned what was vicious. The holy father began to hope that the prince would become a convert himself. The prince went on: "I grant you your liberty, and your companions may go also: worship your God and preach His law; but do not preach it in my country. It is an excellent law; but it forbids stealing and polygamy, so it will not suit my subjects. If you dare to disobey me, depend upon it I will cut off your head." Thus De Britto obtained his liberty; and as he thought it best to obey the prince's injunctions, he left Marava.

When Father Rodriguez, Provincial of Malabar, heard of the liberation of De Britto, he summoned him to the pearl-fishery coast, to regain his strength after there labours. He obeyed, though he would rather have continued in the mission while any life or strength remained to him. But his journey to the coast had been ordered by God. Father François Palo, who was returning to Europe in his capacity of procurator of Malabar, had been shipwrecked; and Father de Britto was sent home in his place. He left the fishery in 1687; and after a voyage of ten months, including a stoppage at Goa, he reached Lisbon in September 1688, having been absent fourteen years and a half.

CHAPTER VI.

FATHER DE BRITTO'S STAY IN EUROPE, AND RETURN TO INDIA.

On the news of his arrival, the whole city rose to greet him, for the fame of his sanctity and heroism had reached Portugal long before. The king, whose page he had been, the infanta Isabella Louisa, the ministers of state and the grandees, the people and the religious orders, all showed him a thousand marks of respect and honour.

He maintained in Portugal the same mortified habits which he had formed in India, wore the same dress, used the same food, and slept on the bare ground. He set about the work upon which he had been sent home with great diligence; and in the college of the Jesuits which he visited, he awoke an extraordinary enthusiasm among the young men: even old priests were seized with the same fervour. Of the volunteers, Father de Britto selected six, and to that number he added several who had been missionaries, but were now occupying chairs in different universities, and whom he wanted to argue with the Brahmins.

Having once selected his band, he commenced instructing them in the details of their work; and when all things were ready, and he had obtained larger funds for the support of this increase to his mission from the king, they set sail for India in 1690: but not without great opposition; for the King of Portugal would have retained him at home, first to superintend the education of his son, and then to be promoted to a bishopric—both of which *persecutions*, however, as he called them, he happily surmounted. They started with a favourable wind, and the voyage was at first prosperous; but presently they were detained by a calm, when their provisions became tainted, and fever broke out. The holy father fell ill, and two of his missionaries died. De Britto, writing home, gave a horrible account of that voyage, and the miseries they endured from the sickness of the crew, the stench of the vessel, the heat and cold, the contrary winds, the incessant fatigues which they all had to suffer: his great humility attributed them all to his own sins.

On their arrival at Goa, his return was celebrated by the whole college of Santa Fé and the Christians there with rejoicings. After a short stay, he passed on to see the Provincial at the pearl-fishery, with whom he held a council on the plan of his future campaign. In consequence of the maturity of judgment which the father displayed on this occasion he was nominated visitor of the mission, and immediately after Easter he set out for Madura on his new charge. Then he visited in succession all the stations, encouraged the missionaries, confirmed the faithful, and converted a great number of idolaters to the faith of Christ. But his chief longings were in the direction of Marava, where he hoped to find that palm and crown of martyrdom which five years before had fallen from his grasp. Thither accordingly he bent his steps.

The kings of Marava and Madura were still at war; and all the sufferings which he had formerly experienced under the same circumstances awaited him now upon his second arrival. Soldiers and banditti were ravaging the country, and he and his flock were compelled to skulk about in the woods. It is difficult to realise the sufferings which the holy father endured for several months with so much joy and resignation. It was his zeal for the salvation of sinners, and the numerous conversions with which God accredited his mission, that supported him under all. We should scarcely be able to credit the fact, if it had not been asserted on oath by one of the catechists in the processes of Beatification. In the short space of ten days the blessed father administered Baptism with his own hand to twelve thousand idolaters; and more than once his right hand fell powerless through fatigue.

He established his head-quarters in the principality of Mouni, on the borders of Marava. In order to obtain for the Maravians a proper place for celebrating the holy mysteries, he chose a thick forest not far from Mouni, and there constructed three chapels, to which catechists were attached for the instruction of the converts in Christian doctrine; and at night the holy father came to administer the Sacraments. In a short time he gained to the faith a vast number of the heathen,—not the vulgar only, not mere pariahs, or even Shusters, but Brahmins of the highest class, and nobility about the royal court. And Almighty God deigned to confirm the faith of these converts by the most extraordinary miracles. By the mere touch of the father devils were cast out, and the sick cured. The same power was possessed even by the catechists and neophytes. They read the Gospel over the sick, and made the sign of the Cross, and God restored them to health.

The report of these wonderful cures reached the ears of Prince Teriadeven, the real heir to the throne of Marava, now in the possession of Prince Ranganadeven the Usurper, a young man who had before shown some signs of favour towards Christianity. Being taken ill, he sent to the blessed father to come and heal him. The father did not go at once himself, but sent one of his catechists, to instruct the prince in the elements of Christian doctrine, and exhort him to put his whole trust in Jesus Christ, as at once the Saviour of soul and body. The catechist went and read the Gospel to him, made him repeat the Apostles' Creed, and that instant his sickness left him.

Awed by the sudden miracle of which he had been the subject, the prince no longer delayed his resolution, but expressed his readiness at once to be baptised. He sent to the father and desired to be made a Christian, and was the more confirmed in his desire when he had witnessed on the feast of Epiphany a large assembly of the faithful, and the holy sacrament of Baptism conferred upon two hundred catechumens. But the missionary, who knew him to be possessed of five wives, replied that he could not conscientiously grant him so great a favour until he had put away all except one, with the firm resolution of adhering to her alone for the remainder of his life. The noble Indian upon the spot sent for his wives, selected the first of the five, who wished herself to be a Christian, and informed the others of the resolution he had taken in consequence of

his miraculous cure by the holy missionary. "Since,"
said he, "the holy law of Christ will not permit me to
retain you all, I give you four the choice of returning
to your parents or of remaining in the palace, where
you shall be treated as befits your rank." Stupified at
this announcement, they scarcely knew what to answer,
and assailed the prince, now with tears and caresses,
then with threats and reproaches; but nothing could
change his resolution,—that he said was irrevocable;
and they went away transported with fury against
Father de Britto, whom they looked upon as the author
of their calamity.

Teriadeven received baptism solemnly with two
hundred of his court. This was in the beginning of
1693, in which year the holy father celebrated Epiphany in the palace of Teriadeven. Immediately after
the ceremony he returned to Mouni, where a great multitude were waiting to be baptised. The joy of the
Church was raised to its highest pitch by these glorious
conversions, and by the prospect of greater still, when
suddenly there burst out the most terrible persecution
that had yet fallen upon them. It confused in its fury
the whole of that infant society, and tore from them
their sole support, the holy father, to whom they owed
their birth unto Jesus Christ, and whose hour of martyrdom had at length arrived.

CHAPTER VII.

THE MARTYRDOM OF FATHER DE BRITTO.

THE fury of heathen bigotry was now to be fanned
by the excitement of female jealousy. In every one of
the four wives put away by Prince Teriadeven, Father
de Britto had raised up an enemy, who would be satisfied with no sacrifice short of his life. But among them
all the youngest, who happened to be the usurper's

F

niece, was the most furious. In a transport of rage she
ran to Ramanadabouram to see her uncle, all dishevelled
and in tears, and told him of the outrage she had suffered from the European pandarish.   Then she appealed to the Brahmins, who hated him too bitterly to
remain deaf to her cries. They had long nourished
their thirst for revenge, and now they saw an opportunity of slaking it. A solemn consultation was held as
to the best course to be pursued, and it was decided
that they should go in a body to the king, and make a
formal complaint against Father de Britto.   They
selected Pomparanam to be their spokesman, an old
man, and very spiteful, who pronounced a set speech on
the occasion. He first urged upon him the danger of
the vengeance of the gods; then he pleaded the disgrace to himself, if during his reign the ancient religion
should pass away; then he inveighed against the enor-
mity of the doctrine itself which could thus violate the
most sacred ties, and interfere between husband and
wife. "Ah!" cried Pomparanam, in conclusion, "down
with this enemy of the gods, or we and you will perish
together."

The king saw perfectly well through the motives of
the Brahmins in thus taking up the woman's cause;
but as the honour of his own family was concerned in
the person of his niece, he acceded to their request.
He ordered the Christians to be fined, and their houses
to be burnt. The father had foreseen the storm that
was gathering, and had warned his flock of the danger,
but they all refused to fly.   They determined to stand
by their dear master, upon whom they knew the great
fury of the persecution would fall, and if God required
it, die with him.   The king despatched four companies
of soldiers to seize the missionary. Three of them advanced to the chapels which he had built in the woods,
where they arrested the catechists who were in charge
of them. The fourth hastened to Mouni, and there they
found the holy father.   It was the morning of the 8th
of January, and he was offering, as was his wont, the

Holy Sacrifice, when God revealed to him what was coming; and after Mass he addressed the people, and said that those who had not courage to give up their lives in testimony to the faith of Jesus Christ, had better depart at once and hide themselves. He pronounced these words in so decided and significant a manner, that they all perceived he had received some definite intelligence, and, seized with a sudden panic, they all dispersed except one Brahmin, a convert, and two children, who preferred remaining with him. The evening of that day warning came of the approach of a troop of mounted soldiery. He knew their errand, and raising his eyes towards heaven, he offered up his life as a sacrifice to God, and went forth to meet them. They seized him violently, and after heaping upon him blows and insults, they led him off with his three companions.

At Anoumandacouri, a neighbouring village, there was being celebrated, in the presence of 10,000 heathens and idolaters, a grand festival to one of their gods. Hither they drag the Christian victims, and when they arrive, harness them to the triumphal car on which the idol is being carried. Loaded with chains, they are forced to accompany the procession all the day, exposed to the jeers of the multitude, and fainting for want of food and loss of blood; and then they are left the whole night. The next day they are taken eleven miles to the royal city of Ramanadabouram, and here the saint is incarcerated in a filthy hovel, and with him the three catechists who had been arrested in the forest chapels. The holy father embraced them, and with tears of joy kissed their chains, and exhorted them to continue firm to the end. They, like him, rejoiced at the near prospect of martyrdom. The heroism of the two children is especially recorded. They animated each other to suffer torments and give up their lives for Jesus Christ.

They were all kept in prison for several days, and treated with great rigour. Teriadeven only heard of their captivity when it was too late to avert it; but he gave orders that they should be treated with kindness till the king's wishes should be known. Those orders, however, were not attended to, and the brutal jailors amused themselves with their sufferings, and fed them with food which the soldiers rejected.

At last the prisoners were brought before the chief minister of state. A small crucifix had been found upon De Britto, and the judge asked him what that image represented. "It is the image of my God," said the father, "who being immortal and impassible in his own nature, was made man, and died upon such a cross as that to rescue us from the slavery of the devil and from sin." At these words the impious wretch threw it down upon the ground in contempt, and stamped upon it with his feet to crush it in pieces. The holy man, although chained and bound, fell upon his knees, shuddering at his sacrilegious wickedness, and crawling with difficulty up to the crucifix, pressed it to his breast, and watered it with tears in reparation of the insult. There was a great crowd of spectators present, who regarded this action as a contempt of court, and they loudly demanded sentence. But the judge, not knowing what to say, ordered the confessors back to prison, and there they remained for a month, suffering as much as ever.

Prince Teriadeven boldly pleaded their cause before the king, in face of the personal danger he incurred by his advocacy of the Christians. Rangadaneven, in a rage, ordered him at once to adore the gods. The prince refused, and said he would rather die than again offer the worship to idols which was due only to Jesus Christ. The tyrant answered that he would soon show which religion was the most powerful, and forthwith gave orders to the magicians to prepare a certain incantation considered infallible in its operation, by which the missionary should lose his life without visible agency. The incantation failed, to the shame of the king, and the discomfiture of his idolatrous priests; and Father de Britto was sent for, and asked whether the failure of the sorcerers was owing to the enchanted book, meaning the breviary, which he was still allowed to retain in his possession. The missionary replied that that book was devoted to the praise of God, and to nothing so hateful as sorcery. The tyrant, in a rage at him, ordered the book to be hung round his neck, while the executioners shot at him in the market-place: "And we shall see," said he, "whether your God can deliver you." He was led away, and the soldiers were taking aim, when Teriadeven broke through their ranks, and ordered them to desist. They obeyed, knowing him to be the true owner of the crown; and as he was very popular, the tyrant feared a revolt if he should persist in the execution, especially as on the blank leaves of the breviary were written the names of the converts who had been baptised. The king feared that having so many thousand Christians on his side, the father was depending on their rescue. His death was accordingly again deferred; and the tyrant ordered him to be sent to Oureiadeven, his brother, who lived at Orejour, a distance of two days' journey from the court, with instructions to put him to death as soon as he arrived.

The father rejoiced when he heard where he was going, for he knew that it was to die; but he wept at leaving his dear companions,—they separated, never more to meet again in this world. So touching was the parting scene, that the very pagans could not restrain their tears. Prince Teriadeven accompanied him a good part of the way. He had to travel barefoot, tightly bound and surrounded with guards, who hurried him on beyond walking pace, over rocks and briers, through sand and brushwood. The blood gushed from the wounds he had received in his prison, and from his torn and blistered feet; and instead of receiving pity from these wretches, they added railleries and taunts. On his journey, the Christians assembled to see him pass, and receive his blessing. He exhorted them to take courage and stand firm, and then turned towards his executioners, and preached the faith to them.

He arrived at Orejour on the last day of January,

and was immediately taken before Oureiardeven, the
king's brother. This prince laboured under an incurable
leprosy, and other loathsome diseases. Now he knew
of the missionary's gift of miracles, and doubted not
that he would gladly purchase his life by exerting it.
The father replied, that it appertained to God alone to
cure diseases; all that he could do was to apply the
remedies, and entreat Almighty God to bless them;
and he added, that if he desired to be made whole of his
bodily disease, he must first heal the sickness of his
soul, by abjuring his false gods, and accepting the true
faith. The prince mastered his passion at this reply,
and went on to offer the missionary all sorts of rewards,
if he would give up Jesus Christ and worship Sheeva.
When he saw that nothing could move the holy man,
he turned to one of his suite named Margharittei, and
bade him cut off his head upon the spot. Margharittei
answered, that he was a Christian himself, and nothing
would induce him to imbrue his hands in innocent
blood. Then the prince's own wife rushed in, and
threatened her husband with the judgments of heaven if
he dared to execute the sentence of the king. Moved
by these remonstrances, he ordered the servant of God
to be carried back to his dungeon.

As soon as this got abroad, the Brahmins, fearing
that their prey might escape their hands, went to the
governor of the town, who was a bitter enemy of the
Christians, and represented the case to him. Mourou-
gapapoullei, for that was his name, instantly demanded
an audience of the prince, and in the strongest terms
reproached him for his weakness and lukewarmness in
obeying the commands of the king. That was sufficient;
the cowardly prince gave in for fear of the king's
displeasure, and granted the governor leave to execute
the sentence of death. It was on the morning of the
4th of February, being Ash-Wednesday, that the servant
of God was apprised of his immediate death. At the
joyful news, so long and ardently desired, his whole
countenance lighted up; he fell on his knees, and re-

turned thanks to God. Then rising up, he said to the
executioners, " See, I am ready to go ;" and he began to
walk towards the place of martyrdom. He had neither his arms tied behind his back nor gyves upon his
wrists ; he walked without restraint, and with his breviary hanging from his neck ; he walked thither en-
tranced with joy, almost beside himself with rapture at
the glory before him, with his eyes fixed on the skies,
and his steps so rapid that his guards were compelled
to stop him more than once that they might not be left
behind. All along the road a multitude of the faithful
were waiting to see him pass, and greeted him with
tears. But when they saw him they were comforted :
a calmness so unutterable, a joy so heavenly, sat upon
his face. The heathens themselves were astonished,
and said one to another, " One would think he was
going to a feast, and not to a terrible death."

  · The spot which had been selected for the martyrdom was a little hill by the bank of the river, not
far from the city. When arrived here he was allowed
by the guards an unexpected boon, to retire for a short
time to pray. The executioner arriving by accident
just at that moment, and seeing the servant of God absorbed in prayer, was afraid to disturb him, and let him
pray on. More than a quarter of an hour had elapsed
when the son of the prince ran up and reprimanded the
executioner for his delay in executing the sentence.
Then the holy man approached the side of the river,
and, after embracing the executioner, knelt down, and
holding out his head, he said, " I am ready ; do as you
are commanded." The executioner drew his scymitar,
and raising his arm, was about to give the fatal blow,
when he perceived the martyr's reliquary hanging by
a cord from his neck. Taking it for granted that it
was some charm which would ward off the stroke, he
had first to remove it ; but he durst not take it away
with his hand, lest he should be bewitched. He therefore severed the string with the scymitar, and made a
frightful gash on the breast and shoulder. The holy

martyr offered to God the first fruits of his sacrifice;
and then the executioner, no longer fearing any amulet
to turn the edge of his weapon, raised the scymitar, and
hewed off his head.   At that moment Almighty God
testified by a miracle to the holiness of his servant.
The head and body, instead of falling forward as they
would naturally have done, fell backwards, to the great
astonishment of the spectators.

This glorious triumph of the faith of Jesus Christ
took place at Marava on the 4th of February, 1693.

After Father de Britto's death the executioner
drove a stake into the ground, on which he impaled
the body; and having cut off the hands and feet, he
hung them, along with the head, from the waist; and
this ignominious spectacle was kept up for several days
as a terror to Christians, and a warning to all not to
forsake Sheeva.   The faithful tried hard to obtain possession of the relics, but in vain; they were too well
guarded by the soldiers.   His crucifix the martyr had
given to a faithful convert, who transmitted it to Father
Laine, and from his hands it reached his professed
house in Paris.   And all that could be collected of the
clothing, writing, objects of devotion, and instruments
of penance were forwarded to the same father, by whom
they were laid up in the Jesuit Church at Pondicherry,
and thence they found their way to Goa.   But it was
some time before any fragments of the body fell into
the hands of the Christians.   Even the cassock and
staff, the cord and scymitar which had been used in the
execution, were jealously kept by the idolaters; they
kept them, as they said, because they were so valuable
against the attacks of evil spirits and against diseases.
The soldiers, as we said, kept guard over the body
while it remained impaled on the stake; but at last a
violent storm came on, and the cord which supported
the head and hands broke; the head rolled into the
river, and was saved; but wild beasts preyed upon the
body.   It is remarkable that this was the very desire
of the martyr himself.   When the soldiers had retired,

the catechists came and gathered up all they could find of the body. In the river they discovered the head; they bought the stake on which his limbs had been impaled of the soldiers, and the scymitar of the executioner: this scymitar Father John de Corte brought with him to Europe a few years afterwards, and presented it to the king of Portugal, Pedro II. And these are all the relics that remain of the Blessed Father John de Britto.

V.

THE NUNS OF MINSK.

OR three centuries there has been established in Poland a Greek Church in connection with the Holy See; and bitter is
the hatred with which it has been uniformly regarded by the Russian government. Of late years more strenuous efforts
than ever have been made to oblige or to
persuade the Roman Catholics to forsake
the true fold, and unite themselves to the
national establishment of Russia, — the
Greek Schismatics. In some instances these
efforts have unhappily been successful;
and about ten or twelve years since, even
three bishops apostatised, taking with
them a considerable portion of the people. These
bishops were immediately rewarded with high honour
and emoluments; and they spared no exertions to ir-
gratiate themselves still further with their imperial
master, by bringing over, if possible, the faithful
remnant of their late flocks. Siemaszko, the apostate
bishop of Minsk, especially distinguished himself in this
unhallowed labour; and the following narrative may
be relied upon as supplying details of the almost incredible brutalities of which he was guilty in his endea-

vours to overcome the constancy of a religious community in his diocese.

CHAPTER I.

EXPULSION OF THE NUNS FROM MINSK, AND SUFFERINGS AT WITEBSK.

AT the time of the apostacy of Siemaszko there was a convent of Basilian nuns in the town, who employed themselves, under their rule, in the service of God, the instruction of children, and the relief of the poor. They were called the Daughters of the Holy Trinity; and the Superior was the reverend Mother Irena-Macrina-Mieczyslainska, or Mother Macrina, as we shall more briefly call her. Their piety, goodness, and charity had endeared them to the country round; but Siemaszko only hated them the more on account of their very virtues, and was determined to gain them over to the schism at any cost; for he well knew that to gain them would be to gain the whole town. The emperor had empowered him to deal with his refractory diocese *as the interests of religion might require,* a phrase, the true significance of which will appear from the sequel; and he had issued an ukase, or decree, putting at the disposal of the bishop military force, if it should be required.

Mother Macrina saw in this decree the death-warrant of her community, either in this world or in the next, according as they should have courage to hold out for the love of Christ, or the weakness to yield; and she assembled her nuns and put before them the choice. They were not long in deciding; and when Siemaszko summoned them to surrender their faith, they with one voice refused to obey. He was furious at their refusal, but said that the emperor would allow them three months to reconsider their determination.

Mother Macrina proposed to the Sisters that they should seek some safer asylum till the storm blew over. "And you," said they, "what will you do?" "I," she replied with angelic sweetness, but invincible determination, "I will die at my post, if I am not snatched from it by force." "Then let us hear no more of flight," they rejoined; "for our duty is to die at your side." So they all resolved to bear patiently the worst.

Three days had scarcely elapsed when Siemaszko, accompanied by the civil governor of Minsk and an armed troop, broke into the convent at five o'clock in the morning, just as the nuns were leaving their cells to assemble in choir. The soldiers placed themselves at the doors of their rooms to prevent their going back into them, and then Siemaszko harangued them as follows: "By his majesty's order I gave you three months; but I come at the third day, for the evil might become worse. This is the last moment of liberty you will have. You may still choose between the riches you now possess, in addition to those which the magnanimity of the emperor is ready to add to them, if you join the orthodox religion; and the hardship of Siberia if you persist in your refusal."

"Well then, we choose the best," was the immediate answer; "namely, labour in Siberia rather than abandon Jesus Christ and His Vicar."

"Wait a while," he replied, with a sneer, "and you will tell a different tale: when the knout has taken off the skin you were born in, and another skin has covered your bones, you will have become more tractable."

After kneeling to take leave of Jesus in the blessed Sacrament,—a consolation granted them by the civil governor, although refused by Siemaszko,—the nuns rose to depart: one only remained upon her knees; her Sisters proceeded to raise her, but she was dead; her heart had broken at being driven away from her peaceful retirement, where she had served God for thirty years.

On leaving the church, Mother Macrina threw herself at the governor's feet, and entreated his permission to carry a crucifix away with them. Siemaszko tried to prevent it, and had himself snatched from their hands a crucifix of silver, and enriched with precious stones, which contained the relics of St. Basil; but the governor allowed them to take one made of wood, and which they ordinarily used in the processions. Notwithstanding its weight, Mother Macrina carried it, resting on her left shoulder, from Minsk to Witebsk; and the more she suffered from the pressure, the more she loved the sacred wound on the left shoulder of Jesus, where the Cross rested during His passage to Calvary.

The nuns were chained two and two together. The first day they were driven fifteen leagues, and most of the Sisters sank again and again from exhaustion; nevertheless they were urged on, and in seven days they arrived at Witebsk. There they were lodged in a convent of "black nuns," as they were called. These were mostly widows of Russian soldiers, and women of abandoned character. The house itself had belonged to a community of Basilian Sisters, who had been turned out to make way for these "black nuns;" and fourteen of them were now found in irons by Mother Macrina. At their request she adopted them as her own daughters, and from that time they shared all the sufferings of the Nuns of Minsk. Their daily life was in this fashion: Before six o'clock in the morning they had to sweep the house, light the fires, and prepare the wood and water for the house; then for six hours they had to break stones, and wheel them away in barrows, to which they were chained; from twelve to one they were allowed to rest; then hard labour again till dark, when they were required to attend the cattle and finish the household work. Their sufferings were greatly aggravated by the wanton cruelty of the "black nuns," who purposely soiled the house and upset the water. The labours of the day over, they were shut up in their prison without having their irons taken off. It was cold and damp, and their only bed was a little straw; but to make up for all, they had their crucifix. At its

feet they knelt at night, saying their office, and praying for the conversion of the emperor, allowing themselves sometimes only two hours for sleep.

Their food was so miserable, that in summer they
lived on herbs, and in winter on what was given to the
animals. But the "black nuns" grudged them even
this, saying that "they did not deserve even pigs'
meat." Nor was this all: notwithstanding the severity
of a Polish winter, they were allowed no fuel, so that
their limbs were often frozen, and their wounds became
more and more tender.

Not the least part of their sufferings was the loss of
holy communion; and they lamented the absence of their
old director Michalewicz, whom they had not seen since
they left Minsk; when, therefore, one day he entered
their cell, they ran to meet him with cries of joy. But
they were immediately repulsed by the strange expression upon his countenance. They did not know that
he had apostatised, and that he came not to administer
the comfort of the sacraments, but at Siemaszko's bidding,
who had counted much on his influence to persuade them
to desist from their opposition. They received his sug-
gestion with the more horror that they had once regarded
him with so much love; and he became, as we shall
presently see, the most bitter of their persecutors.

Siemaszko was determined to put an end to the
struggle by some decisive step. With this view he
ordered them to be scourged. Michalewicz, to whom
the execution of the order was committed, increased the
severity of the torture. Instead of thirty lashes, he
made the number fifty, and had the floggings repeated
twice a week. On every Wednesday and Saturday all
the Sisters underwent this fearful infliction; and he stood
by and watched for some sigh or groan, in token of
submission, but in vain. He heard nought but the
prayer, "By Thy cross and passion, Jesus, save my soul!"
which each Sister uttered at every lash. When he heard
it not, it was because heaven had opened its gates to
receive another martyr.

The Sisters prepared themselves for the scourging by meditation on the Passion of Jesus Christ: they were compelled to witness each other's sufferings; but all the while the torture lasted, they thought they saw Him scourged, and gathered strength rather than terror from the sight. Their greatest pain was, that this scourging was carried on in the presence of the Russian clergy and other men. But even this grief too only united them the more closely to the shame of Jesus.

"What," said some one to Mother Macrina, "did you not utter a single cry during all these horrible tortures?" "No," she replied, "we were too much engaged in prayer: only at first we prayed at the top of our voice, then in a more subdued tone, and at length sometimes," she added with tears, "not at all; and then we knew that the blows fell upon a corpse." "But did not nature sometimes rebel?" "Yes; but with the help of God, we became used to every thing; at first the scourging *was* terrible to look forward to, but after a time we all came up, each in her turn, to receive the lashes without being called." And yet pieces of flesh adhered to the scourges, and the torture continued for a whole month!

The first who died from the scourging was Sister Columba; she was dragged from the torture to her labour, and died immediately. Sister Susan expired under the lash, and Sister Sitauva the following night, with her eyes fixed on the crucifix, and her head resting on the knees of Mother Macrina. Nor were these three the only martyrs. Sister Baptista was burnt alive by the "black nuns," who, it is believed, were in a state of intoxication at the time; and Sister Népomucene was killed by a blow on the head; another Sister, Coletta, had her ribs broken, and died in consequence.

But still the constancy of the survivors remained unshaken; and Michalewicz, who had promised Siemaszko that in a short time he would bring them all over, began to receive reproaches, not unmixed with threats, for his delay. Accordingly, he hit upon another plan: he

divided the Sisters into four different bands, and shut
them up separately, in the hope that he should then
have less difficulty with them.   The place in which he
confined Mother Macrina, with eight of her nuns, was a
cave so damp that the whole place swarmed with worms,
which crawled all over their persons, and into their
mouths, ears, and noses, if for a moment they tried to
compose themselves to sleep.   They had only putrid
vegetables given them to eat; but yet they were happier
than they had been since they had left Minsk, and they
composed a hymn, which they sung continually, and of
which we venture to offer a translation :

" My God, it is Thy will: the burden sore
                        Thou dost ordain;
    For Thee we suffer: still, to suffer more,
                        Our strength sustain.
    Torn from Thy house by traitors, where so sweet
                        The toil each day,
    Whom shall we ask for pity? at whose feet
                        Our sorrows lay?
    My God, look down upon our country; turn
                        To joy our care,
    And schism from her people bid her spurn:
                        'Tis all our prayer.
    Suffer! ye servants of the Lord.   Who, staunch and true,
                        Still perseveres,
    One day the triumph of the faith shall view,
                        And dry his tears.
    Then shall we break our bands—then burst the chains
                        That bind us fast.
    Thy blessed will be done.   In heaven remains
                        Our crown at last."

Michalewicz wrote to Siemaszko that they were all
ready to recant, and he promised to come immediately
and receive their abjuration.   In the meanwhile he
redoubled his efforts to make his words good, going
round to all the dungeons with a paper for the poor
inmates to sign, to which he declared that the others
had already given in their adhesion.

"He lies," said Mother Macrina; "the wretch, he
lies!   No one has signed; of that I am certain.   Give

me the paper!" and she tore it from his hands. Not a signature was there. Pale with shame, Michalewicz clutched up a handful of filth, stuffed it into her mouth, and then slunk away.

The next time that they found themselves altogether with their wheelbarrows, they saluted each other with unspeakable joy, and fell on their knees to thank God for another victory, singing the *Te Deum*. " Now, my children," said Mother Macrina, cheerfully, " we have had a good rest; let us try and work hard. To work! to work!"

When Siemaszko arrived to pay the Sisters the promised visit, he addressed Macrina as mother-general, and brought with him a superb cross from the emperor; but when he went on to say that he came at their invitation, they thought he was raving; at the same time an involuntary feeling of alarm came over them, lest there should be a traitor among them. The Sisters gazed silently on one another, but at last all eyes rested on Mother Macrina. " Infamous creature!" she exclaimed, " what have you said? who has invited you hither?" " You yourself," he replied. At these words the Sisters uttered a cry of distress, and the most sullen silence succeeded; when Mother Macrina snatched from Siemaszko's hand the pretended petition, opened it in the presence of the Sisters, and at once recognised Michalewicz's writing, and with indignation and contempt she flung the paper back in his face. He attempted to brave out the forgery with another lie.

" Blood of a Polish dog!" he exclaimed, " have you not all licked my feet, asking me as a great favour to make in your name this humble supplication?"

" And do you not fear God, whom you offend by so barefaced a falsehood?" said the holy mother. " You know better than any one that we neither fear death nor martyrdom; how could we then beseech you to bring us your accomplice to receive our apostasy." Then to Siemaszko she said: " That cross which you bring me from the emperor, suspend on your own breast, already so richly decorated: once a thief hung upon a cross; now a cross hangs upon a thief. Go! never will you succeed in tempting God's servants."

No sooner had Siemaszko left them, than they she l tears of joy, and thanked God for the grace He had just given them. All the Sisters pressed around Mother Macrina, and gave that vent to their feelings which the presence of the apostate bishop had so long prevented.

The following day, before he left, Siemaszko caused them to be scourged under his windows; and Michalewicz revenged himself for his disgrace by fresh cruelties. The heavy copper pitchers of water which they had to carry, Michalewicz now obliged them to bear at arm's-length, in order, as he said, that the Polish spirit might not get into the water. It was a great distance, particularly in the winter, when they had to take a long round to get at the river. If, exhausted with fatigue, they drew the pitchers nearer to them, the " black nuns," who accompanied them everywhere, would snatch the pitcher from their hands, and empty the contents on their head; they had then to begin over again.

When Siemaszko came again, it was to reconcile a Uniate church to the Russo-Greek rite; and he was determined that Mother Macrina and her nuns should assist at the ceremony. This they firmly refused; and the apostate bishop accordingly gave orders that they should be brought in by force. Bleeding and bruised, they were dragged to the door of the church, where a great crowd had assembled, much to Siemaszko's confusion, who would rather have been without so many witnesses. Mother Macrina, whose head was streaming with blood, caught up an axe which was lying by, and laying her head upon a block of wood, entreated Siemaszko, as he had been their pastor, to be now their executioner. " Cut off our heads and roll them into your church, for never shall our feet walk in. Here is the axe!—here are our heads!"

Siemaszko only replied by knocking the axe out of

her hand. It struck one of the Sisters on the leg, and inflicted a severe wound. He then struck Mother Macrina on the mouth, and knocked out one of her teeth. She quietly picked it up, and presented it to him, saying, "This is the noblest action of your life, monster; and in remembrance of it take this diamond, and set it in your stony heart. Believe me, it will outshine all the jewels for which you have sold your soul." Siemaszko was so stung by these words, that he went into a fit with excess of passion, and was obliged to be taken away. The Sisters, with fresh blows, were sent back to their labours, singing as they went the *Te Deum*, in which many of the people joined.

Siemaszko consoled himself that night by a drinking bout with the "black nuns," and the house resounded with convivial songs and cheers in honour of the emperor. Michalevicz joined in the debauch: he who had never known the taste of strong drink before his apostasy was now seldom sober; and he doubtless sought to deaden the reproaches of his conscience; but the day of retribution was at hand. The wretched man fell drunk into a pool of water, and was drowned.

CHAPTER II.

THEIR SUFFERINGS AT POLOCK AND SPAS.

AFTER two years the Sisters were ordered off to Polock, to assist in building a palace for Siemaszko. They were tied two and two as before, and had to walk in chains. But this was not their greatest trial: their dear crucifix was taken from them. On arriving at Polock, they were placed in a convent, which, like their late prison, also had once belonged to their own order, but was now occupied by "black nuns" and Russian "popes." They were put under the power of the protopope, Juan Wicrowkin, a drunken fellow, who always carried about with him a knotted chong, with which he struck the poor Sisters whenever he met them. The "black nuns" were much more numerous here than at Witobsk, so that their prisoners had each ten tyrants instead of one. Here too, as at Witobsk, some of the old Catholic sisterhood were kept in confinement. There had been twenty-five; but when Mother Macrina arrived, fifteen had perished in the persecution, and she found only ten Sisters and one corpse; two of these had lost their reason from blows on the head, yet they were compelled to labour with the others. One of them died soon after the arrival of the Nuns of Minsk; the other, six months afterwards. She was found a bloody corpse in her cell, and no doubt she had died under the blows of her executioners.

The Sisters were not suffered to remain long at Polock, because the town's-people used to throw them bread over the wall. So they were moved to Spas, and were made to carry all the furniture of the convent to their new abode. Then they were set to level the ground for Siemaszko's palace. Being new to the work, constant accidents happened, which cost the lives of many of the Sisters. Five of them were buried alive by earth falling upon them as they were making an excavation. The danger was known beforehand, but no precautions were taken; and when the horrible catastrophe occurred, the witnesses of it were not allowed to do any thing for the deliverance of the sufferers; and there perhaps they would have remained to this day, but that some brave inhabitants of Polock came by night, and having dug them out, gave them burial; and the bodies of the martyrs rest in peace.

Their most painful task was breaking stones; for they had no hammers, and were obliged to break one stone against another. The labour was so great, that their arms were frequently put out of joint; but they were not on that account relieved from the necessity of breaking the required amount, and the Sisters had to replace the bones in their sockets for each other. What-

ever inflammation ensued, they had still to go on with
their work; and they were soon covered with ulcers
and tumours, that broke out all over their bodies.
Their clothes (one scanty petticoat was all they had)
were soaked in blood; and, faint from want of food,
racked with pain, and ready to drop with fatigue, they
passed the hours of labour, expecting every moment to
die. Then, when night came, they could not sleep: in
no position could they find rest, so covered were they
with painful wounds; and they were fain to lie in each
other's arms, and rest aching heads on no less aching
bosoms. But that God gave them strength to endure
that cross, they must all have sunk beneath its weight;
as it was, three of them died in eight days. One was
crushed to death by stones which she had not strength
to draw to their appointed place. Obliged to let go the
rope, the bucket fell, and the poor labourer was killed;
the other two sank from exhaustion. The nuns were
not generally allowed to help each other; only Mother
Macrina might exchange work with any sister who was
exhausted. In this way she saved her life on one occasion, when nine sisters were killed by the falling of a
wall. She was on a high scaffolding, when one of them,
who was wheeling a barrow below, cried out, "Mother,
I can do no more." She accordingly came down, and
the other went up to take her place; almost immediately
afterwards came a great crash and a piercing cry, and
on looking round, Mother Macrina saw nothing but a
cloud of dust. But when the dust had cleared away,
she saw that the wall had fallen down, and that her
nine sisters had disappeared under the ruins. She
fainted at the sight; but they scourged her till she recovered, and then drove her to her work again.

This misfortune put a stop to the works for some
time, and the surviving sisters were employed in breaking stones, carrying wood, and digging; but after a
few weeks the building re-commenced, as Siemaszko
was expected. He had been again informed that the
sisters were at length ready to recant; he hastened

thithei to receive their recantation. Meanwhile they lost two more sisters from scourging. Some indignant persons had scratched on the walls of the Russian church the following doggrel rhyme :—

> " Here, instead of monasteries,
>   Are Siberia and the galleys;"

and the poor nuns of Minsk were accused of it. They were all flogged, and with such barbarity that two of them died.

When Siemaszko arrived, Mother Macrina asked him who had sent for him to tempt them again. "You yourself," said he. " I !" said the Mother indignantly. "Yes, you, or some of your Sisters." The nuns burst out into a cry of horror. "Apostate!" said the heroic woman ; "traitor to Jesus Christ and His Church, by God's help we will die for the faith as our Sisters have died !" At these words Siemaszko struck her on the cheek, upon which she turned to him the other. Indeed this seems to have been a favourite pastime of his, for in different visits he knocked out nine of her teeth. He then took from his pocket the emperor's ukase, of which we have already spoken, and made her read it aloud.

It approved as "holy, holy, and thrice holy," all that the Archbishop Siemaszko had done or might do for the promotion of the orthodox Greek religion, and commanded all persons, including the military, to assist him. After she had read it, he took from his pocket a petition which Mother Macrina had written to the emperor, renouncing all their temporal possessions, provided they might die quietly in their own faith; and showing it to her, struck her such a blow on the face as to break the cartilage of her nose. " I'll teach you to write to the emperor," said he. Then he struck her again, and taking her by the shoulders and shaking her, he threw her down and stamped upon her. At last he inquired who had written that petition. " I," said the Mother. " All of us," said the Sisters. "Who gave you the paper?" "We got it from some

poor persons." "And who wrote it?" "We did ourselves." His rage at this passed expression. "When
I have taken off three skins, one that you had from God,
and the other two from the emperor, you will tell me
the truth." The Sisters were all scourged; the lashes
fell without being counted, and still he stood by and
asked, "Who gave you the paper?—who wrote the
petition?" But he could find out nothing more, and at
length they desisted. One of the Sisters died that night,
like so many others, on the Mother's knees, and the
next day they were driven to labour as usual.

From that time forward the poor were not allowed
to come near them; and but for the Jews, who gave
them "brandy grains," they must have perished with
hunger. They could not exclude the Jews, because
they owed them money for brandy. Siemaszko came
again the next morning, and with curses urged them
to apostatise, and insisted upon knowing who had helped
them with their petition. Not succeeding in obtaining
the desired information, he went away, enjoining Feodor
to torment them more and more; and this winter
(1841-1842) their sufferings were greater than ever.

Next spring the floggings twice a week were resumed, and they received fifty lashes each time. Sister
Seraphine, who was seventy-two years of age, died
under the infliction. At the thirtieth lash the name of
Jesus was no more heard, her soul was already in
heaven. Twenty yet remained to complete the sentence, and they were given to the corpse. Two other
Sisters also died, one two hours afterwards, and the other
not till midnight. "O my Jesus," said Sister Nathalie,
"come and console me, for I love you with all my
heart;" and so saying she expired. After the sixth
scourging, the Russian general, moved by the entreaties
of his wife, interfered. They went to the house just
as the flogging was about to commence; when his wife
saw all the preparations, she swooned away; and the
general told the protopope that if he obeyed the orders
of the apostate bishop, he would have him hanged, for

the emperor could not be aware of their horrible cruelty. He had them taken back to prison, and sent them 100 roubles (about 4l.), in order that they might be enabled to procure themselves some food. They, however, did not enjoy the benefit of this charity, for the protopope appropriated the whole of it. Nor were they much the better for his interference; for although the floggings were discontinued, Siemaszko was so enraged with the general, that he devised yet worse torments than any that had gone before.

One evening the Sisters were brought home from their work earlier than usual; and the deacons, the popes, and a number of savage men, mad with drink and every evil passion, were turned in upon those defenceless women, with full license to work their will with them. God preserved them through that fearful night: He alone knows how; but the morning dawned on a bloody heap of dead, or mutilated though still bleeding bodies. Two of the sisters were no more: one lay crushed with the iron hoof of one of those wild beasts; the other was one mass of wounds, so that the fatal blow could not be distinguished. Eight sisters, though alive, had had their eyes forced out and their faces torn; one had her nose bitten off: all were horribly bruised and bitten, and gashed and trampled on, and the floor of the prison was slippery with their blood. Mother Macrina was stabbed in the side in three places and in the arm, besides a gash on the head; yet when she asked to be allowed, wounded as she herself was, to dress the wounds of her children, they bore her away from the cell because she would not purchase the boon by deserting her faith. When Feodor came to remove the dead bodies, his only remark to the nuns was, "See how God punishes you."

This outrage did not pass without comment either from God or man. That night nine cattle belonging to the "black nuns" died in the field, and their four horses were found dead in the stables the next morning. It was a judgment from God in token of His displeasure,

and even under Russian tyranny the populace were
roused. The excitement gathered strength, though the
authorities adopted every possible expedient to arrest
it. One gentleman was taken in his own house, and
without a trial sent to Siberia, for having had a requiem
said for the dead nuns; and a convent of Dominicans,
which had long been recognised in the country, was
broken up and dispersed at a moment's warning, for saying prayers for the martyred sisters. But Polock was
not intimidated, and Siemaszko thought it safe to change
the scene of his operations. There was another house
of "black nuns" at Madzioly, and thither the sisters
were dispatched. First, however, they received a visit
from a Franciscan father named Feolosci, who had sold
himself to the schism, and become the bosom friend of
Siemaszko; the nuns did not know this, and when they
saw a Catholic priest their hearts leaped with joy, in the
hope of confession and communion: they remarked it
as somewhat strange that he only gave them alms and
no spiritual consolation. But he seemed ashamed of
his apostasy, and it was not till his second visit that he
ventured to recommend their giving up their faith,
when he employed the following notable argument.
If union and orthodoxy be one and the same thing,
then what more holy than Siemaszko's desire that
under the same monarch there should be but one religion? The sisters were stupefied; and the Mother
asked, "Who sent you?" "I am sent by God," he
said, "to save your souls, which you have steeped in
hell by your obstinacy." "Ah," retorted the holy
Mother, "if our souls are in hell, then your own place,
Judas, is in heaven." At these words he was going to
strike her, when one of the sisters seized him by the
shoulders, and with the help of the others turned him
out of the door. His rage against them was extreme;
and some time afterwards, before they left Polock, he
found means to gratify it. At his instigation, Siemaszko had them shut up for six days and fed on salt
herrings, without a drop of water or atom of other

food; the raging thirst they at first endured exceeds description. The two first days the agony was insupportable; a burning fire devoured their inside, and the skin of their tongue and palate peeled off with fever. But still the Passion of Jesus sustained them; they thought of His thirst upon the Cross; they thought also of the thirst of the souls in purgatory, and they fell on their faces, offering to God their sufferings in their behalf. God had pity upon them; from that moment they felt neither thirst nor hunger; and on the seventh morning, when they were taken to their labours, they made a vow to abstain from water for that day also, in honour of the seven dolours of Mary.

When Ivan saw that they were not yet conquered, he said, "You must have a devil within you who suffers in your stead."

CHAPTER III.

THEIR SUFFERINGS AT MADZIOLY, AND ESCAPE OF MOTHER MACRINA.

It was in the spring of 1843 that one day they perceived the courtyard of the convent full of armed men. As the presence of soldiers always intimated a change of abode for the Sisters, they knew they were going to leave Polock, and they felt convinced that they were destined for Siberia. "So much the better," said they all; "we shall suffer the more;" and they sang a hymn in honour of the Archangel Michael.

But in this expectation they were deceived; one more attempt was to be made to break their resolution, and their present destination was to Madzioly, a town in the government of Minsk. They set off at night; and all had to go on foot, except those who had lost the use of their limbs; even the poor blind nuns, and those suffering from undressed wounds, had to march with

the rest: it was a ghastly procession; yet they bore
the sufferings of that toilsome journey for ten days with
the same heroic patience As they were crossing the
Dnieper their conductor seemed uneasy lest they should
jump into the river to rid themselves of their torments:
"Is the river heaven, that we should jump into it?"
said one of the Sisters, divining the cause of his agita-
tion.

On arriving at Madzioly they were delivered into
the hands of the protopope Daniel; the "black nuns"
there received them with jeers and laughter: "How
fat and fresh you all are! but you have had nothing to
try you yet; wait a little, we will find out how to pull
you down;" the Sisters were then set to the most disgusting offices. To their shame they found there two
Basilian monks who had apostatised, and were among
the most cruel of their tormentors; they stole the linen
which the Sisters had to wash for the household, and
pawned it to the Jews for brandy, and the Sisters were
accused of the theft and beaten.

They had not been long here when they were again
divided into four parties and separated, and each was
then told that the others had recanted; the miserable
falsehood, however, availed nothing; they had too
much confidence in each other's constancy, and when
they all assembled again, they found their number
complete.

Siemaszko paid them a visit in the autumn, and in
the presence of the convent and a number of children,
assumed a gentle tone, spoke in their own language,
offered to put the children under their care; and after
reasoning with them, pointed to a small packet on the
table, and said, "That is ready for you as soon as you
embrace the orthodox religion." They replied, "that
they feared neither torments nor death, for Jesus
Christ, for they would live and die for Him; nor
would they teach the children of schismatics, except to
bring them up in the Catholic faith." Siemaszko in a
rage swore they should be beaten: "Just what we

wanted to ask for," said Sister Marsecka. "You will go to hell if you persist," cried Siemaszko. "O my God," was the answer, "how merciful art Thou to endure the presence of such an apostate!"

Siemaszko then ordered that they should be tortured in a new way: they were tied up in sacks with large ropes round their necks, and taken to the side of one of the lakes surrounding the convent. "Now," said he, "embrace our religion, or I will drown you." "We will not give up Jesus Christ," said they all; "so, demon, do as you are bid." The assistants accordingly jumped into a boat and rowed from the shore, pulling the sisters into the water, and towing them behind. Before they were out of their depth, the rowers stopped and made the old offer, to receive the same indignant refusal; then they went into deeper water, and rowed them about for three hours, the cord all the while nearly strangling them.

After this they were taken back to their prison; they were kept all night in their wet clothes, and the water running off made mud of the prison floor; all their old wounds festered from the cold and damp, and new ones broke out all over their bodies. This punishment was repeated twice a week for three weeks, and was only discontinued on account of the freezing of the water: on the third occasion three of the sisters died in the water; their bodies were put into a hole by the side of the lake, but the inhabitants of Madzioly gave them a more decent burial the same night.

The ensuing winter was a very severe one for the poor Sisters: their wounds opened afresh with the ice, and they grew weaker and weaker; they were allowed to get wood from the forest; but chained as they were, they could scarcely bear the weight; and when they had it, their stove would not carry off the smoke, and one of the Sisters was suffocated; another was frozen to death in the forest.

The winter after was still more severe, and at its close only four remained (who were not either blind or paralytic,) out of all three of the united sisterhoods; nevertheless, it was determined to send them to Siberia to end their days there.

Had this intention been carried into effect, nothing would have transpired of all this history; but Almighty God designed that the world should know what schismatic barbarity can perpetrate: Mother Macrina, with three of her companions, at length effected their escape.

On the occasion of the protopope's fête, the whole of the inmates were intoxicated for three successive days. On the evening of the third day Mother Macrina found her guards asleep in their places; she passed them, and roused the three sisters who still retained the use of their limbs; they reached the top of the wall by the help of the trees, and, notwithstanding its height, after commending themselves to God, let themselves drop on the snow. When they found themselves all uninjured, transported with joy, they knelt down and recited the *Te Deum*. In order to baffle pursuit, and to secure at least the escape of one to tell the tale, they separated, appointing to meet at a certain town on the frontier.

Mother Macrina pursued her difficult journey, or rather wanderings, amid the Lithuanian forests for three months, begging her way, beset with spies, and enduring the greatest extremities of cold, hunger, and thirst. From many persons she received great kindness; but the names have been carefully concealed, that they might not incur the vengeance of the czar. At length she arrived at the town where she was to meet the Sisters, but only one was there—Sister Marsecka. At a later period she ascertained that the other two had reached Gallicia. After eight days she set off, and having crossed the frontier, crawling on her hands and feet among a herd of cattle, and so escaped the last Russian sentinel, she reached Posen in safety, where she only wished to live a retired and humble life of devotion; but the Archbishop obliged her to draw up a circumstantial account of her sufferings. Through the grand duchy of Posen she passed *viâ* Paris to Rome, where, by the command of the Pope, she dictated to three officials the startling history which her own humility would have concealed.

She carries on her person the marks of her seven years' martyrdom : her neck is seamed by the rope with which she was dragged in the water at Madzioly, her feet are galled by the chains, and her head retains the scar which she received on the dreadful night at Spas. She is still living at Rome, where she has now established a house of her order. She is more than sixty years of age, but her mind is as vigorous as ever, and the truth of her narrative is stamped upon her features.

The Russian government has attempted to refute the whole story, and has had recourse for this end to the most contemptible subterfuges. But the czar, when he visited his holiness in 1845, was unable to deny to the face of the Vicar of Christ what he had not scrupled to deny in official documents : he was speechless, went out abashed and confounded from his presence.

Of the blind and paralytic Sisters who were left behind, two died a few days after Mother Macrina's flight; and all the others were placed in a hospital, after a long resistance on the part of Siemaszko, who would only give his consent on the condition of their receiving communion once at least from the hands of a schismatic. At last he gave in, when he found he could not prevail ; but he strictly charged the officers of the hospital never to let a Catholic priest have access to them.

This is the true history of one convent of Basilian nuns ; but the whole order endured the same persecutions; and of the 245 religious of whom it was composed, not one fell away. There is no reason to suppose that the government had any special hatred to this community ; and as all were as constant as they, it is probable that the story of the Nuns of Minsk is the story of every other convent of the Basilian order.

VI.

A CONFESSOR OF THE FAITH DURING THE FRENCH REVOLUTION, 1793-5.

HERE died, not long ago, at Tours, an aged canon, universally respected, but of eccentric habits. He had preserved an old-fashioned simplicity of manner, in which there was a certain mixture of abruptness, freedom, and liveliness that was not unfrequently very amusing. He was a stranger to the modern refinements of language and manner, and troubled himself little or nothing for the opinion of the world. He might be met in the most frequented quarters of the elegant city of Tours, passing through the midst of the gay throng without taking any notice of them, bareheaded (for he was never known to wear a hat), and quietly repeating his Rosary. He had several other eccentricities of the same kind, upon which it is not worth while to dwell. Nevertheless, the old canon was an object of veneration to the whole diocese. It was not his age only which was the cause of this veneration, nor yet his ecclesiastical learning, which was considerable; nor yet his whole life, given up to the functions of the ministry, which he every where exercised with great zeal for the service of God, and an ardent charity for his neighbour: for all this—this crown of the priesthood—is the honourable distinction of many of the French clergy; only in the person of M. Leproust it received an especial dignity from the fact that he had been, at the end of the last century, a confessor of the faith.

At the age of twenty-five, being then only in minor orders, he quitted the seminary and the town of Tours,

in order that he might not be present at the installation of
Michael Suzor, formerly parish priest of Loches, but who
had now been nominated constitutional bishop of the department of Indre-et-Loire. And yet M. Leproust had
had before his eyes several very sad examples. The principal of the College of Tours—the apostate priest, the
representative of the people, Isabeau—has left a name in
the annals of the Revolution. During his direction of
the college, he had particularly distinguished the young
Leproust, who thought himself much honoured by this
notice, and endeavoured to improve and cultivate the
affection which his superior professed for him, and which
that superior afterwards took advantage of to endeavour
to deceive him, and to draw him into the schism

Having refused to assist at the installation of the
constitutional bishop of Indre-et-Loire, M. Leproust refused also to hold any further communication with the
curé of his parish, who had taken the oath. Accordingly,
in the month of March 1793, he was arrested, and condemned to transportation for this breach of the law; he
•was taken to Bordeaux in order to be embarked for
French Guiana; and with this expectation he was detained for two years at Bordeaux, at Blaye, and upon
the hulks. The history of this captivity he has written;
and we here lay a sketch of it before our readers, not
doubting but that they will find in its simple and touching recital much that will both interest and edify them.

"On the 20th of March," he says, "I was arrested
at Vernon, my native parish. I had then only received
the tonsure, and had lived in retirement at my father's
house since April 1st, 1791. The National Assembly
was at that time endeavouring to establish a schism in
France, by requiring of all bishops and priests who were
engaged in the active performance of their functions,
that they should take an oath to support the civil constitution of the clergy, which the Assembly had decreed,
and which one hundred and thirty-two bishops had rejected: which, moreover, Pope Pius VI. (by a brief of
the 1ᵗʰ h of March, 1793) had condemned as heretical

and contrary to the general discipline of the Church. I had determined to take no part in the schism; nevertheless, they had no just pretext for calling upon me to take the oath, since I was not exercising any ministerial functions, and was not even in holy orders. Being denounced, however, by six citizens of the village—the number required by law to authorise the transportation of any obnoxious ecclesiastic—I was arrested on the charge of being dangerous to the Republic, inasmuch as I would hold no communication with the curé of Vernon, who had had the weakness to conform to the oath, and to submit to the intruded bishop; that see being in the meanwhile lawfully occupied by the archbishop, M. Conzié, and having been so occupied ever since the year 1785.

The authorities of Vernon examined my papers and books, but found nothing contrary to the laws of the state; nevertheless, having drawn up a legal statement of my case, they sent me to Tours under the escort of ten national guards. These men, being men of my own village, with whom I was personally acquainted, treated me very well; they even defended me from several persons who were disposed to insult me. By and by two men chose to attach themselves to our company and go along by our side, vomiting forth the most violently abusive language. On our arrival at the bridge in Tours, these two ruffians began to cry out that it was useless to take me any further, and that it would be better to throw me at once into the river; they even endeavoured themselves to force me over the parapet. My guards had to use some exertion in my defence, in order that they might fulfil the order they had received of bringing me before the committee of inspection. It was the evening of Palm Sunday, and there was a considerable crowd upon the bridge and upon the open space in front of the town-hall. This crowd joined in the cry of the men, and menacing vociferations began to arise on all sides, the most frequent of which was, " Here comes another for the guillotine!"

H

M. Barbier, curé of St. Georges, had passed ·by the same route some minutes before, conducted like myself by the national guards of his parish, and had met with the same reception.   It was not without difficulty that I was saved from being very roughly handled by the crowd which filled the Rue Neuve and the house where the members of the revolutionary committee were then sitting.   A number of young men followed me almost into the presence of these worthies, crying out, "To the guillotine!" and adding significant gestures to their words, they even went so far as to mark upon my neck the place where the knife ought to strike.

When brught before the revolutionary committee, I was first of all examined as to the causes which had prevented my assisting two years before, when a student at the seminary, at the installation of the intruded bishop.   I answered, that my conscience forbad me to do so, inasmuch as there being already an archbishop who had been canonically instituted, I could not recognise another.   I expected that for this answer I should be sent to prison, thence to be dispatched to the guillotine; they contented themselves, however, with ordering me to a place of confinement, which proved to be no other than my old seminary.   There I had the honour and the joy to find myself in company with more than a hundred venerable priests, imprisoned on account of their refusal to take the sacrilegious oath, and their constancy in maintaining the unchangeable truths of our holy religion; and these priests were still permitted to say Mass within the house.   In this way I had the precious privilege of being able to indemnify myself, as it were, for the long time I had passed in my own village without being able to assist at the divine mysteries even on Sundays and on the great festivals.

But this happiness and tranquillity were not of long continuance.   The members of the directory of the department wishing to exhibit the fervour of their patriotism, began to increase the rigour of the decrees of the convention · so that whereas that body had sentenced

to transportation only those nonjuring priests who were
in good health and had not yet reached the age of sixty,
the department of Indre-et-Loire determined to extend
this condemnation to those who were seventy.　The
magistrate who came to announce this decree to us,
assembled us on the terrace of the seminary, and addressed us in these words: "Whereas you have not
chosen to take the oath, and whereas you are men dangerous to the republic, whose laws you despise, your
country declares to you, by my mouth, that she vomits
you forth for ever from her bosom; your sentence is,
that you be transported to French Guiana."　Having
bowed to him, we returned to our rooms; and those
among us who had not attained the age of seventy, or
had no serious infirmity, commenced our preparations
for departure.　The day was fixed for the 22d of April.
We hired, at our own cost, some carts to take us to
Bordeaux, and at eight o'clock in the morning they
were drawn up in the court of the seminary.　There
were eighteen of them; and ninety-four ecclesiastics
were to find places in them—seventy-four from the
diocese of Tours, and twenty from the dioceses of Blois
and Le Mans.　A national guard of horse and foot had
been ordered to accompany us.　We had great difficulty
in getting out of the town, for the streets were crowded
by ill-disposed persons, who did their best to prevent
our departure, crying out continually, "To the guill -
tine! to the guillotine!　Transportation is too merciful
a punishment for them; they deserve to die!"　We were
detained in this way for half an hour in the midst of
the frantic populace, whose cries grew fiercer and fiercer.
At last the officer who had the charge of us ordered the
soldiers to draw their swords, and so a passage was
cleared, through which we passed on, amid an abundant
shower of stones from all sides.　We proceeded at full
gallop as far as Grammont, where we halted to bind up
the wounds which five-and-twenty of us had received,
some from stones and some from bayonets; for a large
number of the volunteers assembled at Tours had joined

the populace, and tried to stab us. Our escort behaved pretty well, except that one of the national guards, hearing one of our party address another as " sir," became perfectly furious, and threatened to kill him for using a forbidden title, instead of addressing his companion as "citizen." He actually levelled his musket at him three times; but another guard, more humane and less touchy, prevented the ruffian from doing any real injury; and when the officer was informed of it, he removed the offended soldier to another post, warning us at the same time to be more cautious in our language.

Our first night was spent at Sainte-Maure, where the authorities lodged us in the cellars of the old salt-magazines, which they humanely furnished with fresh straw for us to lie upon. We were not insulted either on our arrival or on our departure from this place; and our journey the next day passed quietly enough, excepting that we were not allowed to refresh ourselves by walking occasionally instead of riding. When we arrived within half a league of Chatellerault, we were met by the authorities and national guard of the town, who conducted us to the prison through a dense but silent crowd. Here we were placed in a lofty hall, from which the ordinary criminals had been removed to make way for us; but as the straw had not been changed, the dust was so intolerable, that instead of sleeping, we were consumed with thirst all night long, and continually asking for water. The gaoler apparently had not even taken the trouble to lock up the thieves; but mixing themselves among the servants of the prison, they contrived to steal several articles from some of our party whilst the surgeons were attending to their wounds. The next morning the national guard of Chatellerault took the place of that of Tours; and these treated us with greater kindness, allowing us to leave the carriages when we liked, and to walk by their sides as friends. At Poictiers we were decently lodged in the old Convent of the Visitation; and as part of the national guard of this town was in Vendée, that of Chatellerault continued to guard us; and escorted us also the following day to Couhé, a little Protestant town, where we spent the night in an old ruined castle, of which only the walls were standing, and where we had not even straw to lie upon. Fifty men of the national guard of Couhé were ordered to escort us the next day, and our charitable guards of Chatellerault took their leave therefore; fifteen of them, however, accompanied us as far as Ruffec, fearing lest our new guards, being all Protestants, should maltreat us. This proved to be a special mark of God's care for us; for when we arrived at Ruffec, we found it was the eve of a great fair; the place was full of people, and our Protestant guards insisted upon it that we should be taken to the principal square, and made to kiss the tree of liberty there. Six gendarmes, however, who had been appointed to accompany us from Poictiers to Bordeaux, sided with our guards of Chatellerault in resisting this proposition; and finally, placing themselves at the head of the troop, they declared they would fight rather than allow us to be thus gratuitously exposed to the insults of the populace. The Protestants, therefore, relinquished their design, and allowed our kind friends to conduct us through the less frequented parts of the town to certain inns, where we were quartered instead of being put in prison, our Catholic guards undertaking to be answerable for us. The next day, these excellent men came to take leave of us; they embraced us with tears in their eyes, and begged our prayers, saying that they would gladly have accompanied us all the way to Bordeaux. They need not have asked for this, for they had conferred such obligations upon us that we could never forget such generous devotion.

The national guard of Ruffec also treated us very well; but in the afternoon, when we arrived at Angoulême, there was a great assemblage of people, who made us get down from our carriages and proceed on foot to the prison, using towards us the most opprobrious and scoffing language. In the prison, too, we were obliged to lie upon the floor, without either mattress or straw. At Barbezieux, however, we were lodged in a loft of the castle of La Rochefoucauld, which was stripped of its furniture and uninhabited. But the people of the town being good Catholics would not let us lie upon the boards; they brought us mattresses, feather-beds, blankets, and sheets, excellent bread, and all other necessary provisions. These good people did their utmost to evince the compassion they felt for us; and the next day, as we were leaving, surrounded our carriages with tears in their eyes. At length, after journeying on for another day or two, we arrived at the post of La Bastide, on the Garonne. Here we embarked upon some lighters, and remained there in the open air all night, expecting to be landed the next day at Bordeaux. So many priests, however, had arrived there from different dioceses, condemned like ourselves to transportation, that the authorities there refused to receive us, and sent us on to Blaye, a little town upon the Gironde, seven leagues from Bordeaux. At Blaye we were received with hisses and insults, and were conducted by the national guard to the strong and extensive citadel, situated on a considerable eminence. The rooms of the prison in which we were shut up were large enough, but we were packed in them like a flock of sheep, and obliged to sleep on the boards without mattresses or blankets. Every evening the officers of the garrison came, with drawn swords in their hands, to count our numbers and see that no one was missing; but they did not insult us. Divine Providence, which never ceased to watch over us, interfered to take us away from Blaye sooner than we expected, thereby delivering us from the greatest danger we had yet encountered. A regiment of 1200 men, destined for Vendée, arrived at Blaye on Ascension-day (6th of May), and were allowed to enter the citadel for the purpose of seeing it. Among the 200 men who composed our garrison these soldiers found some comrades, from whom they learnt that we were priests who had been seized with

arms in our hands in La Vendée. Not one of us, indeed, had ever set foot there; but this report was
constantly circulated concerning all the arrested priests,
in order to make them odious to the people. These
soldiers then assembled at eight o'clock in the evening
before the prison, and began to discuss among themselves the question of our execution. It so happened,
however, that the directory of the department of the
Gironde was federalist,—that is to say, they were opposed to the bloody tyranny of that portion of the
Convention which was called the Mountain, and of
which the two brothers Robespierre were the heads;
and as they knew that the department of Indre-et-
Loire had gone beyond the law with respect to us by
condemning sexagenarians and others still older, they
sent two commissioners to Blaye with orders to receive
the complaints of any of the imprisoned clergy. One
of these gentlemen was the son of a surgeon of Tours,
and consequently rejoiced at this opportunity of seeing
his countrymen; the other was a citizen of Blaye.
They happened to have fixed on Ascension-day for
their visit, and this circumstance was the means of
saving our lives; for whilst they, in the company of
the mayor and another official (the constitutional curé
of the parish), were interrogating each one of us separately as to any appeal we might have to make on the
subject of our condemnation, the 1200 soldiers assembled in front of the prison were shouting and threaten-
ing violence, the priests meanwhile hearing each other's
confessions and preparing for the worst. At the very
time that I was with the commissioners, both they and
I being quite ignorant of the disturbance that was
going on around, the gaoler entered to announce that
he could hold out no longer; that the soldiers insisted
upon having the prisoners given up to them, and that
they were about to burst open the doors. The commissioners, the mayor, and the curé, all behaved very well,
promised to protect us, and rushing out into the midst
of these furious ruffians, exclaimed, " My friends, what

atrocity is this that you are going to perpetrate? These
priests are not from La Vendée; they are from the department of Tours, and have been sent here to be embarked for French Guiana, a place of transportation,
they have submitted to the law which condemned them;
and you, soldiers, ought to respect the law, and to protect and defend those whom it punishes, not to insult
and injure them." God, who destined us for more
protracted sufferings, enabled these men to succeed in
calming the volunteers; they were got out of the citadel, and the next day removed from Blaye. But certainly, if the commissioners had not come on that day,
they would have found nothing but our corpses.

The mayor, not considering that the 250 soldiers
who still remained in the citadel were very much better or more trustworthy than their companions whom
he had succeeded in ejecting, determined on sending
us to Bourg, a little town on the Dordogne, two
leagues from Blaye. One day, while the soldiers were
at exercise behind the citadel, without their arms, we
were removed in great haste and in the most profound
silence. A numerous national guard had been summoned to escort us to the port, where ten lighters were
waiting for us. Whilst we were still on the quay, the
soldiers saw us, and immediately quitting their exercise, spite of the prohibition of their officers, they rushed
down upon us like madmen; fortunately they had no
arms, but they hurled a shower of stones at us, by
which several of the national guards were struck.
During this tumult we were hurried on board; several
aged priests fell from the narrow planks, which we had
to cross, into the water, which caused some delay, so
that the stones reached us also; and they did not cease
till we were fairly launched.

Bourg is the native place of the illustrious St. Pau-
linus, bishop of Nola; and the kind hospitality with
which we were received there made us think that the
inhabitants had inherited the charity of their saintly
countryman. On our arrival in the evening we were

conducted to an old Ursuline convent, entirely dismantled; but the people brought us beds, mattresses, chairs, furniture, and all the food we required. We slept two and two in the nuns' cells, and felt ourselves as it were in another world, in a terrestrial paradise. The day after our arrival, the commissioners of the Gironde came to pay us a visit; we were assembled in the choir of the convent, and one of them, M. Mangeret, made us a short discourse, recommending us to love one another and to live in perfect union! Our union indeed was such that I could almost have fancied myself back again in my old seminary. We established a rule of life for ourselves, meeting in the choir at certain hours of the day to perform our devotional exercises. But, alas! this peaceful life lasted but one short week.

There was one among the municipal corporation of Bourg, an impious republican surgeon, who formed a plot for our murder. All the neighbourhood of Bordeaux is given up to the cultivation of the vine, and the peasants grow no corn; consequently they are obliged to come every Sunday into the towns to buy bread. This surgeon then persuaded the vine-dressers that our presence in the place would raise the price of bread, and thus expose them to the danger of starvation. He inflamed their passions by means of these representations, so that they agreed to assemble on Whitsunday, to the number of near 3000, in order to burst open the doors of the convent and massacre us. The mayor of Bourg, who was a good Christian, and two of whose uncles were priests who had refused to take the oath, discovered this plot, but was conscious that he had no means to hinder its execution, inasmuch as all the guard he had at his disposal for our defence did not amount to more than a dozen old soldiers. He came to arouse us, therefore, at midnight on the eve of Whitsunday, and begged us to make all preparations for embarking as quickly as possible, for that he should be in despair if any harm should happen to us. We descended the

Gironde to Blaye, where the municipal authorities, fearing to expose us to the dangers we had already incurred there, sent us over to the fort Pâti, which is an island in the river, opposite to the town. Here we were lodged in damp dark rooms, to which light was admitted only through small slits in walls fifteen feet thick, and which were full of rats, mice, and fleas. They gave us the same bread as was distributed to the soldiers,—a mixture of bran and flour. A boat brought our rations from Blaye three times a week; and at the same time wine, meat, and other eatables, were brought for those who chose to buy them. They gave us also military beds, sheets, and blankets, which had evidently been used for soldiers suffering from the itch, for several of our number were presently attacked with this malady. Fortunately there was a pretty large bundle of hay here, whereby we were enabled to raise our mattresses from the damp ground. However, spite of these disadvantages, we enjoyed here very tolerable tranquillity; the detachment of soldiers who guarded us behaved with kindness; we were allowed to walk about upon the island when it was not covered by the tide, which happened at the times of the new and full moon; we performed our devotional exercises together, and even held ecclesiastical conferences, in which M. Rabotteau, canon of St. Gatien, and M. Simon, canon of St. Martin, were the most skilful and interesting disputants; the consolation of hearing or of saying Mass, however, we did not enjoy.

Those amongst us who had completed their sixtieth year were now sent back to their several departments, according to the law, which enjoined imprisonment only in their case, not transportation. The sick also were next removed to Bordeaux to the former convent of the Carmelites; so that in the month of September we were only twenty-eight left at Pâti. The popular commissioner of Bordeaux continued to treat us with humanity, and would not let us, therefore, pass the winter on the island: they brought us to Bordeaux, where we were first examined at the hospitals by the physicians, and those of us who had the itch were properly treated. Those who were in good health were removed to the fort of Hâ. Here we were tolerably comfortable, placed in a large room with a fire-place; had curtained beds, each to be shared by two; and we were able to say our prayers in peace. But at the end of a fortnight came yet another change.

Tallien and Isabeau, the representatives of the people, had succeeded in causing the party of Robespierre to triumph at Bordeaux; they replaced the members of the popular commission by the partisans of the Mountain, who were taken principally from the working-classes and from the dregs of the people. These men were naturally, for the most part, very ignorant, of which we soon had a sufficient proof. The National Convention had just promulgated a new decree, whereby all non-juring priests, who should not deliver themselves up in ten days, were ordered to be guillotined within twenty-four hours after their arrest, together with all the persons in the house where they might be seized. The wise members of the Bordeaux Commission imagined that this decree had reference to *all* non-juring priests, and condemned them all to death, consequently they transferred us to another tower, where we were confined in rooms almost dark, crowded together, with nothing but the boards to lie upon; and at first they even left us for twenty-four hours without food or water, saying that there was no use in feeding us, since we were condemned to death. But God was not unmindful of us. Opposite the tower in which we were confined, there was a very high house inhabited by a good Catholic, the father of six children. This man had a priest concealed in his house, who said Mass every day. At a given signal, we used to mount upon the platform, and the windows of the upper-story of the house of this courageous servant of God being opened, we were able, in spite of our gaolers, to unite ourselves to the Holy Sacrifice which was being celebrated before our eyes: we here found abundantly the strength and consolation of which we had need.

During our two months' sojourn at Bordeaux, the room of the prison over our own was occupied by Federalists; for the most part worthy people of the town, who had endeavoured to take no part in the tyranny of the two Robespierres. Among these gentlemen was the lord of one of the parishes of Médoc, named De Vormesel; he had been a member of the popular commission, and had been found concealed in the house of the constitutional curé. When brought to prison, he was placed in our room, because the other was too full. He was a deist and philosopher, and maintained that all religions were equally good. He used to compare them to forms of dress; saying, that each people was free to choose that which seemed best to them; for that God paid no more attention to differences of worship than to changes of fashion; and that, provided He was served and adored, He took no heed to the particular manner in which this might be done. I had frequent conversations with this poor man. I asked him whether he, when he was master of a large house, was indifferent to the conduct of his servants; and whether he allowed them to wait upon him according to their own fancies, without any regard to his wishes? Whether a ruler was indifferent to the laws which he had made? Whether a general allowed each regiment to adopt the flag, the discipline, and the military tactics which they pleased? Our philosopher was obliged to admit that the master of a house, under such a system, would be very badly served, a province very badly ruled, and an army impossible to be led. I then said to him, that if the great ones of this world imposed certain regulations upon their servants and subordinates, surely God had a right to prescribe to His creatures the manner in which He would be adored, loved, and served. With these and many other arguments I tried to open the eyes of this poor philosopher; but the spectacle which he witnessed in our prison struck him much more forcibly than any

argument of words. All of us, both priests and Federalists, were in expectation of the same fate—the guillotine was every thing we had in prospect; but while
the priests, under these circumstances, preserved perfect
tranquillity, and an evenness of temper not unmixed
with gaiety, the Federalist prisoners were plunged in
sadness and profound despair, and only thought of
escaping the scaffold by poison. M. de Vormesel
brooded over these frightful thoughts continually, as
he walked in a gloomy and abstracted state of mind
up and down our room; he used to say that he could
not understand our calmness and peace of mind. But I
explained to him that it arose from the very cause of
our imprisonment. Contending for the true religion of
Jesus Christ, we could desire nothing better or more
noble than to die in such a cause. Our Divine Master,
having assured us that those who generously give up
their lives and fortunes in order to remain faithful to
Him, shall be brought to the enjoyment of a heavenly
kingdom, how could we fear the scaffold, which was to
put us in possession of this eternal happiness? In this
way I endeavoured to show the unfortunate man the
difference between the two masters whom we served.
He had been in the habit of spending fourteen hours
a-day in the service of the Republic, which now rewarded him with a prison and a scaffold. "Believe
me," said I, "if you will but return to God with sin-
cerity of heart; if you will throw yourself, like the prodigal, at the feet of this tender Father, He will raise
you up and will pardon you; and if you die upon the
scaffold, you will draw down upon yourself the mercies
of God, who renders to each one according to his works."
Under the influence of these words and counsels, M. de
Vormesel each day grew more and more calm, and became more accessible to the thoughts of religion and of
the Church; morning and evening he prayed with us,
and we daily gave him to read the life of a Saint and a
chapter of the Imitation of Christ; God did not permit
us, however, to finish our work, for he was hurried off

to Paris, and there guillotined. Before he left, he asked M. Simon to give him a copy of the Imitation; wishing, as he said, to strengthen himself in the good sentiments with which we had inspired him. God grant that he may have had the grace to persevere!

During our two months' sojourn at Bordeaux we had a visit one day from Isabeau, the representative of the people, who, as I have already mentioned, had been for several years principal of the college of Tours; so that most of us were known to him. In the first room which he entered, he saw M. Simon, and immediately launched forth in invectives against him. A few days afterwards, he ordered us to be sent back to Blaye, to fort Pâti. This was in the month of December, and the cold was most intense. We packed up what few things we had, and they were even carried down into the court; for we expected to leave the very next day. The officer, however, who had been charged with the execution of the order, made a mistake. Instead of coming to take us, he went to the prisons of the palace, and fetched some of our companions, who had been transferred to the Carmelite convent; thus the very persons who had been removed from Pâti precisely because they could not stand the damp of that fortress even during the warm weather, were now sent back again to the same place in the depth of winter. They suffered greatly from the cold and the high tides; the water filtered through the vaults in such abundance, that some of them were even obliged to keep their umbrellas open over their beds, in order that their heads at least might be kept dry. Meanwhile, not knowing what had been done, we remained in daily expectation of our removal; we had no change of linen, for the gaolers would not allow us to go down to the court to re-open our boxes. At last, after a fortnight's delay, we were re-embarked for Blaye; not, however, to join our companions at Pâti, but were again taken to the citadel. This time we were not lodged in the prison, but in the story above that occupied by the soldiers, in little boarded rooms, without beds, sheets, or blankets, and we had to pay even for straw. Our rooms had no ceiling, and were immediately under the tiles; but there were fire-places, so that by purchasing from the soldiers what wood they could spare, we were enabled to have fires. Happily we were able to perform all our exercises of piety with tolerable tranquillity, and even succeeded in having the holy sacrifice of the Mass; for some charitable souls at Bordeaux had contrived to send us all that was necessary for that purpose. Every morning, therefore, about four o'clock, while the soldiers who guarded us were still asleep, we got up in silence, and one of our number, in the name of all the rest, offered to the God of strength and mercy the heavenly Victim.

At Bordeaux we had been allowed a pound of bread a-day; but on our arrival at Blaye they gave us only three-quarters of a pound, and by and by this was still further reduced to half-a-pound until Mid-Lent. Moreover, at Bordeaux the bread was made of millet; but here it consisted of pease and beans ground into flour, and generally spoiled on board the merchant-vessels which brought it. This bread was of the colour and weight of earth, and had a most detestable taste and smell; we could not have eaten it but for the frightful hunger by which we were tormented. At Mid-Lent our ration was again reduced to four ounces; and finally, from Easter until our embarcation, we only had a pound given us every ten days. To supply the deficiency, those who had money bought wine, meat, fruit, &c. The soldiers received daily a pound of good brown wheaten bread; they put aside a little to sell to us; but as we were obliged to give them whatever price they chose to ask, we could not all indulge in this luxury. The rest of us endeavoured to do as well as we could by the help of some fermented and almost rotten herrings dressed with leeks, which we procured from some women of the country, who were allowed to come to the citadel; to this we added nettles, also beet, and any other herbs we could pick up in the courtyard, and the whole was seasoned with vinegar and coarse brown sugar, made to supply the place of butter. During the Lent of 1794, I ate more than sixty of these herrings; and the unwholesomeness of the food corrupted my blood, and produced so bad a sore in my foot, that I was prevented from walking for a considerable time.

In the month of May, Isabeau came to visit the citadel. He was dressed in the uniform of a general, with a plume in his hat and a sword at his side, about fifty officers and others accompanying him. He chose to see again the priests from Tours; and turning furiously to M. Simon, he told him that the citadel was too good a place for such as he was, and ordered him to be forthwith conducted to Pâti; an order which was executed the following day. This worthy priest had so won the affections of every one, that even the members of the committee shed tears at his departure. During the seven years that I spent in the college of Tours, I had been particularly honoured by the friendship of Isabeau. He was not aware that I was here, and evinced great surprise when he saw me. "What!" said he, "are you here too, you? this is very astonishing."

"It is indeed astonishing," said I, "that we should both of us be here; you in the situation and costume in which I see you, and I in the state in which I am."

"If you had trusted me and taken the oath, you would now be happy, like those of your companions who followed my advice."

"Such happiness as that," I replied, "I do not envy; the tranquillity of my conscience is more precious to me than every thing else."

"What can I do for you?" he then inquired.

"All I ask of you," I replied, "is to let us have some bread; for we have had none for ten days."

"I will send you some. Adieu;" and so he took his leave, he and all his suite.

The Abbé Royer, who had also been under him in the college, cried out, as he was going away, "Citizen Isabeau, give us some bread!" He turned round, and answered, "You have chosen to follow the Pope; go and ask him for bread." For this we were rather disposed to grumble with M. Royer. Isabeau, however, kept his word, and sent us daily a quarter of a pound of good oat-cake each; but this only lasted for three weeks: at the end of that time we were reduced to our pound of bean-bread every ten days; and this went on till the 15th of November for those who did not work. Those who were employed on the works had a special allowance of food assigned to them after the 4th of August. On Friday, the 1st of that month, the members of the committee of inspection, accompanied by several officers, came to examine our trunks and bags; they made the most minute search; and took away our breviaries and other books, our pictures and crucifixes; these last they tore in pieces, broke, and stamped under foot before our eyes. They also took away our money, and what few articles of plate we had been able to keep until then. Not even our chalice could be concealed from them; we had buried it; but after they had found every thing else, they felt confident that we had some sacred vessels, and the soldiers turned up the earth with their bayonets until they discovered it. Immediately they seized upon it, together with a small ciborium, and carried off these precious treasures in triumph, as though they had gained a glorious victory over the God for Whom they knew that we were fighting with so much perseverance. The next day we were called together upon the terrace; our letters of holy orders were demanded from us, and if not voluntarily given up, were forcibly seized. When this had been done, they gave us notice that instruments would be brought to us to-morrow, for that we were to be set to work. We observed to them that to-morrow was Sunday.

I

"That is precisely the reason," they answered, "that we shall make you work on that day."

"And precisely because it is Sunday," we replied, "we refuse to work. Is it possible that you are not acquainted with the cause of our confinement here? Is it not for the defence of the holy religion of our fathers? and how then shall we do any thing which that religion forbids?"

"If you don't work to-morrow, you will be taken to the dungeon."

"To the guillotine, if you will! We are ready to suffer any thing, even death itself, rather than violate the laws of God and of His Church! Besides, has not liberty of conscience been decreed?"

"Oh!" answered a Jew, a captain of artillery, "he who decreed the existence of a Supreme Being is guillotined."

It was thus that we learned the death of Robespierre. He had issued orders to guillotine, on the 5th of August, all the priests confined at Bordeaux and Blaye, in all about twelve hundred. A large hole had actually been dug for the burial of the bodies; and a guillotine had been constructed with four blades, to cut off four heads at once. The executioners had promised to transact this matter in two nights; but He who knows how to curb the fury of the waves, showed us on this, as on so many other occasions, that He is able also to defeat the machinations of the wicked. It seemed to us as though He had renewed for us what He did of old for Mardochai and the other Jews who were in captivity in Persia, when the proud and cruel Aman was hung on the gallows which he had destined for Mardochai. This terrible Robespierre, who intended to guillotine us in the beginning of August, was himself guillotined, together with his brother, on the 27th of July.

When the members of the Vigilance Committee saw that we would not consent to work on Sunday, we were sent back to our rooms, and left till the next evening without food or water. In the afternoon, however, about five o'clock, we were again brought out upon the terrace, and the commissioners inquired of us, in a milder tone, whether we would commence work the following day; to this we agreed, adding, that we were willing to work every day except Sunday. This matter being thus settled, they brought us, the next morning, spades, shovels, and wheelbarrows. We were employed at first in collecting the filth of the fortress, and carrying it to a hole which the commandant wished to have filled up. Some of us cleansed the streets, the spaces round the cannons, and did other things of the same kind. All who were engaged in this work received a few ounces of bread as their sole payment; but twelve of the strongest drew an instrument called the *diable*, a small cart, upon which were piled large stones, to be hauled from the port up to the citadel, on the top of the hill. Those who consented to this occupation were allowed a pound of bread a-day. Twelve workmen of the town had been previously employed at it; and they used to think that they had done a good day's work when they had been three times between the port and the citadel. The priests, however, made twelve journeys to and fro the first day they were set to work, which astonished the master-carpenter so much that he could talk of nothing else. "I was told," said he, "that the priests were all idle, and good for nothing; but I never had such diligent workmen as these." The engineer also said that he wished he could always have priests to work in the dockyards, for the work would be much more quickly done. Others of our number were employed in levelling, wheeling barrows, and bringing earth from the subterranean passages which were being constructed. Those who were old or infirm scraped the streets and open places of the citadel, which covered as much space and contained as much building as a town of six thousand inhabitants; and for this labour they received a quarter of a pound of bread a-day. We worked in this way as common labourers

during three months and a half, both in the interior of
the citadel and on the port; and the public feeling o₁
the people of Blaye became much changed towards us
in consequence : they were astonished, both at the humility and the activity of our labours, and began to
speak of the imprisoned priests with admiration and
respect; they could not understand how men delicately
brought up, and unused to hard work, should be able
to endure such fatigue during the great heat of August.
And, in truth, it was not easy to understand how the
greater part of us had escaped death from privation
and hunger; it was the almighty power of God alone
that enabled us to bear up against it His providence
preserved us to labour hereafter in His vineyard. He
still looked with mercy upon France, and destined us
to contribute to her salvation.

The women, who brought their baskets to the citadel on Sundays as on other days, used to do justice to
our conduct, even at the cost of condemning themselves. "The priests do not mind being hungry," they
said; "they are determined not to work on Sunday;"
for it ought to be mentioned, that on the days when we
did not work we had no allowance of bread. The commandant of the citadel, a violent red republican, had
been dismissed on the fall of Robespierre, and had been
succeeded by one more gentle and humane. As on
week-days we went out of the citadel to work on the
port, so this man allowed us on Sundays also to go out
for a walk. By this means we were able to see some
good Christians in the town, who were still attached to
the Catholic faith, and who procured for several priests
the power of saying Mass in their rooms, at which a
number of the faithful used eagerly to attend. The
commandant told us that he trusted to our honour,
being well assured that none of us would abuse his
kindness by effecting our escape, and so compromising
his responsibility. He certainly did not err in trusting
us; not one of us would have been base enough so to
abuse his generosity ; and besides, we felt too much

honoured in being prisoners for Jesus Christ's sake to think of escaping.

This happy state of things, however, did not last long. Isabeau, always violent against us, ordered that we should be put on board certain vessels which had been used for the negroes; none but those who were seriously ill or infirm were to be exempted. Moreover, fearing lest we might be too well treated in French Guiana, on his own responsibility and by his own arbitrary will he violated the law of the Constitution, and changed the place of our transportation. He gave instructions that we were to be disembarked on the desert shores of the west of Africa; hoping doubtless that we might either become the slaves of the Turks or the prey of wild beasts. With a view to the execution of this order, the authorities ordered us to undergo a medical inspection; the result of which was, that all the sound and healthy priests, to the number of six hundred, were embarked on board three vessels, *le Gentil, le Dunkerque, les Associés.* These vessels descended the Gironde to Blaye; and on the 15th of November 1794, the *Gentil* completed her cargo by taking on board all the priests of fort Pâti and of the citadel. Thus we were two hundred and fifty on board, crowded between decks not more than three feet high, so that we were unable to stand. On the day of our embarkation all the inhabitants of Blaye came to see us, and accompanied us to the port. Their feelings and demonstrations were very different from what we had experienced eighteen months before, on our first arrival. Instead of shouting and throwing stones at us, they now wept, pressed our hands, and recommended themselves to our prayers.

Our floating prisons were furnished with flour and wine for the passage, as also with implements for the cultivation of the barren deserts upon which we were to be landed. At first we were put upon the same rations as the sailors—a pound and a half of bread daily, with half a pound of salt pork or hard beef, or

occasionally dried cod-fish, for our morning meal. At
night, for our supper, a large cauldron was filled with
beans, which were served out to us half-cooked, without
being shelled or having undergone any sort of cleansing,
in buckets, a bucketful among ten of us. All our food
was prepared in a most filthy manner. The cook, after
having taken our morning meal out of the cauldron,
would step into it himself, and sweep it out with the
same besom as was used to remove dirt from the deck;
and when we had had cod-fish in the morning, he did
not take the trouble to throw away the water in which
it had been cooked, nor to remove a number of fish-
bones which were always sure to remain in it, but he
tossed the beans in upon the top of them, together with
some fresh water and a pound of oil, and so cooked
the whole mass. Notwithstanding this disgusting want
of cleanliness, this bad cooking and bad seasoning, we
were so hungry after our twelve months' fast at Pâti
and the citadel, that we devoured what they gave us
with great avidity. When the cook saw this, he dimi-
nished the quantity, and made us pay when we wanted
more. I have seen canons of cathedrals, who had been
accustomed in their own homes to the most scrupulous
cleanliness, give this wretch an assignat of five francs
for a spoonful of his beans; so much power has hunger
in overpowering delicacy. At the end of a fortnight
we had become a little less ravenous, and were propor-
tionately more disgusted with the dirt of our food; so
the captain gave us leave to prepare our own food for
the future, which, though it was of the same bad quality, certainly rendered it more eatable. The officers
themselves kept an excellent table, furnished with all
kinds of luxuries. Twice a-day they had what they
called prayers; that is to say, they assembled all the
crew upon deck, and, with their heads uncovered, sang
the *Marseillaise* in chorus, with all the outward show
of devotion, raising their eyes to heaven, as if to implore the benediction of that God Whom they refused
to acknowledge, and Whom they were insulting by

their profane song. During the five months and a half that we were on board we were obliged to hear this horrible and disgusting melody twice every day, accompanied by the most ridiculous gestures; but happily these brave singers never invited us to join in the ceremony. They did not even disturb us in our own exercises of piety, but allowed us to pray aloud, and all together, twice a-day; for a general officer who had come to visit us on board before we set sail, and with whom one of our party happened to be personally acquainted, had kindly made his interest with the authorities of the town to restore to us our breviaries and other books that had been taken away on the 1st of August. They were now sent out to us in a boat; and although it proved that many of them had been lost and damaged, yet by using them alternately, all of us were able to say office. Those who were lodged on the deck or between decks were able to enjoy this consolation from eight o'clock in the morning until suppertime; but the greater number, being in the hold, were in almost total darkness.

From Christmas to Candlemas the cold was most intense, and accompanied with violent gales of wind; and as our oven and cauldron were upon deck, those who prepared the food were exposed to all the inclemency of the weather, and several of us were seized with violent colds and inflammations on the chest, until at last we were really unable to brave it any longer; and for several days we were obliged to live upon our hard sea-biscuit alone, those whose teeth were not very strong crushing it with wooden hammers. We were obliged to go on deck for every thing we wanted, and to return by an uncovered winding staircase, which the rain and snow rendered so slippery as to cause us many a fall. Night commenced with us at four o'clock, and lasted until eight in the morning, during the whole of which time we were shut up without lights, and lying upon the bare boards. Moreover, we were infested with rats and mice, which were continually running over our bodies and faces, and even entangled in our hair.

At last, on the 6th of December, we set sail and went as far as Royan; and of course many of us soon suffered much from sea-sickness. On the 17th, we set sail again for the island of Aix; a passage which, under ordinary circumstances, is only of six or seven hours; a strong north wind, however, delayed our progress, so that we did not reach it before the morning of the 18th. Here we remained for a fortnight, the captain not venturing out to sea on account of the English cruisers. On Christmas night, so violent a storm arose, that we were in great danger of perishing. The vessel had been secured against the fury of the tempest by four anchors; three of the cables broke; had not the last and strongest remained firm, we should certainly have been lost. But the Infant Jesus, whose birth the Church was that night celebrating, again calmed the winds and the sea, and on Christmas-day we assisted the sailors in working the ship. The captain seeing no chance of being able to put to sea, so as to take us to Africa, and not wishing to expose himself to be taken by the English, determined to go up the river Charente, beyond the battery which defends the passage. Here we found two vessels at anchor, upon which had been crowded, in the month of July, eight hundred priests, condemned, like ourselves, to transportation, and sent with this intent to Rochefort. The members of the department of Rochefort not being federalist, like those of Bordeaux, these priests were much worse treated than we had been. Their trunks and every thing else had been taken from them; so that they went on board with nothing but the clothes which they were actually wearing. These vessels were scarcely larger than our own, and yet four hundred had been stowed upon each of them; whilst we, who were only two hundred and fifty, were suffering great inconvenience even from that number. Death, however, soon set free many of these poor captives. They had been taken on board during the greatest heat of summer;

the captains, most inhuman red-republicans, confined them in the hold during the whole of the night, and during almost the whole of the day also. They were only allowed to come on deck to take their meals. Thus, overcome by the heat, crowded together, without change of linen, and devoured by vermin, scurvy and other maladies had swept off a great many of their number. About a dozen died every night from suffocation; the survivors implored their jailers to open the hatches, in order that they might have a little air, and told them that there were already a dozen dead; to which the only answer they received was, "So much the better; that is not enough yet." In the morning they went on deck to receive their rations, and were then obliged to bring up the bodies of their deceased brethren, which were thrown into boats; the strongest amongst them were sent ashore with the corpses, to dig the graves and bury them. During the seven months they remained on board these vessels more than six hundred died; by the month of December scarcely two hundred had been able to withstand the effects of such barbarous treatment, and even these were so pale and emaciated that they looked more like skeletons than living men. Our captain, who was far more humane than theirs, allowed us to go and visit them, twelve at a time; and we could hardly restrain our tears at the sight of their pitiable condition. As our clothes had not been taken from us, we were able to provide them with the means of changing their miserable filthy rags. They were kept on board till the 2d of February, when the authorities of Rochefort, having been changed, behaved with less barbarity, and sent them to be confined at Saintes and at St. Jean d'Angely, where they were well treated, and soon set at liberty.

As for ourselves, our captivity was prolonged until the month of April; but the captains of the ships became much more merciful towards us. At first, they had often placed us in irons; if we ventured to make the slightest complaint, we were immediately brought

upon deck, loaded with chains, and exposed for twenty-
four hours to the most severe cold. Latterly, on the
contrary, these same captains talked to us with civility,
sometimes even with friendliness; they occasionally invited us to their table, and what was far more precious
and more pleasing to us, they allowed us to say Mass
on board our vessels on Sundays and holidays, and even
assisted at it themselves with all their crew. The vessels
being in the Charente were not inconvenienced by the
motion of the sea; and we were consequently able to
celebrate the Holy Mass without difficulty, and even
to make our Easter communions. Notwithstanding all
these relaxations, our position remained always the
same; there were many annoyances inseparable from
our condition, not to mention that we had momentarily
before our eyes the prospect of our departure for Africa.
Providence, however, watched over us, and without our
knowledge found a wonderful means for restoring us
to liberty.

France had been governed since the fall of Robespierre by the Conventional Assembly, which had established a commission of public safety, composed of twelve
of its members. Every fortnight each one in turn became president, and thus exercised sovereign power in
the republic. During the presidency of the butcher
Legendre, one of the most cruel republicans, God permitted that a young man from Rochefort, very well
disposed towards us, should be nominated secretary for
the fortnight. This secretary wrote at once to a Catholic of Rochefort, to inquire the names of the priests
who were confined on board the ships, in order that he
might give them their liberty. This good Catholic
hastened to us with the news, and asked our names;
but as we feared that there might be some intention of
representing us as having taken the oaths, we refused
to give them, being resolved rather to die on board our
vessels or in exile than to take, or appear to have taken,
the oath. Our scruples were reported at Paris; and
the secretary answered, that we might be quite easy,

'or such was not his intention; that all he desired was to set us at liberty. M. Dupuy des Chapelles, canon of St. Gatien, then prepared a list of the priests of the diocese of Tours, which was sent immediately to Paris, and our liberation took place on Low Sunday. In the haste with which the lists were made out, several names were omitted; four of our brethren of Tours were in this predicament, and altogether about a hundred were obliged to remain on board. Their names were afterwards sent to Paris; but it was too late, the presidency of Legendre had expired, and our friend the secretary could do nothing for them. Some time after our departure, as the number did not suffice for three ships, they were put ashore and sent to the little port of Brouage, three leagues from Rochefort, a marshy and unhealthy situation, where most of them died. We who had been set at liberty were allowed at once to leave Rochefort, and passports were given us for our own province. Those who were able took places in the public conveyances; the others performed the journey on foot, like pilgrims, carrying their bundles on their backs. We found the disposition of the people was very much changed towards us. The pillage of the churches, the total interdiction of the pretended constitutional worship, the scandal given by the majority of the priests who had taken the oath, the abolition of Sunday, and the establishment of decades and pagan festivals, instituted by Robespierre in honour of the Supreme Being, of Reason, of Liberty, of Old Age, of Youth, &c.; the destruction of all the public crosses; the prohibition to all teachers to speak of God to the children under their care, to instruct them in their praye s, or to make the sign of the cross; all these horrible impieties had at length opened the eyes of the people. They now understood that the non-juring priests had been right in affirming that what the republicans really wanted was no priests at all, not even constitutional priests, of whom they made use only in order to deceive the people, and to persuade them that

their religion was not being changed; intending, however, as soon as they should find themselves strong
enough, to dismiss these complaisant priests, and to
abolish every kind of worship.   The people were filled
with dismay at the realisation of these sinister predic-
tions, and at finding themselves deprived of the bread
of the divine Word and of all religious service.   They
no longer, therefore, cried out after us, " To the guillotine !" nor insulted us, nor threw stones ; but regarded
us with admiration, as men who had escaped so many
dangers, who had passed through so fearful a storm ;
they recognised the finger of God in our preservation
and unexpected return despite the efforts of the wicked,
who had destined us for perpetual banishment.   Everywhere, therefore, we were most cordially received.   At
La Rochelle the townspeople came out to meet the
priests who arrived there, and contended for the honour and pleasure of conducting them to their houses,
and of providing them with lodging and entertainment
to the very best of their ability.   But it was, above all,
on our arrival at our native places that we were most
extravagantly *fêted;* even those who had persecuted us
before being now the most forward to welcome us home
again.   All our neighbours were at the doors, and
seemed scarcely able to believe their eyes.   They shed
tears of joy on recovering in safety those whom they
had supposed to be lost to them for ever.

VII.

THE MARTYRS OF THE CARMES.

HE history of the Church of Christ scarcely exhibits more sublime pictures of Christian heroism than arose out of the French Revolution. With a devotion to the faith worthy of primitive times, the great body of the priesthood of France refused the oath on the civil constitution of the clergy, and persevered in refusing it, although confiscation and death were the consequences of their resistance. This constancy, little expected from the ministers of a wealthy and privileged Church, struck at the root of the design for the extinction of Christianity, which the republican leaders had from the beginning entertained, and the brave ecclesiastics became the objects of the most violent persecution. In Paris the citizens were immediately and personally engaged in a struggle with the crown, so that at first the priests suffered less in the capital than in the provinces; but the respite was short. On the 10th of August, 1792, the Tuilleries were stormed; and that act of violence was the signal for a fiercer onslaught on the champions of religion than they had yet sustained. Robespierre, Danton, Marat, Manuel, and other sanguinary leaders of the people, were then at the zenith of their power; and a horrible scheme for the wholesale massacre of the insubordinate clergy was deliberately arranged. Some of the details of this awful catastrophe we now propose to relate, as illustrative of the grace and courage with which in every age and under all circumstances the Christian faith inspired its martyrs.

On the night of the 10th of August lists of the proscribed bishops and priests were sent to the different sections of Paris, with orders to arrest them at once, and commit them either to the convent of the Carmes or to the seminary of St. Firmin. The alleged ground for this illegal act was, that the clergy named had been seen with the Swiss guards of the palace firing upon the people. The accusation was false; but as the clergy of Paris had uniformly abstained from the slightest interference with political questions, it was necessary for their enemies to invent a charge in order to accomplish their ruin. The more to excite the fury of the populace, they caused a head to be carried through the streets on a pike as the head of the Abbé Rengard, curé of St. Germain l'Auxerrois; and the bearers were made to cry as they went, "So does the nation punish the refractory priests and traitors who dare to take part against her with the Swiss." Yet even this decree was based on a lie, for the Abbé Rengard was alive, and a month after, to the confusion of the authorities, applied for his passport.

The arrests began in the section of Luxembourg. Armed bands were sent into the parish of St. Sulpice to hunt out, as the people were told, the enemies of their country. With list in hand, these soldiers traversed the quarter and knocked at the priests' doors, and led their victims off in triumph amid the hootings of the people. Ecclesiastics the best known for their learning, piety, and zeal, nay even for their kindness to the poor, were the chief objects of their search. Such were the brothers De la Rochefoucauld, bishops of Beauvais and Saintes. Such also was the Abbé Sicard, who had devoted himself to the instruction of the deaf and dumb. But of all the nonjuring clergy none were more hateful to the republican authorities than the Archbishop of Arles, on account of his high rank, his unbounded influence, his great holiness, and his quiet but firm defence of his persecuted brethren. He had displayed throughout the troubles a prudence and a moderation which ought to have placed him beyond the reach of injury; for, opposed as he had been, like all his colleagues, to the civil constitution, he had never been known to mount the tribune ; and, after the closing of the Constituent Assembly, he had remained in Paris rather than give a pretext to fresh disturbances by his presence at Arles. But in an address to the king he entered a solemn protest against the law for the deportation of the clergy, and by this act of mercy he incurred the vengeance of the authorities. He was among the first to be arrested, and was imprisoned in the Carmes.

One hundred and twenty priests were confined with him, most of whom were arrested in the parish of St. Sulpice. No accommodation had been provided for the prisoners, nor had they any means of obtaining even the necessaries of life. Touched with their forlorn condition, a sectary, who had been up to that point one of the most violent against them, gave orders to the guards to admit whatever might be brought for the use of the prisoners, provided all precautions were taken against the clandestine introduction of arms ; and he even went himself to the neighbouring houses to solicit charity in their behalf. As soon as it became generally known to the faithful that they might offer to the necessities of the priests, comforts of every kind, beds, linen, and food, were liberally sent in. Arrangements were also made for their regular maintenance. One munificent lady, who would not allow her name to transpire, made herself responsible for the support of twenty priests so long as their confinement should continue. Alas! the call upon her charity was of short duration. The prisoners were also permitted to receive the visits of their friends at certain hours; and at the desire of the physician they had liberty to take exercise in the convent garden. Here they used to walk for an hour in the morning and an hour in the evening, either all together or in separate divisions, according to the caprice of their keepers. At the extremity of the garden was a little oratory, which in winter served for an orangery. There they used to pray before an image of the Blessed Virgin. Little thought they, as they

prayed, how soon that very spot was to be watered by
their blood.

Their situation was not always equally grievous; for
their guards were frequently changed. From the national guards they received nothing but kindness during
their imprisonment, and in the subsequent massacre;
but the federated Marseillais and Bretons considered it
a sign of patriotism to abuse all ecclesiastics. In all
their troubles, the presence of the three bishops was
their chief consolation, who preserved in the heart of a
prison a tranquillity of soul which sustained the courage
of the weakest of their brethren. The Archbishop of
Arles especially set the example of dignified patience
and resignation. Though more than eighty years of
age, and with daily increasing infirmities, he steadily
refused to avail himself of his interest to secure his removal to his own dwelling. " No, no," he used to say,
" I am too well off where I am, and in too good company." Indeed, so far from claiming any relief, he
took advantage of his superior dignity to see that others
were supplied with necessaries before himself: on the
third night of his imprisonment he lay upon the floor,
that the mattress reserved for his own use might be
given to a prisoner who had just arrived. The highest
in rank, he bore the largest share of the sufferings which
the priests had to endure from an unbridled soldiery,
and with such patience as excited the admiration of his
brethren, and even disarmed the cruelty of the guards.

One day a gendarme sat down by his side, and began to invent all sorts of sarcasms and railleries, to
move, if possible, the anger of the meek bishop. He
spoke of the guillotine, congratulating him upon the
worthy manner in which he would do the honours of
the scaffold. Then he rose from his seat, made a low
bow, and in a mocking tone called him Monseigneur,
and by all the other titles which the Assembly had
abolished. The prelate answered not a word. Then
the man lit a pipe, and smoked it in his face: still he
was silent; but as the smoke of the tobacco made him

ill, he changed his place. The man followed him from seat to seat, till at length the brutal pertinacity of the soldier yielded before the unconquerable patience of the archbishop, and he desisted out of very shame. His courage was equal to his patience. On one occasion, in the middle of the night, a priest started up at some noise, and woke the archbishop, exclaiming, "Monseigneur, the assassins are coming!" The prelate, perfectly collected, quietly answered, "Well, if the good God demands our lives, the sacrifice must be made." And with these words he calmly went to sleep again.

The other bishops contributed no less to support the courage of the generous band of confessors, especially the Bishop of Saintes, whose lively disposition suffered nothing from confinement. He received the new arrivals, which came in day after day, as if he had been in his own palace, and with a gaiety which made it difficult for them to believe that he was as much a prisoner as they were. The priests distinguished themselves also by their devotion to the new comers, especially two young curés, Fathers Auzurel and Fronteau.

The priests observed a religious silence in their prison, if prison it can be called, which was a church, rendered yet more august by the presence of so many confessors. But the guards polluted the holy precincts by the most scandalous language. It was indeed a grand spectacle; a vast number of priests habitually on their knees before the altar, rendering to God the worship of angels in the midst of the blasphemies of devils. But their prayers were often interrupted by alarms from without, and the prisoners lived in perpetual expectation of immediate death. One day they heard far off the cries of a large crowd and the reports of musketry. The tumult came nearer, and they could distinguish the popular airs of the Revolution, and the fatal Ça ira. From these cries and menaces they felt certain that their last hour was at hand. From all parts of the church they took refuge in the sanctuary, and upon their knees implored the protection of the Queen

K

of Martyrs, while they offered to God the sacrifice of their lives. They watched with anxiety the opening of the gates; but instead of murderers they saw enter, to their great astonishment, all the aged and infirm priests who had been placed in the house of St. Francis de Sales. These priests had no public duties to discharge, and were exempt from the oath; but they had the sacerdotal character, and that was sufficient ground for their incarceration. After them arrived the directors and professors of St. Sulpice with a number of their pupils. The prisoners could scarcely believe that violent hands had been laid on the old men of St. Francis's. "It would be impossible to describe," says the Abbé Pannonie, who was one of the first prisoners, "the shock we experienced at the sight of these reverend old men. Some of them could scarcely support themselves. The treatment they had received on their way was frightful. Decrepid as they were, they had been urged on to keep pace with their cruel conductors by blows from the butt ends of their muskets. As soon as we had recovered from our surprise, we hastened to give these new guests such assistance as lay in our power; and we were well repaid by the bright examples which those holy solitaries gave us. The serenity of their countenance, their patience and resignation, gave fresh strength to our own resolution. Many thanked God for having prolonged their lives so far that they could now offer them up for the faith." The number of the prisoners was further augmented by priests from several quarters of Paris; and by the Eudistes, many of whom had been arrested before; among others M. Hebert, their superior, and confessor to the king,—a priest greatly distinguished by his learning, zeal, and charity.

The legislative assembly, witness of these illegal and arbitrary arrests, claimed no obedience either for the laws or the rights of humanity. On the contrary, it proceeded with all despatch to dispose formally of the ecclesiastics, in defiance of all law. Its movements were not animated simply by personal animosity to the

priests as opponents of the Revolution, but as the mainstay of Christianity in the country. The only question
that remained regarded the method to be pursued.
The Jacobins already fully contemplated a general
massacre of the clergy; but they durst not propose this
horrible scheme till the other parties were prepared to
concur in it. However, the insufficiency and inconvenience of any other plan was urged with great success.
To banish 50,000 bad citizens into the neighbouring
countries would be the worst possible policy; to transport them to a penal settlement would require at least
100 ships, and would be expensive; to imprison them
in France would be no less costly, and would not effect
the object in view, the extinction of Christianity. The
result of these arguments was, that their extermination
was tacitly consented to. But for the sake of appear-
ances a very stringent law of deportation was passed.
The whole Catholic priesthood were to leave their
country within fifteen days. However, long before
that period had elapsed, hundreds of priests were seized
and thrown into the Carmes and elsewhere. Meanwhile,
the steps of the authorities became more daring, and at
length what had been tacitly arranged was openly decreed. The prie ts were to be murdered.

However, it was deemed expedient to keep the decree as yet a secret from the people, and its execution
was deferred till some opportunity should occur of stir-
ring up the popular mind to the necessary degree of
fury. The victims themselves were also kept in ignorance of the doom which was in store for them, and
were even buoyed up with delusive hopes of a speedy
liberation.

On the 29th, Manuel, the procureur of the commune and a prime mover in the massacres, went to the
Carmes to examine what room remained for fresh prisoners. Many priests approached him, and addressed
him with confidence. He told them that the decree of
the municipality relative to their deportation was concluded, and would be announced to them on the morrow.

" You will have," he said, "to evacuate the department in the space prescribed by law. You and we
shall both gain by that. You will enjoy your religion
in peace, we shall have no more occasion to fear you.
For if we let you stay in France, you will be like Moses
—you will be lifting up your hands to heaven while we
fig t." Some of the priests asked if it would be permitted them to take away their effects with them into
exile. Manuel answered them, " Do not distress yourselves ; you will always be richer than Christ, who had
not where to lay His head." To the priests confined in
La Mairie he said he had come " with words of peace
and consolation ; in thirty-six hours they should receive
the details of the law of deportation, and twelve hours
after they should be set free, after which they would
have fifteen days to make ready for their journey ; but
that it would be necessary for each to show that he
was a priest, for the advantage of leaving France at
that moment was a favour which many would envy."
Detestable hypocrisy ! with these flattering words upon
his tongue, he knew that he had himself joined in de-
creeing their massacre. Few of the priests, however,
believed him ; and their worst prognostications were
confirmed, when two days afterwards commissaries
were sent to the Carmes to ascertain that there were no
arms concealed in the church. They visited the cots
and every corner of the church, turned over the beds,
removed what was on the altar, even the sacred symbol
of our redemption ; they found no arms, but they took
away the very table-knives ; but still, to buoy up the
priests with the hope of deliverance, messengers were
sent to them at night after they had retired to rest
with fresh illusions ; yet at that very moment their
graves were being dug, for the massacre was arranged
with all the coolness and regularity of an act of administration. Cut-throats were formally enrolled, and
their salary fixed at a livre a-day ; ten waggons were
hired to carry away the corpses, pits were ordered to
be dug, and overseers appointed for the work ; not even

the water, vinegar, and brooms to remove the blood were forgotten, and lime was provided to hasten the decomposition of the corpses.

Meanwhile the conspirators were waiting for an opportunity of carrying their purpose into effect. Such an opportunity speedily offered itself. On the 1st of September intelligence was received at Paris that the Duke of Brunswick had laid siege to Verdun. The cry was at once raised that the priests were the betrayers of their country; and the danger was exaggerated by false reports to increase the general indignation. The citizens were summoned to take up arms against the Prussians; but it was openly said that their greatest enemies were at home. There was heard a rumour that a conspiracy had been discovered, by which the prisoners were all to be set loose by their accomplices. As soon as the patriots had left Paris, they were then to rush through the streets, take horrible vengeance upon the inhabitants, restore the king, and deliver Paris to the enemy. The people believed this absurd lie; a panic seized the city, groups of citizens formed in the corners of the streets, and whispers were heard, "We must not leave behind us alive one of our enemies to break out in our absence and massacre our wives and children."

This was the moment for which Danton and Marat and their party had waited. The prisoners at the Carmes were happily ignorant of what was passing outside. Saturday, the 1st of September, found them still hopeful, and was spent by them in the ordinary exercises of religion. Sunday dawned on the same security. However, the morning promenade was put off, and some of the prisoners remarked that they were more closely watched, and that their guards were changed sooner than usual. "Fear not, sirs," said one of the new guards; "if they come to attack you, we are strong enough for your defence." But at that very moment all was ready for the massacre. The assassins had been hired, and the porters of the prisons had been warned; the convent of the Carmes was now to present one of the most horrible scenes that the Revolution had produced, yet at the same time the most splendid that had ever glorified the Church of France. One knows not whether most to admire in their holy retreat the heroism of the martyrs or their generosity; for each desired to die, and so save the life of another. There were confined the very flower of the French clergy. Besides the three prelates, the rest were vicars general, canons, directors, and professors of seminaries, superiors of religious communities, learned Jesuits, zealous missionaries, distinguished writers; in a word, priests of the highest merit, who had remained to that moment invincible in their devotion to the faith. Nor were they shaken now that they anticipated their approaching fate. The horrible plot had got wind, and those who had friends or relations in the prisons ran trembling to the authorities, and besought their release, not always unsuccessfully. Robespierre saved the Abbé Berardier, principal of the college of Louis the Great, under whom he had himself studied. Even Marat and Danton saved some of the prisoners. The latter had promised a friend that he would set the Abbé Bousquet at liberty; but he thought no more about him, and his forgetfulness cost the prisoner his life. But those who had no interest with the authorities could only visit their friends for the last time, wring their hands, and bid them farewell with tears. And thus the prisoners obtained a knowledge of the dreadful truth. Every moment removed their hope of deliverance. "The hasty movements of our guards," said the Abbé Bourthelet, "the shouts which reached our ear from the streets near, the report of the cannon, all confirmed our fears. But our confidence in God was perfect." At two o'clock a commissary came to call over their names, and they were sent into the garden. Some went up to the farthest extremity, where was an alley between an elm hedge and the wall of partition that divided the Carmes from the Benedictines of the Blessed

Sacrament; others took refuge in the little oratory, and said Vespers; so that the prisoners were in two parties.

They were upon their knees at prayer, offering to God the sacrifice of their life, and mutually giving each other absolution, when all at once the garden-gate was thrown open with a great noise, and seven or eight young men rushed in, each with a belt of pistols at his girdle, and brandishing a naked sabre over his head. The Archbishop of Arles was by the oratory, and the Abbé Pannonie said to him: "This time, Monseigneur, I believe they really are come to assassinate us." "Well, my dear friend," replied the archbishop, "if the moment for our sacrifice has arrived, let us submit; and let us thank God that we have to offer our lives to Him in such a noble cause."

The assassins rushed upon the prisoners with frightful cries. Some turned towards the oratory where the archbishop was, others to the alley. The first priest whom these latter met was Father Gerault, the director of the Ladies of St. Elizabeth. He was reciting his breviary, undisturbed by the cries of the assassins, when a blow with a sabre from one of them laid him upon his back, and he was despatched by others with pikes. He was the first of the martyrs at the Carmes. His breviary, pierced with a ball and stained with blood, was discovered on the spot at the restoration of the Carmes, and it is still preserved as a precious relic. The second martyr was the Abbé Salins, the same to whom Manuel had given the promise of a speedy deliverance. Several others were wounded; but in their eagerness to arrive at the bottom of the garden, they would not give themselves time to put them out of their agony.

The other assassins who had turned towards the oratory demanded the Archbishop of Arles with shouts of fury. When they came up to the group, they addressed the Abbé Pannonie, who was a few steps in front: "Art thou the Archbishop of Arles?" The abbé lowered his eyes without answering, hoping to

draw upon himself the blows which were designed for
the archbishop. But the prelate advanced towards the
assassins with these words: "Let us thank God for
calling us to seal with our blood the faith that we profess; let us ask of Him the grace which we cannot
obtain by our own merits—the grace of final perseverance." M. Hebert, the superior-general of the Eudistes,
demanded a trial for himself and his brethren; but the
assassins replied by a pistol-shot, which wounded him
in the shoulder. Then they shouted again, "The Archbishop of Arles!" The venerable prelate, crossing his
hands upon his breast and raising his eyes towards
heaven, with great dignity approached those who called
him. The priests surrounded him, to hold him back,
and to conceal him. "Let me pass," he said; "if
my blood will appease them, what does it matter if I
die?" Then to the ruffians, like our Saviour on a like
occasion, he said, "I am he whom you seek." "Ah,
wretch, then! art thou then the Archbishop of Arles?"
"Yes, I am he." "Thou art he that shed the blood
of so many patriots at Arles." "I have never shed
any blood," he replied; "I never injured any one." A
blow with his sabre upon the archbishop's forehead was
the assassin's only rejoinder. The meek old man uttered
no complaint; and almost at the same instant his head
was struck from behind with another blow from a sabre,
which laid open his skull. He raised his right hand to
cover his eyes, and the same instant he received a third
blow, and then a fourth, and he sank into a sitting posture, supporting himself by one arm; a fifth stretched
him senseless on the ground. A pike was driven into
his breast with so great violence that the iron could
not be drawn out again; and the body of the holy
prelate was trampled under the feet of the assassins.
After having slain the archbishop, they turned themselves against the group of priests who crowded round
the scene of martyrdom, and now remained immovable
with admiration at the manner in which the holy prelate met his death. Some of them were slain, others

wounded; the rest, under an instinct of self-preserva-
tion, dispersed themselves over the garden. Some of
the youngest rushed forward and scaled the wall, in the
hope of saving themselves by the Rue du Cherche-Midi;
others climbed up into the trees or hid themselves under
the hedges; a great number took refuge in the oratory,
where they joined their brethren, who were already there
at prayer. The assassins hunted them down, firing as
they ran, and singing and laughing heartily when the
shots took effect on any of the fugitives.

The priests, at first surprised, soon recovered their
courage and tranquillity. They offered their breasts,
and fell upon their knees to seek pardon, not of their
murderers, but of God. Some of those who had crossed
the wall returned, lest their flight should make the
assassins more furious against their brethren. They
were thus besieged in the oratory, and the assassins
fired their muskets and pistols upon them through the
railings with which the place was enclosed. Crowded
together into a very narrow space, the victims fell one
upon the other, but no complaint was uttered by any
one. The Bishop of Beauvais when upon his knees
received a ball in his leg which broke his thigh, and
was supposed to be killed. Those who were not wounded
were covered with the blood of their dying brethren,
and the pavement was running with gore. The stains
yet remain; we need not say how religiously they are
preserved: it is the blood of martyrs, and who can look
upon it without the deepest emotion?

The garden and the chapel were now strewn with
corpses; a great number of priests had perished in that
frightful chase, and the assassins were running hither
and thither after their victims. At length there arrived
a commissary with fresh assassins, who stayed the mur-
dering with these words: " Stop, stop! it is not so that
you must set to work; the vengeance of the people is
just, but the innocent must be spared!" Upon this the
commandant of the porte, who had remained at the
other extremity of the garden, ordered the priests back

into the church. They betook themselves into the sanctuary, and near the altar they confessed each other, said the prayers for the dying, and commended themselves to the infinite mercy of God. Shortly afterwards the assassins arrived to seize them and drag them away, notwithstanding the representations of the commandant, who reminded them that the priests had not been judged. Again they replied that they were all guilty, and must perish. But they were in the nave, and separated from their victims by an iron grille; and though they tried twenty times to force the barrier, they were unable to break it down. In the midst of the uproar, the Bishop of Beauvais was brought in from the oratory in the arms of his murderers. There was a dead silence as they laid him on a mattress in the nave. Till then the Bishop of Saintes had been ignorant of his brother's fate. On entering the sanctuary, he had eagerly inquired after him, and now the Abbé Bardet pointed out to him the spot where his brother was placed. He instantly ran to embrace him, but he was not allowed to remain by his side.

While these things were going on in the church, a party of assassins were searching for such of the priests as had taken alarm at first and escaped from the garden. However, they did not discover all. Some were hidden in the rafters of the roof; and one, M. de Keravenant, curé of St. Germain de Pres, in the bell-tower. In the garden also partial massacres were still going on. One touching scene is recorded by the Abbé Pannonie. The Abbé Dutillet, with some of his brethren, being shut in by a wall, remained firm, and offered his breast to the assassins. A Marseillais in jest raised his piece three times to take aim, without firing. "An invulnerable priest!" said the Marseillais; "I shall not try a fourth time." "You are too tender-hearted," said another; "I will kill him." "No," said the Marseillais, "I take him under my protection; he has all the appearance of an honest man." And so saying, the republican assassin covered the priest with

his own body. It was on account of the abbé's Marseillais accent. The good abbé having thus found
favour with his townsman, interceded for the lives of
his brethren who were close by, and was on the point
of gaining his request, when two of them stepped forward, and said: "We ask for no mercy; if our brethren
are guilty, so are we; their religion is ours, and like
them we are ready to die for it." "Let them die for
it by all means," replied the assassins, and at once put
them to death. The Abbé Dutillet then repaired to
the church, and was about to be murdered in his turn,
when the same Marseillais recognised him, and saved
his life a second time.

The assassins then all met in the church, where they
were separated from their victims by the grille. Thirsting for their blood, they were maddened by the sight
of the priests kneeling before the altar, and praying for
their very murderers: they shouted to them to rise;
the priests obeyed; and then, like wild boars whetting
their tusks, they began to get ready their weapons for
the slaughter. The commissary urged upon them the
indecency of shedding blood in the holy place, and
their chiefs promised them a prompt judgment; but
they could with difficulty be appeased. But presently
the commissary, by means of a table, contrived a sort of
tribunal near the corridor, leading from the left of the
high altar by a flight of steps to the double staircase.
At the top were posted the assassins who were to consummate the holocaust. The priests, summoned two
and two, came before the terrible tribunal to be asked
simply whether they still adhered to their refusal to
take the oath. At the answer in the affirmative,—and
without a single exception the whole glorious band of
martyrs remained constant to the last,—they were conducted through a doorway, of which the steps exist to
this day. Here the two martyrs descended, and fell
under the pikes and poignards of the first assassins. They
were then passed on to other murderers below, by whom
they were despatched; and then the cry was raised,

" Vive la Nation !" and fresh victims were summoned from the church.

Those who were still in the church kneeling before the altar heard the death-cries with unshaken courage, and marked their numbers thinning, each with the certain knowledge that his own name would be called sooner or later; yet not one of them wavered. When their turn came, the priests who were summoned to die rose with transports of joy, as if invited by angels to the marriage-supper of the Lamb, or with the calmness of a soul assured of a speedy embrace in the bosom of Jesus. One disdaining to break off the course of his prayers, went with his eyes fastened on his office-book, and met his death-blow breathing out the praises of God. Some with a noble and majestic bearing cast on their executioners an eye of sorrowful pity, and the moment they were called hastened to secure their crown. Others lingered to take one last glance at the crucifix, and went their way praying with the Crucified, "Forgive them; they know not what they are doing." The Bishop of Saintes, when his name was called, kissed the altar for the last time, and passed through the door as calmly as if he had been engaged in the ceremonies of his cathedral. He was followed in perfect composure by Hebert, the general of the Eudistes, who had been already wounded by the side of the Archbishop of Arles. The younger priests were not less intrepid. When the Bishop of Beauvais heard his own name called, he was lying on his mattress in one of his chapels in the nave. " I am perfectly willing to go to die," he said, " with my brethren; but my thigh is broken, and I cannot support myself: help me to walk." What heart would not have been melted by these words? But the savages raised him by his arms and dragged him along to the place of slaughter, and murdered him with their pikes. He was almost the last. There were a few more priests to seal their faith by their blood, and then this awful massacre ceased for lack of victims.

Such was the spectacle which the Carmes presented

for nearly three hours. How dreadful, and yet how
glorious! More than two hundred priests had died for
the faith with all the courage, calmness, and constancy
of the primitive martyrs. The world understood it not,
for there was no sign of fanatic enthusiasm in their noble
contempt of death.

"I am confounded," said the commissary; "I am
lost in amazement. These priests went forth to death
with all the joy, all the eagerness of a bridegroom to
the marriage-chamber."

The Catholic understands it well: with the history
of eighteen centuries in his mind, he is at no loss to
account for the heroism of confessors.

After the massacre the doors of the church were
thrown open, that the people might enter and give a
popular sanction to the atrocities of the commune.
Many rushed in to pillage the bodies of the slain. The
executioners then established in the church a drinking-
stall and a dancing saloon, and celebrated their crime
with drunken orgies. In the midst of their revellings
one of the mattresses which the prisoners had used was
seen to move. They lifted it up, and found the Abbé
Dubray concealed beneath. Almost stifled by his
covering, he had raised it a little to breathe, and the
action cost him his life. They dragged him out and
slaughtered him before the altar. This was the only
blood shed within that sacred spot.

Some of them were voluntary martyrs. M. Galais,
superior of the little community of St. Sulpice, had
climbed a tree, from which he was about to escape from
the garden, when he saw the Abbé Bardet and the
Bishop of Saintes pass beneath on their way to the
church. Blushing at having thought of separating
himself from the company of martyrs, he descended,
followed them into the church, and when he left it to
be murdered, counted himself happy to have obeyed
the inspiration which had conducted him to martyrdom.
Another volunteer was M. de Valfons, an old officer of
he regiment of Champagne, the only layman in the

Carmes at the time of the massacre. He was devotedly attached to his director, the Abbé Guillemenet, and when that venerable priest was arrested 'he followed him into captivity. He assisted during their confinement in all the exercises of the priests, and edified them all by his eminent piety. Often he was told that he might escape, but he preferred captivity. He was in the garden when the massacre commenced, and followed the priests into the church. When his director's name was called, he rose joyfully to accompany him to death, the abbé reading his breviary, and M. de Valfons the holy Scriptures, and they received their crown together. The Bishop of Saintes might have escaped if he would have left his brother.

In different ways many priests escaped: some by the interest of their friends; some by concealing themselves in and about the convent; some were protected by individuals among the assassins themselves, and some by the national guards. Several made their way out of the garden; but some of them afterwards returned to join their brethren, and suffered with them. Fourteen, however, escaped; among them, M. Vialar, the private secretary of the Archbishop of Alby. The details of his escape are recorded. When the assassins entered the garden, he was at the bottom near the wall. After kneeling down with all his brethren to offer to God the sacrifice of his life, if it should be required of him, he rose, and judging the wall to be not insurmountable, he began to scale it. The Bishop of Saintes was passing at the time, and he invited him to follow. The prelate, however, simply answered, shaking his head, "My brother!" and M. Vialar, knowing that he would never forsake his brother, scaled the wall alone. He then found himself in a kind of court-yard belonging to the hôtel opposite. In the yard was a small nook under the oratory in the Carmes, from which he could distinctly hear the groans of the dying priests and the execrations of their murderers. Frightfully agitated, he wandered up and down the court, not knowing where to go next. The wall on the hôtel side was higher than the convent-wall, but half-way up was a projection, which he caught, and so reached the summit. From this point he succeeded in effecting an entrance into the house over a grated doorway, when he found himself in the upper story, and there, overcome with fatigue, he fell asleep. Fortunately the house was uninhabited, and he slept on undisturbed till nightfall. Hearing voices at the coach-gate, he went downstairs, and met a woman, to whom he related his adventure. By that time the massacre had been accomplished, and the woman gladly let him out, and he escaped into a hiding-place in the city, at a distance from his old residence. He remained there two months, when perceiving the persecution to be on the increase, he fled towards Senlis. On his way he met the Abbé de Rochemure, who had been his companion in prison, and whom he thought dead,—indeed the name had appeared in the official list of the massacred. Not being secure at Senlis, M. Vialar returned to Paris, and attempted to procure a passport; but failing in that endeavour, he disguised himself as a *colporteur*, and, with a knapsack upon his back, traversed France and Switzerland, and at length arrived at Rome. Afterwards he became chaplain to the Neapolitan ambassador at St. Petersburg. From the narration of his escape we obtain a glimpse of the unrelenting animosity with which the Catholic priests of France were hunted down.

The Abbé Saurin was saved, like the Abbé Dutillet, by his Marseillais accent. He was quietly waiting his hour to be massacred in a chapel of the church of the Carmes, when one of the assassins passed by speaking with the Provençal accent. The abbé approached him, saying,

"My friend, you are of Provence!"

"Yes," he replied, "of Marseilles."

"I am of the same town," said the abbé.

"What is your name?"

"Saurin."

"Oh, your brother is nearly related to me."

"Well, then, if we are bound by family ties, you ought to save me; for my only crime is that I am a priest."

The Marseillais instantly turned to his comrades and said,

"Citizens, this man is my relation, and as such he must not perish by the sword of the law."

"Bah!" they replied, "he is as guilty as the rest, and must perish like them."

"No, no," said the Marseillais; "and if I say no, I have a right to say it. Was I not at the taking of the Bastille? was I not at Versailles on the 5th and 6th October? and again at the Tuilleries on the 21st June? and at this last affair on the 10th August? See," he added, uncovering his breast, "see the wounds I have received."

The Abbé Saurin declares that there was not a scratch to be seen; but the stratagem succeeded, and the priest was handed over to his countryman. However, this act of mercy was not so purely generous as it seemed. When they got into the street, the Marseillais made him give up his new redingote, and take in exchange his old habit of the national guard. He then demanded some money in return for his services. The abbé gave him an assignat of two hundred livres,* and they separated. This priest afterwards succeeded in reaching Rome.

The Abbé Pannonie, whose generous attempt to save the Archbishop of Arles has already been mentioned, was saved, but by a miracle. After having escaped the massacre in the garden, he returned to the church with his brethren, and had made up his mind to die. Indeed, he was on his way, when one of the national guard approached, and said, "Save yourself, my friend!—save yourself!" Thinking it his duty to

---

* Many of the priests had money upon their persons when they were slain, which had been given them by friends to defray the expense of their journey in the event of their deportation.

avail himself of the means of escape, he gained the corridor leading to the cloister. However, he was immediately pursued by the assassins with fixed bayonets, from which he received nine wounds, and it is wonderful that he was not killed on the spot; but in the narrowness of the place the soldiers could not use their weapons. At length he ran towards a part of the garden called the Parc-aux-Cerfs, where he encountered another national guard, who tried to rescue him from his assassins, persuading them that he had been judged and acquitted. But the commandant of the Marseillais ordered him to be put into a doorway till he should be judged again. There the abbé remained, bleeding profusely from his wounds, under the guard of his faithful friend.

"Have you any hope of saving me?" he said to the soldier.

"If I had not, could I endure such a spectacle?"

He had upon him assignats to the value of several hundred livres, but the good soldier absolutely refused them.

"I shall be well paid if I can save your life," he said.

They waited till the massacre was over and the people were admitted.

"Now," he said, "mix with the crowd. They will be too eager to pillage the dead to think of you."

Trusting to Providence, he did so, and escaped into the street. After twenty minutes' walk, he reached a lady's house, by whom he was taken in and concealed. But how he escaped observation it is impossible to explain, for, wounded and bleeding as he was, he encountered numbers of persons talking about the massacre,—some applauding, others lamenting it; and it was not yet dark. Eventually he reached London. On landing in England he received great kindness from an English clergyman of the name of Strickland, who gave him a new suit of clothes, and kept the old ones, slashed with the bayonets and bloody, as a relic.

Even those whom the commissary had saved, or

L

whom certain generous citizens had claimed, were removed with great difficulty; for in passing through the streets they scarcely escaped being torn to pieces by the mob of furious women. And on their arrival at the church of St. Sulpice, where the Committee of the Section held its sittings, they had to undergo another examination. At midnight they were remanded into the hall of the Seminary; while they were there, one of the cut-throats came in complaining that they had been promised three livres for their labours, and had only received one. The commissary replied that there were still two days' work at the other prisons, which would make up the three livres; besides, there were the clothes of the victims. The assassin said, that not knowing they were to have the clothes, they had spoiled them with sabre-cuts. The next morning, the prisoners were again examined; and at length it was ordered that they should be set at liberty. However, their perils were not yet over: assassins were in waiting to murder them as soon as they left the church. But a sufficient body of the national guard conducted them to the Community of Priests at St. Sulpice, and there inquiring their different residences, separated into as many smaller parties, one of which escorted each prisoner to his home, with a recommendation to him not to show himself abroad for several days.

The massacres were not confined to the Carmes. Wherever priests were confined, there they were murdered,—at the Abbaye, at La Force, at St. Firmin,—and they displayed every where the same devoted courage. As soon as the massacre at the Carmes had ceased, Maillard, the delegate of the commune, was heard to cry, " There is nothing more to do here ; away to the Abbaye, there we shall find game!" Covered with gore and dust, fatigued with carnage, sated but not satiated with blood, he and a party of his assassins flung themselves into the committee-room, crying, " Wine! wine! or death!" The members of the committee gave them wine, and they drank until they were intoxicated. Then they went to the Abbaye, and regarded with savage delight the corpses which lay strewn about in the street; for the massacre had already been going on. Twenty-four priests had been moved, in six coaches, from the prison of La Mairie to the Abbaye; on their road, their guards themselves incited the populace to attack them; and they traversed the streets amid the cries of the rabble. The accusation against the priests of having betrayed their country at Verdun had been industriously circulated; but not content with that, the committee announced, by firing of cannon, the actual capture of the place. The announcement was a fabrication, Verdun was not actually taken for some days; but the reports of the guns served a double purpose,—at once to raise the fury of the people, and give a signal to the assassins when to commence the massacre. The slaughter was to begin at the third report, and the cortège arrived at the Abbaye gate as the fatal sound was heard. As the priests stepped out of the carriages, they were, with one exception, slaughtered; and their corpses still lay where they had fallen when Maillard and his assassins arrived drunk from the committee. Moreover, other assassins had assembled at the little gate of the Abbaye (for those who had murdered the twenty-four priests in the street had gone straightway to the Carmes), and yelling for victims, had threatened to burst into the prison. To put them off, and save the mass of the prisoners, the concièrge had thrown them one at a time to murder, —as a traveller, with his wife and children attacked by wolves, had been known to throw out first one child and then another to the famished beasts, in the hopes of saving the lives of the rest. These partial executions were still going on when Maillard arrived. He brought with him a despatch from the commune commanding all the prisoners to be judged except one, the Abbé Lenfant, who was to be kept in a safe place. Fearing lest the abbé should have been already murdered, an assassin was sent round with a damp sponge to wash the bloody countenances of the slain, in order to ascertain the fact. The abbé was not among the dead.

Maillard then established a tribunal as at the Carmes. In order to avoid bloodshed in the interior, it was arranged that the death-warrant should be "To La Force!" The unhappy prisoner hearing these words thought himself acquitted, or at least remanded, and left the tribunal comforted, only to be massacred as soon as he reached the street. By a concerted arrangement at La Force, the verdict of condemnation was "To the Abbaye!" By this outrage upon the feelings of humanity sixty priests were slain either in the street or in the Abbaye court. The Abbé Sicard gives a touching account of the whole scene. He had been one of the twenty-four priests brought from La Mairie, and he had been saved by his own presence of mind in declaring his name to the people. Every one knew the Abbé Sicard as the great friend of the poor deaf and dumb, and for a wonder he was spared, but still confined in the Abbaye; and he saw sixty of his brethren massacred before his eyes. "What a night," he exclaims, "I passed in that prison! The massacre took place under my window. The shrieks of the victims, the blows of the sword which fell on their innocent heads, the execrations of the murderers, the applause of the witnesses of the horrible spectacle, made my blood curdle to the heart. . . . . I heard the questions which were put to the priests, and their answers. It was demanded of them whether they had taken the civic oath. By an untruth they might all have escaped death; but they preferred to die; and as they died they said, 'We submit to your laws, we die faithful to your constitution; we only except what regards religion and affects our conscience!' They were instantly pierced with a thousand wounds, in the midst of the most frightful vociferations. Clapping their hands, the spectators cried 'Vive la Nation!' and then the savages danced their abominable dances round each corpse. . . . . Then there was a long pause, and the assassins

commenced a carouse. But between three and four
in the morning the same murderous cries were raised
again. Two more priests had been discovered hidden,
and they were being dragged on to death. They entreated a few hours to confess themselves to each other,
and the assassins granted it; not, however, out of any
mercy, but because they had no more priests, as they
thought, to massacre the next day for the amusement
of the people. They were accordingly locked up again;
and at length, wearied with slaughter and drunk with
wine, after a disgusting repast spread for them in the
midst of blood and corpses, the assassins took a few
hours' sleep. But the following morning at ten o'clock
the terrible tribunal commenced its sitting again. The
coolness with which arrangements were made for further butcheries is perfectly appalling. As the previous
victims had been too soon despatched, and all the assassins had not had the pleasure of aiming a blow at
every victim, it was resolved that in future only the
back of the sabre should be employed, and the assassins
were to stand in double rows, and the victims passed up
the middle, so that each might have the opportunity
of striking in his turn. The first who were slain in
this new fashion were the two priests who had been
remanded. Meanwhile others had been discovered,
among them the Father Rastignac; they too perished
immediately; and the whole of that day was spent in
searching out more priests, and massacring them in the
same place. The number who perished thus is not
known."

The reader will be curious to know what became of
the Abbé Lenfant. He was brother to one of the members of the committee, who had interposed to save him;
and at the Abbaye he was confined till the 5th, when
he was released. But his brother's precautions were
too carelessly taken to ensure his safety. On his way
through the streets a woman cried, "There is the confessor of the king;" and he was seized and brought
back again to the Abbaye. He raised his hands to-

wards heaven, and said, "My God, I thank Thee that I can offer Thee my life, as Thou offeredst Thine for me." They were the last words he ever spoke; and so on his knees, at the door of a house opposite the Abbaye, he received the fatal blow.

At St. Firmin the massacre commenced after the massacre at the Carmes had ceased. In this prison had been confined many of the priests who were arrested on the 11th and following days of August; and with them were a number of the lay brothers of the Lazarites, and an old captain named Villette, who for the last six years had lived withdrawn from the world in that house. A member of the assembly proposed that these laymen should be excepted from the massacre of the ecclesiastics; but the motion was negatived. The General Assembly decreed that the laymen who had made common cause with the refractory priests must share their fate.

The conduct of this massacre was committed to a man named Heriot, who afterwards perished with Robespierre. It appears that he had intended to follow the plan adopted at the Abbaye, of causing the prisoners to be slaughtered in the street; but the inhabitants of the quarter protested against being made the witnesses of so horrible a sight, and the victims were ordered up again into their chambers. Here the butchery was conducted without any pretence of justice or semblance of decency. All night long, with sabres and bayonets, the murderers were engaged in a general slaughter of priests and religious laymen. Some were thrown from the upper windows to be dashed upon the pavement below, and then torn to pieces by the women, or rather the furies, who were gathered together in the street. In this way perished the Abbé Copeine, who was dying in bed when he was taken out to be hurled from the top story. So also perished the Abbé Gros, curé of the parish, whose body was dragged in the gutter, and his head carried about on a pike. On opening his will, it was discovered to have bequeathed all his property to the poor of the very quarter which had thus savagely abused his remains! Ninety-two priests were martyred in the Seminary of St. Firmin.

In the prison of La Force were confined twelve priests, of whom two were saved. The other ten were massacred with the same heathen inhumanity. Nor are these by any means all who lost their lives at this terrible period. The number of victims in the cause of religion is not known. In the various massacres which we have enumerated, more than 400 priests were martyred. At the Carmes 200, at St. Firmin 92, at the Abbaye 86, at La Force 10; and in the isolated murders, which were going on for five days all over the city, not a few.

And for what did these glorious confessors suffer? Not as many other victims of that bloody committee, for any pretended political crimes, but in defence of the faith. They were true martyrs. They died not as Royalists, but as Christians. They died to maintain entire the religion of Jesus Christ, when all the powers of hell were banded against it; and not a drop of their blood fell fruitless to the ground. At no less cost could the integrity of the faith have been vindicated in France; for who can say what might have followed, if the clergy had consented to take the revolutionary oaths? The men who, in the hour of trial, fell away, would scarcely have had the courage to retrace their steps. In more peaceful times they would probably have set up some Gallican establishment on Erastian principles, and the whole country might have been permanently cut off, like other nations of Europe, from Catholic unity; but they were faithful unto blood, and now are seen the fruits of their great courage. To the admiration of all Christendom, the Church is rising again as a giant refreshed. The flood of infidelity is fast receding, and throughout the empire souls are flocking into the true fold. There are not wanting many cheering proofs of this happy change, of which the convent of the Carmes itself presents an instance in point.

On the Feast of Corpus Christi, 1854, the very garden which sixty years before had echoed with the groans of dying priests, rang with the voices of other priests singing the praises of God in the celebration of the *Fête Dieu*. Through the alleys, and beneath the trees, and by the oratory, and down the staircase, all hallowed by the steps and the blood of martyrs, wound the solemn procession in honour of the highest mystery of the faith for which they died. What more convincing proof could the infidel expect of the vanity of his own philosophy, and the inherent vitality and indestructibility of the Church of Christ? After his most daring effort, here, in the very scene of his triumph, his philosophy has passed away, and the Church performs the ancient rites of her ancient faith with all their ancient splendour.

The procession took place under the joint direction of the Dominican fathers and the principal of the "Ecole des Hautes Etudes," who share the use of the garden between them. In front marched a numerous body of old *militaire*, followed by young men, representatives of the first families in France. After them came many religious in the old habits of those long-tried orders that have at once built up and adorned the Church of God. Besides the Dominican fathers, there were the Fathers of the Oratory, the Marists, the Capuchins, the Brothers of St. John of God, and the Brothers of the Christian Doctrine. Then followed a numerous body of the clergy, and twenty priests in chasubles, before the Most Holy, borne beneath a splendid canopy by the curé of St. Sulpice. A multitude of men of every rank—for women were not admitted—many of them distinguished persons, brought up the rear: the music of the 33d regiment of the line alternating with the chorus of the "Ecole des Hautes Etudes." It is easy to conceive the impression which such a spectacle in such a spot must have produced on all that witnessed it.

Little children were strewing flowers before the Lamb of Peace, along the paths through which the assassins rushed, and under the trees, where now Our Saviour was borne in triumph by His priests. There was not a spot of which it could not be said, "There happier priests died for the same Saviour." The Dominicans established their altar by the side of the staircase where the massacre was completed. The altar of the Seminary was dressed at the foot of the yew-tree by which the heroic Archbishop of Arles was martyred. The Oratory, where so many priests were slain, and whose blood is still to be seen, is now the "Chapel of Martyrs;" and there was given, by the curé of St. Sulpice, the final Benediction to the assembled faithful.

But in a more permanent way the ancient convent of the Carmes bears witness to the struggles and the progress of the Church. It is now the "Ecole des Hautes Etudes," a seminary established by the late Archbishop of Paris, to counteract the pernicious effects upon religion and morality of the government system of education.

By the exclusion of all religious teaching from the universities of France, infidelity was being propagated in the most dangerous form,—in connection, that is to say, with the progress of science. For, on account of their high literary attainments, men who had taken university degrees were selected to fill all the great chairs, and preside over the chief seminaries in France; and thus they monopolised the whole training of the rising generation. Mgr. Affre pointed out to Louis Philippe the baneful results which must necessarily follow from this system, but without effect. The King of the French refused to modify his policy, and the archbishop determined to provide the religious element that was wanting from an independent source. In conjunction with his episcopal brethren, he established in the Carmes a preparatory seminary for the universities, called the "Ecole des Hautes Etudes;" in which, as its name implies, the pupils should be instructed in the highest branches of literature, and thus be fitted to take the highest university honours, at the same time that they were trained for the service of the Church, for all are destined to be priests so soon as they have taken their degrees. In this way a body of professors has been provided for the different dioceses, equal to any in point of learning and ability, and superior to all in point of religion; under whom the Church seminaries are more than on a par with those of the government. The result exceeds the best wishes of the original promoters of the undertaking. The Church is gaining ground rapidly on the adversary, where before she lost it. Under the government professor, the pupil became, indeed, a good scholar and an accomplished gentleman, but he also grew up an antagonist of the Church and a scoffer at religion. Under the diocesan professor, before the institution of the seminary of the Carmes, he was trained in the faith and in morals, but he was unable to cope with the other in literary acquirements. The " Ecole des Hautes Etudes" has raised the secular education of the diocesan seminary to a level with its government rival; and in consequence of the high religious character, has surpassed it in favour with the people.

If the blood of martyrs be the seed of the Church, happy indeed was the selection of the Archbishop of Paris when he founded his seminary in the Carmes; and doubtless the success of his institution is due in a great measure to the merits and intercessions of those heroic men whose sufferings we have thus so briefly recorded. Founded by a martyr on a spot consecrated by the blood of martyrs, the school must needs carry with it the blessing of God. And the ancient convent of the Carmes at once awakens hopes for the future of the rising Church, and glorious reminiscences of the Church that has passed away.

XXI.

GABRIEL DE NAILLAC.

ABRIEL PIERRE REBIERE, Seigneur de Naillac, was born of a noble family at the château of Cessac, in the province of La Marche, in 1760. His father, who was of advanced age at his birth, took pains to impress religious sentiments on his mind; but, unfortunately, the taint of an erroneous teaching awaited him in the bosom of his own family. He lost his mother at an early age, and his father was greatly influenced by a brother of his own; a man of acuteness and learning, but who was infected by the then prevailing errors of Jansenism. He had been, indeed, a leader of the sect; but in consequence of the measures adopted for its suppression, had withdrawn himself to Utrecht, not, however, before he had made the château of Cessac a rendezvous for his co-religionists. The worthy seigneur entertained them with the reverence he considered due to persecuted piety, and allowed them to avail themselves of his name and influence to spread their opinions. His son, as might have been expected, imbibed the same views, and they became for a time firmly rooted in his mind, only to be eradicated, as they eventually were, by the gift of divine grace, co-operated with by deep and patient study of orthodox theology.

After passing through a course of study at the college of Tournon, he was removed to that of Pont-le-Voi, in Touraine. Here, at his father's desire, he relinquished awhile literature and mathematics for the acquirement of the polite accomplishments deemed essential to his rank. In these he soon excelled. Then

he entered on philosophy, and devoted two years to its
study; but, unhappily, Pont-le-Voi was under the protection of the philosophic and unbelieving Duke de
Choiseul, who had founded it on the ruins of a religious
house, whose property he had secularised for that purpose.   Here De Naillac had the misfortune to form an
intimacy with one of the free-thinking abbés of that
day—a witty and clever, but unprincipled and super-
ficial character, ever ready with an insidious thrust at
religion and morality.   Under this and the like in-
fluences, it was little wonder if our young student of
philosophy soon came, not perhaps openly to renounce
his religion, but to fall in with the current sentiments
of the time, to regard faith as obsolete, and philosophy
—that is to say, infidelity—as the test of genius, and
the path to honour and virtue.

Now, at his father's wish, he was sent " to see the
world;" to be introduced to the society of the metro-
polis, with a view to his establishment in life.   He soon
fixed his affections on a young lady of family and for-
tune, Mademoiselle de Neuville by name; he was accepted by her parents, and their union took place.   At his
wife's especial desire, they fixed their residence in Paris.
She loved society, and was well qualified to shine in it.
He also could claim a good position by his rank and
mental acquirements.   Their circle included many of
the celebrated characters of the day; and they lived in
the full enjoyment of all the refined pleasures that
affluence, combined with the cultivation of intellect, can
procure.

He was now the world's favourite; but God was
gradually leading and preparing him, in his own good
time, to be a witness to the faith, a model of penance,
and a succour to the afflicted.

A son and heir was born to him, and then three
daughters in succession; but his first-born, after exhi-
biting an unusual degree of precocity, fell a victim to
the stroke of fatal disease,—an agonising blow to the
father, who had fixed all his hopes on the boy.   The
era of the Revolution approached.   De Naillac was a

patriot. The acknowledged abuses, the vacillation of the government, and the democratic leanings of some in high places, had disposed him at first to favour the movement. At the assembly of the noblesse of his own province, La Marche, he espoused the popular side. But as reform grew to revolution, and revolution to rebellion and disloyalty, he became its determined opponent, and resolved on defending to the last the ancient monarchy of France. He remained alike unmoved by the menaces of the anarchists, and allurements of the demagogues in power, while he lent his ready co-operation to every measure for ameliorating the condition of the masses. He gave his wealth for the relief of the populace, though he was cursed and threatened as an aristocrat by the savage mob. Their violence and daily encroachments on his rights and property could not drive him from his post. At length the danger of his prince aroused him to take up arms. He committed himself to a brave but ill-concerted rising in the provinces, which issued in failure—in the flight of some, and the destruction of others concerned in it. He narrowly escaped with life. His zeal for the cause was unabated, and he immediately engaged in another royalist attempt; but this was disconcerted by the king's flight and arrest at Varennes. Louis embraced the constitution, how fatally events soon proved. His tenderness for the lives of men made him discourage and disavow the proceedings taken by the emigrant nobles and gentry in his behalf. These last were now in arms on the German frontier, favoured by the emperor, and headed by the two royal brothers, afterwards Louis XVIII. and Charles X. De Naillac now bade adieu to his wife, children, and friends, and the ancient manor-house of his ancestors, as it proved, for ever, and joined the camp at Coblentz in October 1791.

After some delay, which he spent in the acquirement of military knowledge, the Prussians, with their king, arrived, and the confederates opened a campaign

against the rebels; but no success attended their arms.
The allies were soon in retreat, sorely harassed by
sickness, famine, and the enemy.   Still they disdained
surrender.   De Naillac suffered most from anxiety for
those he had left at home; and as yet religion brought
no balm to his tortured spirit.

When the army was dissolved, he repaired, with
the other emigrants, all dispirited and destitute, to
Liège, then governed by its prince-bishop, a stanch
friend to the royalist cause.   He resolved to labour for
his bread, rather than compromise the safety of his
friends and family at home by any attempt at correspondence.   The prince-bishop of Liège showed great
hospitality to the French emigrants; and these in
return volunteered the defence of his dominions from
the French revolutionary propagandists and their sym-
pathisers amongst his subjects.   In this manner they
rendered him some essential service, and De Naillac
was amongst the most active in the work.   The goodness of heart natural to him had already prompted him
to devote himself, with all the little means at his disposal, to the relief of the distressed amongst his own
emigrant countrymen.   But now it was that religion
began to absorb his attention.   The beautiful churches
of Liège, where the Catholic worship was, and is, carried out in its true majesty, attracted him, and in a
short time he was led to penetrate beyond its mere ex-
ternals.   A preacher of most impressive eloquence, the
Abbé Beaurégard, who had been a court-preacher to
the king of France, appeared in the city; and by his
instrumentality the incredulous philosophical soldier
was converted back to his early belief, and to the devout practice of his religion.   Almighty God was mer-
cifully so disposing the events of his life as to lead him
gradually to Himself.   Certain commercial projects, by
which he had hoped to realise a competence in his
exile, gradually proved abortive.   Some remarkable
preservations from imminent danger occurring about
this time, had likewise a tendency to fix his mind in

the direction it was now taking. He was a constant and attentive hearer of the eloquent abbé. The religious spark early enkindled in his mind had never quite gone out, and now it revived, and enabled him to grasp at least one primary truth, the being and personality of God, all-mighty and all-good. This in due time conducted him to faith and to penance.

Political affairs ceased to engross his mind. He had sacrificed all that gives value to life for his loyal principles; now he sanctified the offering by submitting to the Divine will even the destiny of his king and country.

His progress in the spiritual life was wonderfully rapid. Rich in the gift of prayer, the hours seemed too short for its exercise. Great as was his reserve and humility, yet it became known to his most intimate friends that he enjoyed at this time an abundant measure of consolation. Towards Mary his devotion was most tender and assiduous. One day, whilst adoring before the Blessed Sacrament, an inward voice spoke to his soul in so vivid and distinct a manner, that he could not doubt it to be a direct manifestation of the Divine will, and an intimation as to what the future destiny of his life was to be.

The French revolutionary invasion now became daily more menacing; the allied forces were unable any longer to protect Liège; and it became necessary for the emigrants to withdraw to some securer refuge. Sore was the trial to De Naillac to leave a second home, where he had found religion in her beauty, and been taught her reality and her sweetness, and to know that those sacred aisles would soon witness the profanations of infidel fanaticism. He departed, followed by the deep regrets of the numerous friends he had made in Liège, and proceeded, in company with a large band of emigrants, by way of Nimeguen, to the little town of Essen, in Westphalia. He had resolved this time to withdraw far enough from the troubles of France, and hoped not to be again disturbed. Essen was anti-

revoluuonary and Catholic, and received the emigrants
with an embrace of fraternal sympathy. It was rewarded, during the subsequent convulsions, by a rare
exemption for a long time from the horrors of war; in
answer—may we not believe?—to the grateful prayers
of the strangers for the hospitality they experienced.
Nearly seven hundred found an asylum at this place;
they formed the more religious portion of the body, and
were brought together by a mutual sympathy on this
point. The churches were always thronged, and a
great multitude of French priests daily offered up the
Holy Sacrifice for their unhappy country.

De Naillac found a lodging in the house of a venerable clergyman and his colleague, and spent his time
in listening to their edifying converse, in the exercises
of devotion, and of works of charity. A few other
emigrants joined him, and a little society was formed,
under the direction of the two clergymen, for the practice of charity and of penance. Still his aspirations
ascended to heaven for the welfare of France, and for
the triumph of what he deemed the right cause; and
still was he ready to shed his blood in that cause; but
it was for the altar's sake he wished to raise the Lily
out of the dust. The brave army of Condé had been
prodigal of their lives, as had several other royalist
confederacies; the death-throes of La Vendée had recalled the deeds of the Machabees; a movement in Brittany for the rescue of the Church was now on foot; and
lastly, the king of England was incorporating bodies
of French volunteer officers, with the view of co-
operating with the efforts making for the restoration
of the monarchy. De Naillac joined one of these bodies,
that commanded by the Comte de Tresor, and shared
in the descent on the Ile-Dieu and the subsequent sufferings and disasters. In these events he bore himself
like a true soldier and Christian: his spirit of penance
and devotion amidst the confusion, hardships, and perils
of the war, and his unwearied efforts to alleviate the
miseries of his poorer comrades, were most admirable;

but our limits forbid further details. Eventually he was removed, with his corps, to the Channel Islands, and after their disbanding to England. In Jersey, the devout society was either continued or constituted anew; and on their arrival in London its action was most beneficial. It consisted of gentlemen, late civil and military officers in the royal service of France; all men of devoted piety, and, since the ruin of their country, aspirants to the priestly or religious state. No human record commemorates their rich fruits of devotion and charity, performed in an obscure corner of London. The members had no other occupation, by day or night, than united prayer, the study of religion, and the laborious exercise of the corporal and spiritual works of mercy amongst the crowds of poor French emigrants in the Middlesex Hospital, and in other similar scenes of suffering and misery. Such was the company in which De Naillac was, for some time after his arrival in London, an active member; but now a new field was to be opened to his charity.

At Somers Town, then a village suburb of London, there had been opened, in 1797, a House of Refuge for the aged and decrepit amongst the French emigrant priests, many of whom were now destitute strangers in a strange land. This establishment lasted down to the time of the Restoration, and proved a welcome harbour to not a few venerable confessors, who had practised the virtues of Tobias and of Job, and had endured similar afflictions.

François Després, late a pastor of Rennes in Brittany, was the first director of this establishment, and he, having fallen a martyr of charity in 1802, was succeeded by another exemplary priest, late vicar-general of the same diocese of Rennes. Under the former of these superiors the post of hospital attendant, or infirmarian, became vacant: it had been usually discharged by an ecclesiastic; and the saintly Bishop of Léon, who for the eighteen years of his exile had devoted himself unweariedly to the welfare of his banished countrymen,

M.

was charged with the finding of a successor. He was both delighted and edified to find a candidate in a Frenchman of noble rank and refined education, who solicited, as a great favour, the appointment to an office of the most fatiguing and repulsive kind. De Naillac was the applicant, and was at once appointed; and the good bishop, on all occasions, and even on his death-bed, never omitted an opportunity of testifying his deep admiration of such self-denying charity.

Shortly after entering on the duties of his post, De Naillac wrote as follows to the leader of the little pious confraternity with which he had hitherto been asso-ciated. His letter is dated "The Polygon, Somers Town, July 1798:"

"While I live, I shall never forget your friendship; never shall I cease to feel truly grateful for it. Provi-dence now sees fit to part us : the will of God is, I trust, sufficiently manifest in the approval of the holy Bishop of Léon, and in the desire of the reverend superior of the Aged Priests' Asylum, that I undertake the duties of infirmarian there. I have already commenced their discharge. To depart silently from our society, did indeed some violence to my feelings; but I thought it best to shun the sorrow of a parting scene, though I had to deny myself the pleasure of making a personal acknowledgment of the great kindness I have experienced from you. I would entreat my dear friends to pardon and forget whatever disedification I may have given during our intercourse. I sincerely lament it, if there have been any such defect in me. I would also beg for the continuance of our friendship : it has been most highly valued by me, and will be while I live."

It was on a festival of the Blessed Virgin that he obtained the highly-prized privilege of being servitor to the afflicted. He spent the day in supplications for her patronage. He remarked with gratitude that the chief blessings of his life were received on days that were dedicated to her.

He told it in confidence to a friend, that his aim in

seeking this employment was, that he might vanquish
the extreme repugnance he felt naturally to such duties.
To work as cook and scullion, to wait on the sick, to
dress festering ulcers, were labours nothing but the
sternest resolution could have enabled him to attempt:
yet for these things he was needed; and prizing the
opportunities they afforded of penance and of merit, he
accepted them with joy, and persevered in them for
upwards of eleven years. In the garb of a servant, he
would sweep the house and the court-yard, and work at
the meanest offices till the perspiration streamed from
his brow. Nothing was too hard or too lowly for his
zeal; and this not by a fitful impulse, but by the uniform tenour of his life. He bore, with the tenderness of
a son, the infirmities, moral as well as physical, of the
afflicted priests: he served them with pious respect:
he knelt at their feet, and like a good Samaritan,
dressed their sores with light and tender hand; and
showed no disgust, but most compassionate sympathy,
at sight of the most dreadful maladies. As the patients grew more and more helpless, the severity of
his labours increased; but his cheerful energy increased
with it. His one discontent was, that he was not
permitted to serve all the night whenever a night-
nurse was required. His daily labour commenced at
five, and ended at eleven, even in the depth of winter;
and he had the sole charge not only of nursing five or
six generally of his beloved paralytic and helpless old
priests, but likewise of the kitchen and the whole domestic management. Sometimes nature seemed on the
point of giving way. Then his refreshment was to visit
our Lord present in the tabernacle of the little domestic
chapel; where, as he declared to intimate friends, he
found his strength and spirits completely recruited
One instance only we will mention of all that his heroic
charity accomplished. M. de Noan, a venerable pastor
from Brittany, came under his charge afflicted with a
gangrenous ulcer in the foot. The sub-infirmarian had
himself just become disabled, and De Naillac thence-

forward would accept of no assistance. M. de Noan's sufferings were intense : amputation was too hazardous in one of such advanced age, but all that skill could do was done. The ulcer spread, and became most offensive, while the pain forced cries of agony from the patient. The faithful minister, taking example from St. John of God, dressed the horrible sore during a whole hour thrice daily on his knees at the bed-side. He did it as if it were a pleasure, and so tenderly, that the aged sufferer would allow of no other attendance. The gangrene extended and mortified, and the good old priest found repose in death. De Naillac tended him to the last with assiduous care; and when he was gone, mourned him with deep regret as a father and a benefactor. Every feeling was absorbed in love of his brethren; in the struggle after self-denial and perfect charity.

He proved on many occasions that he possessed the gift to speak with wisdom, and in season, the word of consolation and advice; and in so doing to adapt himself to every character, to win the affection and esteem of all. To be praised was his greatest aversion : if by chance any one commended or flattered him, he grew alarmed, and instantly made it a subject of humiliation before his God. In the fifth year of his service as infirmarian to the aged priests, his beloved wife was taken away. He felt the blow acutely, and mourned her long and tenderly. And now, by the earnest recommendation of friends, and prayerful seeking to know the Divine will, he was called to the service of the priesthood. His humility at first made him reluctant; but these scruples overcome, he applied himself with energy to the studies preparatory to his ordination. He was much impressed with that saying of St. Athanasius, " sine legendi studio, neminem ad Deum intentum videas;" that is, " without application to study, no one can be fixedly intent on God."

He celebrated his first Mass with the most tender and elevated sentiments of devotion, and with a fervour

that was unabated during the short residue of his life.
Short indeed it was, for the extreme fatigues he had
undergone, his voluntary mortifications, and the profound grief he suffered at the sight of the calamities
of his country and of religion, had brought on an
internal disease, which broke out with violence in the
month of March 1809. He was aware of his approaching change. " In eight days," said he to a friend, " I
shall be no more: God's holy will be done! Oh, what
a blessing to go to my dear Lord! Pray for me."

His reception of the last Sacraments recalled the
fervour of the primitive Christians. He humbly begged
the forgiveness of all, and especially of the aged friends
to whom he had ministered, for any offence that, through
human infirmity, he might have given. He assured
them of his present happiness, and perfect confidence
in his God. Although his case was known to be hopeless, yet so little was his strength impaired, that those
around could scarce believe him dying; but just as
some hopes had begun to be cherished of his recovery,
on the morning of the 24th of April, as he was attempting to write some last words, he suddenly fell back,
and peacefully expired in the arms of the reverend
superior of the house. The distress at his loss amongst
the inmates of the asylum was indescribable; great too
was the regret of all who had known his virtues and
enjoyed his friendship. He was followed to the grave
by a very numerous train of the French refugees, both
of those highest in consideration and of the poorest.

A modest stone was erected over his grave, with a
Latin epitaph, of which the following is a copy and a
translation:

" Hic jacet Reverendus admodum Gabriel Petrus
Rebiere de Naillac; in proavorum castello prope urbem
Garactum Marchiæ caput pernobili genere natus. Pa-
triis institutis semper fidelis et ubique, in coalitis Bor-
bonidum copiis anno MDCCXCVII. et sequentibus, mili-
tavit strenue. Demisso exercitu in seniorum civium
suorum valetudinario, formam servi accipiens, per XI.

annos, omnibus omnia factus, infirmos et debiles curavit
assidue, ulcerum fœditatem abstersit, advigilavit ægro-
tantibus, sepeliebat corpora eorum. Interea viduus, dilec-
tissimam uxorem luxit amare, et Christi militiæ ascrip-
tus terrena despiciens, dives autem in humilitate sua,
functus est sacerdotio. Obiit die xxiiii. Aprilis anno
MDCCCIX. in seniorum gremio ad Somers Town, an-
num agens L. Hoc monumentum in defuncti memoriam
et ad superstitis solatium amici, addicta utrique posuit
amicorum societas. Plangent eum planctu, quasi super
unigenitum, et dolebunt super eum ut doleri solet in
morte unigeniti. Requiescat in pace."

" Here lies the Reverend Gabriel Pierre de Naillac,
the scion of a noble and ancient house, who was born at
his ancestral mansion of Cessac, near to Guéret, chief
town of La Marche in France. Always and every
where faithful to the institutions of his country, he
served bravely in the allied armies under the Bourbons
in 1797 and the following years. After the disbanding of those forces he devoted himself to the lowliest
work of charity in a hospital of his countrymen, for
eleven years. Becoming all things to all, he there diligently nursed the sick and decrepit, dressed their sores,
and buried them when dead. In the meantime having
become a widower, he bitterly lamented a much-loved
wife; and despising earthly things, but rich in his humility, he entered the ranks of the priesthood of Christ.
He departed this life at the Aged Priests' Asylum,
Somers Town, April 24, 1809, in the fiftieth year of
his age. This monument is erected by a society of his
friends as a solace to survivors, and in testimony of
their affection for his memory. ' They mourn for him
as one mourneth for an only son, and they grieve over
him as the manner is to grieve for the death of the first-
born.' May he rest in peace!"

IX.

MARGARET CLITHEROW,

THE MARTYR OF YORK.

HIS truly Christian heroine was born in York about the year 1556; her maiden name was Middelton. She was brought up a Protestant, and continued such until two or three years after her marriage. According to the old saying, that "the blood of the martyrs is the seed of the Church," it was hearing of the patient sufferings of so many Catholics, both priests and laity, during the bitter persecution of Queen Elizabeth, which first turned Margaret's thoughts to the Catholic faith; and no sooner had a question concerning it suggested itself to her mind, than she set herself to inquire into the matter thoroughly, and was in due time received into the Church.

From this period her whole life was a season of preparation for the act of martyrdom which eventually crowned it, for she had to endure an abundant measure of the persecution which raged at that time against Catholics. Several times she was separated from her husband and children, and thrown into prison, where she remained for a space of more than two years, and where she devoted herself to the practice of all holiness, rejoicing in the quiet and seclusion it afforded her, so that she always looked back on the term of her imprisonment as the happiest period of her life, because the most profitable. And she was in truth a model of all Christian virtues of humility, obedience, and the most fervent charity, of all which a remarkable example is recorded by her director. When the statute was framed which made it high treason to entertain a Catholic priest, a Catholic gentleman, a friend of hers, advised her to be more careful than she had hitherto been in this respect, and on no account to adventure such a risk without consulting her husband. She hastened to communicate to her director the advice she had received, saying to him, " May I not receive priests and serve God as I have done, notwithstanding these new laws, without my husband's consent? I have hitherto," she continued, " put my whole confidence in you, that I might safely walk without sin by your direction. Now I know not how the rigour of these new laws may alter my duty in these things; but if you tell me that I offend God in any point, I will not do it for all the world." Her director answered, that her duty to God was in no way subject to her husband's control, and that the new laws made no difference in that duty; so that, if berore they were enacted it was right in her to receive priests, and to serve God after the Catholic manner, it was right still; and that it was for her husband's safety not to know of her proceedings in this matter; that moreover it was an especial duty not to obey these wicked laws, because to do so was to become in a measure partaker of the sin of those who made them, and to carry out effectually the intention of the lawgivers, namely, the abolition of the Catholic faith throughout the realm. This counsel was most welcome. to her devoted spirit.

"Thank you, father," she answered; "by God's grace, all priests shall be more welcome to me than ever they were."

"Then, my daughter," he said, smiling, "you must prepare your neck for the rope."

"God's will be done," she answered; "but I am far unworthy of that honour."

She continued, therefore, as she had begun, in spite of the persecuting laws, zealously to receive any priests who came to her. She had prepared two secret chambers for their reception, and for a place to say Mass; one in a neighbour's house adjoining, but with a very small hidden entrance from her own house, where, therefore, she might resort at any time without being seen or suspected, and the other at some little distance; which last she reserved for more dangerous times. In fitting up these places for the holy service she had spared no expense ; and when afterwards they were given up to pillage, the spoilers were astonished at the quantity and richness of the church-furniture which she had collected.

Though living thus in daily peril of the most deadly kind, our heroine had her reward in an unfailing serenity of heart, amounting even to gladness. Her "discreet and honest mirth," and "mild smiling countenance," are held in affectionate remembrance by her biographer; as also her strength of mind, acuteness of intellect, and quick despatch of business, more especially in any thing concerning the Catholic cause. "If the difficulty," we are told, " appeared ever so great, and the thing almost desperate, by her advice it was commonly brought to pass without danger." Though in her fervour she adventured risks, which seemed to some extravagant, for the spiritual good of others, furnishing them with means of serving God far beyond the measure of their strict obligation, yet the discretion and skill with which she ordered every thing were such as to enable her to carry on these holy practices undetected for a longer time than any one thought possible. She was very popular, too, among even her Protestant neighbours ; so that, though many suspected that she heard Mass in her house daily, they were as careful to conceal the matter, and give her warning of any impending danger, as if the affair had been their own. She did not allow the weighty matters in which she was engaged to distract her from her household duties ; but fulfilled them all with scrupulous exactness, ruling her servants with strictness, and reproving them, if needful, with a sharpness which alarmed those about her, who knew what perilous secrets were necessarily confided to the faithfulness of these very servants, who had thus their mis-

tress's very life in their power. " I should be ashamed
of myself," she said, " if I allowed my house to be
ordered negligently from any danger to myself."

Her biographer has left a short sketch of her rule
of life, which, though it reads like that of an ordinary
Christian, is raised to a very different level when we
remember that all these duties, so easy to us, were per-
·formed by her at the peril of her life. She rose early,
made a meditation of an hour and a half, and heard
Mass. Then set herself to the work of the day till
four o'clock in the afternoon, when, with her children,
she came to what her biographer calls evensong, probably vespers; then to her household duties again, till
eight or nine, when she would visit her "ghostly father" again, to pray with him, and ask his blessing
before retiring to rest. Twice a-week she frequented
the Holy Sacrament of Confession and the Blessed
Eucharist. She delighted in spiritual reading, more
especially the New Testament in the Rheims translation,
and the Imitation. Her early education seems to have
been strangely neglected, in an age when there was so
much of mental cultivation, for we are told that it was
during her first imprisonment that she learned to read;
but in the idea that at some future day she might possibly be called to a religious life, she had learnt to say
the Office of our Lady in Latin.

The priests whose ministrations she so valued were
most of them taken one after the other, and martyred
at a place called Knavesmire, about a mile from York.
This spot therefore became to her a holy place of pil-
grimage, where, as often as she could gain permission
from her director, she would go barefoot by night for
fear of spies, and kneeling under the gallows, meditate
and pray as long as her companions could suffer her.
Thus was stirred up within her a fervent desire to follow their good example, though she thought herself
altogether unworthy of such an honour. "In truth,"
she would say, " I see not in myself any worthiness of
martyrdom; yet, if it be His will, I pray Him that I

may be constant, and persevere to the end." Her being so frequently delivered out of prison was rather a trouble to her, as it made her fear the more that " she was not counted worthy of so great a calling."

Her time, however, came sooner than she looked for it. In the year 1586, we are told that "the Lord Eure, vice-president, Mr. Meare, Mr. Hurleston, and Mr. Cheeke, counsellors at York, sent for Mr. Clitherow to appear before them. Mrs. Clitherow feared that during her husband's absence they would send to the sheriffs of York to search the house, and therefore she gave immediate notice to the priest who was concealed in the secret chamber we have mentioned, and he was conveyed away safely before the arrival of the sheriffs, who came during Mr. Clitherow's absence, as his wife had anticipated. In another part of her house, however, was concealed a Catholic schoolmaster, named Mr. Stapleton, who had lately escaped from prison, and who was engaged at that time in teaching her children, and two or three little boys besides. Whilst he was thus occupied, one of the sheriffs partly opened the door, and, suspecting the schoolmaster to be a priest, shut it again hastily, and ran to call his fellows. Mr. Stapleton, thinking it was a friend, opened the door again to call him in; but immediately guessing the truth, escaped by the secret way to the priest's chamber in the house adjoining, and so got off safely. The searching party came back to the room in great haste, and, enraged at having lost their prey, took Mrs. Clitherow into custody, together with her children and servants; and threatened one of the little boys present (not one of her own children) so cruelly, that at last he yielded, and showed them the priest's chamber, with the receptacle for books and church-furniture which it contained. All these they seized, sent the children and servants to separate prisons, and carried Mrs. Clitherow before the council. After a short examination she was committed to the Castle as a close prisoner: this examination was secret; but from the state in which she reached the prison, bathed in perspiration and utterly exhausted, her biographer surmises that she was put to the torture, which, as we know, was freely used on like occasions. The little boy who had showed the priests' chamber also accused many persons whom he had seen there at Mass, among others a certain Mrs. Agnes Leech, who was also committed to the Castle on Saturday, the 12th of March, and who continued in the same chamber with Mrs. Clitherow until the Monday following, which was the first day of the assizes at York. Her husband was also imprisoned, and she was allowed one or two interviews with him, but only in the audience of the gaoler and others. Her serenity of mind, however, not only did not forsake her, but increased with such gladness of spirit that she was afraid she might thereby lose the merit of suffering. "Sister," she said to Mrs. Agnes Leech, "we two are so merry together, that I fear, unless we be parted, we shall hazard to lose the merit of our imprisonment."

On Monday, the 14th of March, in the afternoon, Mrs. Clitherow was brought from the Castle to the common-hall in York, before the two judges, Mr. Clinch and Mr. Rhodes, several others of the council sitting with them on the bench.

Her indictment was read : "That she had harboured and maintained Jesuit and Seminary priests, traitors to the Queen's majesty and the laws; and that she had heard Mass and such like." Then Judge Clinch stood up and said, "Margaret Clitherow, how say you? are you guilty of this indictment or not?"

She answered, with a mild and smiling countenance, "I know no offence whereof I should confess myself guilty."

The judge said, "Yes, you have offended the Queen's majesty's laws, forasmuch as you have harboured and maintained Jesuits and priests, enemies to her majesty."

She answered, "I neither know nor have harboured any such persons. God forbid that I should harbour or maintain those which are not the Queen's friends."

The judge said, "How will you be tried?"

"Having committed no offence," she answered, "I need no trial."

They said, "You have offended against the statute, and therefore you must be tried;" and often asked her how she would be tried.

She answered, "If you say I have offended, and that I must be tried, I will be tried by none but by God and your own conscience."

"That cannot be," said the judges; "you must be tried by your country." Then they brought out the chalices and vestments, and mocked at them; and asked her in whom she believed?

"I believe," said she, "in God."

"In what God?" asked the judge.

"I believe," she answered, "in God the Father, God the Son, and God the Holy Ghost; in these three Persons and one God I fully believe; and that by the death, passion, and mercy of Christ Jesus I must be saved."

The judge said, "You say well;" and after a while asked her again how she would be tried? and again she refused trial; fearing that by her trial others might be criminated, and so brought into the same trouble. The judge said, "Good woman, consider well what you do; if you refuse to be tried by your country, you make yourself guilty and accessory to your own death; for we cannot try you but by order of law. You need not fear this kind of trial; for I think the country cannot find you guilty upon the slender evidence of one child." She still refused; and then the judge told her that they must proceed against her according to law, which would condemn her to a sharp death for want of trial; but she answered cheerfully, "God's will be done. I thank God that I may suffer any death for this good cause."

That night the judge retired without having pronounced sentence, and she was brought from the hall, "with a great troop of men and halberts, with a most cheerful countenance, dealing silver on both sides of the streets," to the felons' prison on the bridge, which bridge—a noble construction of six arches, on which besides the prison, stood a chapel and the great council-chamber of the city—has been now removed, to the great regret of antiquarians. Here that same night she was visited by a puritan preacher, by name Whigginton, who endeavoured to turn her from the faith.

The next day, at eight o'clock, she was carried again to the common-hall, and the judge thus addressed her: "Margaret Clitherow, how say you yet? Yester-night we passed you over without judgment, which we might have pronounced against you if we would; we did it not, hoping you would be something more con-formable, and put yourself on the country, for other-wise you must needs have the law. We see nothing why you should refuse; here be but small witness against you, and the country will consider your case." "Indeed," said she, "I think you have no witness against me but children, whom with an apple or a rod you may cause to say what you will." They said: "It is plain that you have had priests in your house by these things which are found." She answered: "As for good Catholic priests, I know no cause why I should refuse them as long as I live; they come only to do me and others good." On this Rhodes, Thur-leston, and others, exclaimed: "They are all traitors, rascals, and deceivers of the Queen's subjects." "God forgive you," she meekly replied; "you would not speak so of them if you knew them." After several more speeches of this kind, the judge asked her once more whether she would put herself on her country, and she again declined; on which he warned her that she had nothing to expect but the rigour of the law. Then Whigginton, the preacher who had visited her the even-ing before, spoke in her favour, reminding the judge how slender was the evidence against her, and assuring him that if the Queen's law empowered him to proceed against her to the death, the law of God did not. But Rhodes and others urged on her death; and at last the judge reluctantly passed sentence upon her to this effect, "that in the lowest part of her prison she should be stripped, laid on her back on the ground, and as much weight laid on her as she could bear, and so continue for three days; and on the third day, should she still refuse to plead, be pressed to death, her hands and feet tied to a post and a sharp stone under her back."

The martyr heard this fearful sentence without any change of countenance, and meekly answered: "If this judgment be according to your conscience, I pray God for a better judgment in His presence." The judge again offered her the alternative of throwing herself on her country, but she again refused, saying: "God be thanked; all that He shall send me shall be welcome; I am not worthy so good a death as this is; I have deserved death for my offences against God, but not for any thing I am accused of."

Then the sheriffs pinioned her arms with a cord, and escorted her with halberts back to the bridge again, she all the while bearing so cheerful a countenance, that some of those who looked upon her as she passed said, that it must needs be that she received comfort from the Holy Ghost; but others answered that "it was not so, but that she was possessed of a merry devil, and that she sought her own death." As she walked between the two sheriffs, she scattered money on both sides of her as well as she could, her arms being pinioned.

When her husband heard her sentence, he was like one distracted. "Alas!" he cried, "will they kill my wife? Let them take all I have, and save her, for she is the best wife in all England, and the best Catholic also."

Her friends made every effort to save her; and among other expedients, were very earnest that she should declare herself with child; but she could not be persuaded to say more than the real truth, that she was not certain whether she was so or not. However, the bare possibility that such might be the case was sufficient to make the judge extremely reluctant to order her execution; but he was overruled by the council.

and at last, "like Pilate," as we are told, "thinking *t*. wash his hands of the matter, he referred all to them, desiring them to use their own discretion; and at his departure from the city, he commanded that the execution should take place on the following Friday," the 25th of March, unless they should hear from him to the contrary.

The martyr, after her condemnation, set herself to prepare for death with much fasting and prayer; still fearing that she was not worthy to suffer such a death for God's sake. At this time she sent word to her ghostly father, desiring him to pray earnestly for her; but that the heaviest cross to her was the fear of escaping death.

Again and again Protestant ministers and others came to her in her prison, to try both to persuade her to throw herself on her country, and also to renounce the Catholic faith; but her stedfastness in both was immovable. "Answer me," said one of these to her, "what is the Church?" The martyr said: "It is that wherein the true word of God is preached, which Christ taught, and left to His apostles, and they to their successors, ministering the seven Sacraments which the same Church hath always observed, doctors preached, and martyrs and confessors have witnessed. This is the Church which I believe to be true." Whigginton, the Puritan, who had before visited her, came to see her again, and to urge her to yield. "Possibly," said he, "you think you shall have martyrdom; but you are foully deceived, for it cometh but one way. Not death. but the cause maketh a martyr. In the time of Queen Mary were many put to death, and now also in this Queen's reign, of two several opinions; both these cannot be martyrs. Therefore, good Mistress Clitherow take pity on yourself. Christ Himself fled His persecutors; so did His apostles; and why should you not. then, favour your own life?" The martyr answered: "God forbid that I should favour my own life in this point. As for my martyrdom, I am not yet assured of it, for that I am still living; but if I persevere to the end, then I verily believe I shall be saved." Among others, the mayor of York, who was her step-father, came to visit her, and kneeled down before her, urging her with tears to save her life. Many came to her daily; but her stedfastness was proof against all arguments and persuasion. She petitioned to be allowed to see her husband; but was refused unless she would yield. "God's will be done," she said; "for I will not offend God and my conscience to speak with him."

Two days before her martyrdom, the sheriffs of York came and told her what day was appointed for her death. She thanked God, and requested them that she might go to the place where she was to suffer half a day or half a night before, and to remain there until the time when she should suffer; but they would not grant it.

After the sheriffs were departed, she said to a friend of hers, "The sheriffs have told me that I shall die on Friday next. I now feel the frailty of mine own flesh, which trembleth at these news, although my spirit greatly rejoiceth. Therefore, for God's sake pray for me; and I desire all good folks to do the same." And then "kneeling down and praying a little, the fear and horror of death presently departed from her." From this time her courage never failed her; but she devoted herself unceasingly to preparation for her great trial, spending her whole time in fasting and prayer.

The night before she suffered, she asked her jailer's wife to allow one of her maids to bear her company through the night, "not for any fear of death,—for that," she said, "is my comfort; but that flesh is frail." The woman said, "Alas, Mrs. Clitherow, the jailer is gone, the door is locked, and none can be had." But she herself remained sitting by her till almost midnight, and then went to bed in the same room. At twelve o'clock she saw the martyr rise from her knees, and "putting off all her apparel, clothe herself in a linen

N

habit like an alb, which she had made with her own hands three days before to wear at her death. Then she kneeled down again till three, when she rose and came to the fireside; then she lay down flat on the stones for about a quarter of an hour, and then re-tired to her bed, where she remained till six in the morning."

She asked her jailer's wife to see her die, and said she wished some good Catholic could be beside her in the last agony and pains of death, to put her in remem-brance of God. The woman said she would not see her die such a cruel death for all York; "but," said she, "I will procure some friends to lay weight upon you, that you may be quickly despatched from your pain." This the martyr would in no way allow, but said, "God forbid that you should procure any to be guilty of my blood."

About eight o'clock the sheriffs came for her, and found her ready and expecting them; and so she went with a cheerful step to her death, or, as she called it, to her marriage. Again, as before, she dealt her alms as she passed along the street, which was so full of people that she could hardly make her way through the crowd, who all marvelled at her joyful, smiling countenance.

The place of execution was the Tolbooth, six or seven yards distant from the prison. There were pre-sent at her martyrdom the two sheriffs, some ministers, four sergeants, who had hired some beggars to do the murder, three or four men besides, and four women.

When the martyr reached the place, she knelt down and prayed to herself. Her tormentors bade her pray with them, and they would pray with her. But she said, "I will not pray with you, nor shall you pray with me; neither will I say amen to your prayers, nor shall you to mine." Then she prayed aloud for the "Ca-tholic Church, for the Pope's holiness, cardinals, and other fathers which have charge of souls;" then for "the Christian princes in the world, and especially for

Elizabeth queen of England, that God may turn her to the Catholic faith, and after this mortal life she may receive the blessed joys of heaven; for I wish," said she, " as much joy to her majesty's soul as to mine own."

Then Fawcett, one of the sheriffs, commanded her to put off her apparel. She implored on her knees, together with the other women, that this might be spared her, but in vain; however, the women disrobed her, and put on her the long linen habit which she had prepared for herself. Being thus ready, she lay quietly down on the ground, her face covered with a handkerchief. Then the door was laid upon her, and she covered her face with her hands; but the sheriffs told her that she must have her hands bound to two posts, which was done; " so that her body and arms made a perfect cross." At the first weight that was laid upon her, she cried, " O Jesus, Jesus, Jesus! have mercy upon me!" which were the last words she was heard to speak. A sharp stone was placed under her back, and seven or eight hundredweight at least were laid upon her; and her agony lasted for nearly a quarter of an hour.

Such was the life and death of this blessed martyr of Christ. As it may seem strange to some that she should have scrupled to plead, when so many other holy confessors of the faith have done so, it is right to give, in conclusion, her own touching reasons for her conduct.

" Alas!" said she, " if I should have put myself on my country, evidence must needs have come against me, which I know none could give but only my children or servants. And it would have been more grievous to me than a thousand deaths, if I should have seen any of them brought forth before me to give evidence against me in so good a cause, and be guilty of my blood. Secondly," she continued, " I know well the country must needs have found me guilty to please the council, which seek earnestly my blood; and then all they had been accessory to my death, and damnably offended God. I therefore thought, in the way of charity, for my part to hinder the country from such a sin; and seeing it must needs be done, to cause as few to do it as might be;—that was the judge himself."

X.

THE MARTYRDOM OF GERONIMO

AT ALGIERS, 1569.

BOUT the beginning of the sixteenth century, Spain, then at the zenith of her power, began to establish herself upon the Algerian coast; and in retaliation upon Barbary for the long and cruel tyranny under which she had groaned, took possession of Oran, Boujeiah, and other important harbours; built forts, and in different ways attempted the subjugation of the country. But although she was able to fortify herself in a few strong places near the sea, still the interior of the country continued to be held by the natives, and frequent engagements took place between the garrisons of the different forts and the unsubdued Arabs.

Upon these occasions it frequently happened that prisoners were made on both sides. Those Spaniards who fell into the hands of the natives were carried to Algiers and sold into slavery, with the exception of as many as dared to purchase their liberty at the expense of their faith. Such renegades unhappily were seldom wanting to disgrace the Christian name throughout the whole course of the struggle between the Moors and the Spaniards. Those Mahometans who were taken captive by the Christian soldiers in like manner became the property of the victors, and the attempts which were made to effect the conversion of the prisoners

were not always unattended with success. One signal
instance of the marvellous grace displayed in a youth,
who had been converted and was afterwards recaptured
by the Mahometans, has been recorded. It is an instance of baptismal grace germinating after many years,
and at length producing fruits in martyrdom. The
facts are as follows:

In the year 1538 the troops in garrison at Oran
made a razzia on the neighbouring Arabs, and brought
home with them a quantity of booty, including several
captives. These, according to the custom of the day,
were sold, that the prize-money might be divided among
the conquerors. One of the prisoners was a little boy
only four years of age, whose pleasing expression of
countenance attracted the attention of John Cars, the
vicar-general. The ecclesiastic purchased the Mahometan child, instructed him in the Christian religion,
and baptised him by the name of Geronimo.

The little Geronimo, however, only remained four
years with his new master. In 1542 the plague broke
out at Oran, and in the confusion and distress produced
by the pestilence some of the Arab prisoners found
means to escape. They fled from the city, taking with
them Geronimo, and after a time he was restored to his
parents. It is not known whether at that period, when
he was only eight years of age, he made any objection
to returning to the religion of his father. If he did, it
was overruled, for he was brought up a Mahometan.
But in heart and affection Geronimo must have still
adhered to the Faith; for after seventeen years, moved
doubtless by the special grace of God, he forsook his
own home and returned to Oran, where John Cars was
still living. He at once made a public confession of
Christianity, and was reconciled to the Church by the
same hands which had originally admitted him into the
true fold. Soon afterwards he loved a young Arab
maiden, like himself a convert; and John Cars pronounced over his children in Christ the nuptial benediction.

Geronimo now caused himself to be enrolled in one of the Spanish regiments called the Cuadrillas de Campo, a corps the duties of which lay outside the town. In this service he distinguished himself greatly by his courage and zeal; but at the end of ten years he was unfortunately captured by pirates from Tehran. Cruising along the coast in a small vessel, he and nine of his comrades were overpowered by numbers. Their boat was sunk, and they were bound and brought into Algiers, then under the government of the Calabrese renegade Ali-el-Eudj.

The Dey of Algiers enjoyed the right of choosing for himself two out of every ten captives brought in by the corsairs. It was the condition on which they were permitted to exercise openly their nefarious pursuit. Geronimo was one of the two selected by Ali; and he was accordingly marched off from the market to the Dey's task-house, where he was set to work with the other slaves. These were, of course, most of them Mahometans, and they soon discovered the Moslem origin of the Christian stranger. They reported the fact to their master, and from that moment Geronimo was assailed on all sides by menaces, entreaties, and promises. There were among the other slaves a few Christians, who had been taken captive in battle, one of whom was a priest; and there was a sort of oratory in the *bagne*, where they were permitted to worship. They suffered comparatively little ill-treatment from their master and his overseers. It was Geronimo the convert whose reconversion to the religion of their prophet they were determined to effect at any cost. From the renegade Dey down to the meanest of the slaves, Geronimo received alternately good and bad usage, kindness and cruelty. But he remained firm and unmoved. Nor were the Arab theologians more successful in overcoming his constancy. He was as insensible to argument as to threats and persuasions. Proof against every attack, he declared his unalterable determination to die in the faith for which he had forsaken home and kindred.

In the autumn of the year 1569, the Algerines, for the better security of their town, were engaged in the construction of a fort outside the walls. near the gate Bab-el-oved; and the Dey watched the progress of the work with great interest, superintending the building personally, and animating the slaves employed by his presence and his promises. The fort is the same which is now called the *Fort des Vingt-Quatre-Heures*. It is composed of blocks of pise, a peculiar material commonly used in the fortifications of Algiers. Pise is a compost of stones, mortar, and earth, mixed in certain proportions, trodden down and rammed hard into a compact mass in a huge mould, and exposed to dry in the sun. When thoroughly baked and quite solid, it is turned out of the mould, and is then ready for use. One day Ali was observing the labourers trampling the compost into the moulds, and kneading it close and firm with their heavy rammers, when a sudden idea seemed to strike his mind, and he called to him the foreman of the masons, Michael of Navarre, and pointing to an empty mould which the men were just going to fill, he said, " Michael, leave that box empty till to-morrow. I will take the body of that dog from Oran who refused to return to the religion of Mahomet, and make a block of pise of it." And with these words, without waiting for an answer, Ali left the stupified mason, and returned to his palace.

Now Michael was a Christian, and sorely grieved was he at the Dey's words. Nevertheless, he was compelled to do as the tyrant had said, and he laid the empty mould aside. And when the day's work was over, and the slaves had returned to the bagne, he went with tears in his eyes to seek Geronimo, and told him what the Dey had determined to do, and exhorted him to be resigned, and to die manfully for the Cross.

" Blessed be God for all things," exclaimed the future martyr; "let not the infidels flatter themselves that they will terrify me by the thought of the horrible torture which they have intended for me, and by which they hope to prevail on my fears to renounce the true religion. All that I beg of God is, that He may have pity on my soul and forgive me my sins."

These words of Geronimo filled the heart of Michael with joy; and he gave God thanks for the grace which He had given to His servant. Geronimo, too, gave thanks for that he was counted worthy to give testimony for the faith; and he began to prepare for the morrow. His fellow-slave, who was a priest, administered to him the last sacraments, and he spent the night in prayer, offering up to God the sacrifice of his life, and imploring the grace of final perseverance; and thus fortified, he calmly awaited the summons that was to conduct him to a cruel death.

The next morning, being the 18th of September, 1569, four *chaonces* of the Dey came early to the bagne, and called aloud for Geronimo. He was in the oratory at prayer, but he surrendered himself into their hands.

"Well, dog, Jew, traitor, why dost thou persist in refusing to become a Mussulman?" they vied with each other in exclaiming as soon as they perceived him. But he said nothing in answer to all their revilings. Then they laid hands upon him, and would have dragged him off; but he walked willingly all the way to the Fort des Vingt-Quatre-Heures, where Ali had already arrived, and along with him a large number of Turks, renegades, and Moors, all eager for Christian blood.

"Now, then, dog!" exclaimed Ali, "once for all, wilt thou not return to the religion of Mahomet?"

"Not for all the world," replied Geronimo; "Christian I am, and Christian I will remain."

"Sayest thou so?" howled aloud the exasperated Dey; "well, thou seest that box; in that box I will have thee pounded and buried alive."

"Do thy will," answered the holy martyr with wonderful courage; "I am prepared for all; and nothing in the world will induce me to abandon the faith of my Lord Jesus Christ."

Then Ali, setting his teeth in fury, signed to the four chaonces, who seized Geronimo, and bound him hand and foot. Then they lifted him up, and first placing a layer of compost at the bottom of the mould, threw him upon it, and began to cover him over with pise. Geronimo uttered not a cry while he was thus being laid on the altar.

There was a renegade there named Tamango, a Spaniard, who, after being taken captive at the defeat near Mostraganem, had turned Mussulman, and assumed the name of Djafer. This man, more furious than the Mahometans themselves, jumped into the box, and calling loudly for more and more earth, seized a rammer, and began to pound the poor sufferer with all his force; and other renegades, stimulated by the example of Tamango, and anxious to show themselves as good Mussulmans as he, laid hold of rammers, and leapt into the mould, and assisted at the sacrifice. Closer and closer was pressed down upon the convulsed victim of their cruelty the thick and adhesive compost, long after his blessed spirit had received at the hands of God its great reward. And then such a block of pise was formed as not all the fortifications of Africa could boast. It was laid in its place, and other blocks were built upon it; and not a mark was left to distinguish the resting-place of the martyr Geronimo. And years passed on, and the story was forgotten, except that one Hædo, an author of the period, wrote of the brave Algerine for the information of posterity; and in the year 1847 his memory was revived. But it was not till the 27th December, 1853, that the actual relics of the martyr were discovered. Three whole centuries Almighty God permitted to wile away ere the crown which Geronimo had so long worn in heaven should be acknowledged upon earth. The process of his beatification has only just commenced.

Don Diego de Hædo, author of the Topography of Algiers, and to whom we owe our knowledge of the above particulars, indicated the exact position of the

body of Geronimo in the Fort des Vingt-Quatre-Heures.
He says, " On examining with attention the blocks of
pise which form the walls of the fort, it will be easy to
discover the spot where the body of the saint reposes.
In the north wall will be seen a block, of which the
surface has sunk in, and with the appearance of having
been disturbed.   For the body of Geronimo, in falling
into decay, left in the block a hollow which has caused
a sinking that is very visible.   Confident in the goodness of the Lord, I believe that the day will come when
this martyr will be removed from that spot, to be laid
in another and more suitable resting-place; and not only
he, but all the holy martyrs who have watered that
land with their blood."

The day has come which the good old topographer
foresaw.   But his pious care to point out the martyr's
tomb did not further its recovery, as he anticipated.
The sinking of which he speaks had probably been
smoothed away by the weather; for notwithstanding
the closest search, the block in question could not be
pointed out when the demolition of the fort was commenced under the orders of the French government.
However, the knowledge that the remains of a martyr
certainly did exist in one or other of the many blocks
of which the walls were composed, caused the process
of destruction to be carried on with great care.   Captain Susoni, to whom the work was committed, watched
the proceedings with all vigilance, and every precaution was taken against passing over the precious receptacle of a martyr's relics.   However, course by
course was removed, and block by block separated, and
still no signs of Geronimo appeared.   The discovery began to be considered hopeless, till at length, one day—
it was the 27th December, 1853—a petard, which had
been placed beneath two or three courses of pise near
the ground, exploded, and laid open a cavity, containing
a human skeleton, the whole of which was visible from
the neck to the knees, in a perfect state of preservation.

The soldiers immediately announced the great discovery to their commanding officer, who, after a brief examination, concluded that the bones were the bones of the martyred Geronimo, which they had so long been in search of; and he hastened to communicate the good news to Mgr. Pavy, the Bishop of Algiers. The prelate hastened to the spot with a number of his clergy; and a crowd of people, with civil and military officers, rushed also to pay a visit to the martyr.

He lay stretched on his face, the legs close to each other; the arms had evidently been tied together behind the back, and the cord which bound them was imbedded in the mortar. The feet also appeared to have been tied. Although the fleshy parts had all mouldered away, yet their impress had been faithfully left in the pise, and had formed a perfect mould, such as modellers make in sand; so that it would be merely necessary to run in the proper quantity of plaster in order to obtain an actual cut of the features and figure of the martyr, taken at the very moment of his agony. The very texture of the coarse stuff of which his prison-garments were composed had been transferred to the pise, as well as the strained position of the muscles of the limbs, convulsed under the torture of being buried alive. The head was covered with a *chachia*, with turned-up edges, as if it had been too large for the wearer; the tassel and the button by which it was attached were distinctly visible.

A cast of the head has been taken by M. Latour with the most complete success. It is impossible to look upon this cast without an indescribable sensation of awe. There are the features of the martyr; there is the very expression which they wore while he was being pounded to death: they are full of agony, and yet full of resignation. No sculptor could have produced such a countenance; no art could have so depicted pain and faith. It is the living reality, which is now, after three hundred years, exposed to view.

The bishop, immediately on the discovery, took the

proper steps enjoined by the canons for the verification of the relics. A commission of civil and military surgeons was appointed to examine the body, that they might give an opinion on the sex, age, and race. They pronounced it to be the body of a man of the Berber race. A written account of the proceedings, with an account of his martyrdom from De Hædo, the expectation of finding the body, the search, the discovery, the surgeons' report, and the cast of the head, were forwarded to Rome, where the cause of Geronimo immediately excited the warmest sympathy, especially in the breast of the Holy Father, who received Mgr. Pavy's written statement in lieu of the usual preliminary proceedings. On the 30th March, 1854, his Holiness was pleased to order *de plano*, and on the advice of a commission of four cardinals, the introduction of the clause which confers on the servant of God to whom it relates the title of " Venerable ;" so that there is every reason to hope that in due course of time the glorious martyr Geronimo will be raised upon the altars of the Church.

On the 28th of May following, the block of pisé containing the relics was translated with great reverence and ceremony to the cathedral. At three o'clock in the afternoon, there arrived at the spot where the block was lying, the governor-general with his *état-major*, the prefect and his attendants, all the municipal and military authorities, to take part in the procession. With the Bishop of Algiers came the Bishop of Mahon and the entire clergy of the diocese. The Algerine militia, the gendarmes, and the troops of the garrison, were in attendance to form a hedge round these functionaries ; and beyond was an immense crowd, posted on each little hill, and wherever the ground permitted a view of the ceremony, and forming an imposing amphitheatre round the rock of the Fort des Vingt-Quatre-Heures. When all was ready, the procession began to move slowly towards the cathedral.

First came a picket of mounted militia; then, in two ranks, the ladies of the Pension of Aga, of Babazoun, of Notre-Dame-des-Victoires, of St. Philip, and of the Good Shepherd, with other religious women.

The bust of Geronimo, and then his portrait, carried by youths, followed between two lines of Trappists, and then the car bearing the block of pise advanced between the parochial clergy and the episcopal insignia.

After the block came the shrine, containing the holy relics, of which the cords were held by the procureur-general, the prefect, the admiral in charge of the station, the mayor, the Spanish consul, and the colonel of the regiment. Surrounding the shrine and the bearers of it walked the members of the chapter.

After the holy relics followed Mgr. the Bishop of Algiers, with his vicar-general. On his right walked the Bishop of Mahon, with his canons, and on his left the Abbot of La Trappe and two religious of his house.

Then followed the civil and military authorities, between two lines formed by the men of the archconfraternity, and after them came inhabitants of the town, natives of all the European nations. The gendarmes brought up the rear.

Along the whole line of the procession, the balconies, crossings, tops of houses, windows, all were crowded; even the hospital arches were full of half-convalescent patients; the whole town seemed to have poured into the street to do honour to Geronimo.

On arriving at the cathedral, the shrine, the bust, and the portrait, were deposited in front of the altar, and after suitable prayers and hymns, the bishop addressed the devout throng on the rare and glorious event they had that day assembled to celebrate. Well may the Christians of Algiers cherish the memory of Geronimo, and rejoice in the intercession of so great a martyr; for events more strange, more touching, could not be pointed out in the whole martyrology of the Church, than are exhibited in the narrative of the death of the heroic Algerine;—his long concealment, his discovery after three centuries, and the wonderful preservation and reproduction of his very lineaments.

XI.

MISSIONS AND MARTYRDOMS
IN CHINA.

F all heathen nations on the face of the globe, China has been the chief object of the Church's solicitude. In the conversion of China more martyrs have shed their blood than for that of any other country. And yet there is no people which has more obstinately rejected the treasure of the faith than the sceptical inhabitants of this vast empire. The history of Christianity in China is the history of alternate triumphs and reverses. There have been times when it seemed not sanguine to expect the immediate conversion of the whole population; at others, and such is the present, the gospel has been altogether proscribed. This ebb and flow is, indeed, nothing more than the Church has experienced every where else; but in other countries the faith has survived the fury of persecution, to break out afresh after the storm in greater glory than ever. The hypocrite or the worldling might apostatise; but the faithful who remained firm were the nucleus round which fresh conversions gathered as soon as the pressure was removed. Not so in China. The Chinese, as a people, seem ready to discard the faith as soon as they embrace it. The harvest is just ready to gather in; suddenly there comes a blight, and scarcely a vestige remains of all the goodly show. The seed has to be sown afresh: the labour has been thrown away,—all has to be begun again from the beginning.

There are, of course, many noble exceptions to this general rule. It is not meant to be asserted that there is no Christianity in China; far from it. There are at this moment about 800,000 Christians; and many of them are exposed to the greatest danger for their fidelity to the faith. There are also scattered about all over the country small Christendoms, the relics of old and once-flourishing churches, which have kept their religion for years, unvisited by any priest, and only accidentally discovered by the missionary in his apostolic wanderings. Further, not the least heroic of the many martyrs for Christ which the country can boast have been native catechists and priests. Still, the population of China is 300,000,000, and the conversion of this immense multitude seems as far off as ever. The causes, humanly speaking, of this lamentable sterility, are not difficult of discovery. But before we investigate them, it will be well to glance rapidly over the various attempts which have been made at different times to evangelise the empire.

The first authentic notice which we find of the existence of Christianity in China, is furnished by the very interesting monument that was discovered in the year 1625, near the city of Si-gan-fou, the ancient capital of Cathay, as the empire was then termed. It is indeed alleged that St. Thomas the Apostle made an expedition into those parts from Malabar; but little evidence exists for the truth of the tradition. The Si-gan monument is a marble slab, ten feet long by five broad, surmounted by a pyramidal cross, and containing a long inscription, in the Chinese character, on the state of Christianity in China during a period of 146 years; that is to say, from the year 635 to the year 781.

The inscription commences with this heading: "This stone was erected to the honour and eternal memory of the law of light and truth, brought from Ta-cin, and promulgated in China;" and concludes with its date, "the 2d year of the reign of Tai-tsoung, Nice-Chou being bishop." It speaks of the numerous churches which the piety of the emperors had reared in 635; of the high titles given to the primate or sovereign guardian of the kingdom of the Great Law; of two persecutions which terminated ineffectually, one in 699, the other in 712; of the labours and success of the missionaries; of the arrival of a messenger from Ta-msin, in the Roman empire, and his invitation from the emperor to offer Christian sacrifices in the palace; also of the great devotion of the emperor, and his annual offerings on Christmas-day. The popularity of the priest Y-son, and the universal reverence for the prime minister, Kouo-tze-y, a great statesman and a Christian, at whose death the whole empire went into mourning for three years, being the mourning worn by children on the demise of their fathers. The evidence of this interesting inscription, a fac-simile of which exists in the Imperial Library at Paris, is conclusive as to the prosperity and extent of the Church during the eighth century.

Mention is here made of two unsuccessful persecutions. But it is probable that there were others subsequently, of which no record exists. It is certain also, that at that time the faithful had to contend with the heresy of Nestorius; for towards the beginning of the ninth century, Timothy, patriarch of the Nestorians, sent monks to preach to the Tartars and the Chinese. Indeed the Si-gan monument itself may have been erected by Nestorians; and this circumstance has induced most Protestant writers, as, for example, Mosheim, to acknowledge its authenticity. But however this may be, it appears that before the thirteenth century the lamp of faith had declined. Unlike other nations, the Chinese had not lastingly embraced the truth. But when the Crusades had given rise to freer communication between the East and West, and when the rise of the great Mongol scourge, Zingis-khan, directed the attention of Europe and the Church farther east still, then the cause of religion began again to revive. In the time of Zingis-khan and his successors, missionaries were sent into Tartary and China. Zingis had declared

an absolute toleration of all religions. In the words of
Gibbon : " the various systems of Moses, of Mahomet,
and of Christ, in freedom and in concord, were taught
and practised within the precincts of the same camp;
and the Bonze, the Imam, the Rabbi, the Nestorian,
and the Latin priest, enjoyed the same honourable exemption from service and from tribute." Under these
favourable circumstances, the Catholic missionaries met
with large success. They had brought with them the
ornaments of the altar, that they might attract the
heathen; and they celebrated the ceremonies of religion
before Tartar princes, who gave them an asylum in
their tents, and even permitted them to erect chapels
within the royal precincts. In the year 1250, St. Louis
of France sent a mission into Mongolia, and Rubruk,
the missionary employed, gives many curious particulars of his travels, showing the flourishing prospects of
Christianity at that time. At Khara-Khoroum, the
Mongol capital, he saw, not far from the royal palace,
a building surmounted by a small cross. " Then," says
he, " was I filled with joy; and I entered with confidence, supposing that I should find there something
Christian. And I saw within an altar magnificently
adorned. Hangings, embroidered with gold, displayed
the image of our Saviour and of the Blessed Virgin,
and of John the Baptist and of two angels, whose bodies
and vestments were enriched with precious stones.
There was also a great cross, wrought in silver, having
pearls at the centre and at the extremities, with many
ornaments, and an oil-lamp burning before the altar,
having eight burners. And in the sanctuary was sitting
an Armenian monk." This description of a chapel, so
near the capital, shows an advanced state of Christianity. Rubruk further relates, that there were in
those countries a vast number of Nestorians and of
Greek Catholics, who solemnised the Christian rites in
all freedom. Princes, and even emperors, received
baptism and promoted the propagation of the faith.

Of these missionaries to China during the thirteenth

century, one of the most successful was John de Mon-
tarvin, a French priest, under whose labours the number
of Christians had so much increased by the close of the
century, that Pope Clement V. erected an archbishopric
at Pekin, with four suffragan sees in the adjoining
countries.   And then occurred one of those wonderful
relapses into paganism for which the celestial empire
is so remarkable.   During the fifteenth century communication was entirely interrupted between the East
and West.   China, notwithstanding all that had taken
place, came to be reckoned among fabulous countries,
and the history of Christianity during that period is
lost; but when Father Matthew Ricci, from whom
dates the existence of the present Church in China,
reached the empire, all traces of the flourishing Church
of the early ages, and the splendid revival in later times,
had passed away.   The Si-gan monument had not
then been discovered, and nothing remained to show
that the Gospel had ever been preached in the extreme
East.

Intercourse between Europeans and the Chinese
was just resumed by the Portuguese, when their viceroy
at Goa entered into a commercial treaty with the authorities at Canton.   But the cause of religion was not
much promoted by this step, till the Portuguese, having
rendered the Chinese an important service by ridding
them of a dangerous pirate whose vessels infested their
coasts, were permitted to establish themselves on a
barren rock, where they built the town of Macao.
Macao soon became an important place, although now
its value has passed away.   But for many years it was
the centre from which missionaries went forth into
Japan, Tartary, China, and other pagan countries of
Asia.   Francis Xavier was on his way thither when
he was taken ill and died at Sancian, almost within
sight of the country he had so long yearned to evangelise.   But Almighty God provided others of a like
spirit to follow out the enterprise, of whom the greatest
was Father Matthew Ricci.

Father Ricci appears to have been endowed with all the qualities requisite for the great and arduous work which lay before him ; zealous, ardent, and daring, but prudent, indefatigable, and judicious, with a soul unappalled by the magnitude of the undertaking, and conscious of his own power to execute it,—yet withal so humble and modest as to conciliate the prejudice of a proud and conceited people ; above all, with a heart given to God, and enjoying that intimate union with Him which could alone render supportable the perilous life of an apostle. For more than twenty years he laboured without fruit. His seed seemed to be cast in barren ground, and to die as soon as it touched the soil; but at length he succeeded in making an impression upon the government. His acquaintance with many arts and sciences brought him into favour at court, and he took advantage of this influence to promote the cause of Christianity. Conversions then began to increase, and even churches to be built ; and when he died in 1610, at the age of fifty-eight, worn out with labours, he had the satisfaction of leaving behind him a flourishing mission, and a numerous body of labourers, as zealous and able as himself. The progress of Christianity after his death was very rapid. During the next hundred years several emperors declared in favour of the faith ; and whenever the government smiles upon it, the Chinese are ready to become Christians.

It was at this epoch, during the reign of Khang-hi, that the French began the missionary work in China which they have since carried on with so great zeal. The government of France, under the great Colbert. were engaged in the prosecution of geographical researches in all parts of the world, and, at a loss for scientific men bold enough to venture into the unknown regions of the East, bethought themselves of applying to the Jesuits, a body of men qualified by their learning to undertake the commission, and ready, as was well known, for any enterprise, however hazardous, which could advance the propagation of the faith   In 1685 six missionaries of the Company of Jesus, having been admitted members of the Academy of Science, set sail for Pekin. They soon attracted the admiration and esteem of the people by their virtuous life, their learning, and their apostolic zeal. The Emperor Khang-hi loved them so well that he gave them a dwelling in his own palace, and a large piece of land hard by for the erection of a magnificent church, which he built at his own expense. In a formal decree he declared himself the protector of the Christian religion, and his example was followed by princes, dignitaries, and mandarins; so that in every province the word of God was freely preached. In a short time churches, chapels, and oratories sprang up; Christendoms were formed every where; the empire appeared on the eve of conversion.

In a few short years all these bright hopes were blasted. To Khang-hi succeeded Young-Ching, who persecuted the Christians as diligently as Khang-hi had favoured them; and Father Ganbil, a French missionary, writing in 1722 to the Archbishop of Toulouse, says, " I have been here a month, and am terribly shocked at the sad state of a mission which not long ago looked so prosperous. Every where are to be seen churches ruined, Christendoms dispersed, missionaries exiled. Religion is on the point of being proscribed." Two years later, another French missionary, Father de Mailla, writes word, " What we dreaded a little while ago has actually taken place—our holy religion is entirely proscribed in China. All the missionaries, except those at Pekin, who are retained for their scientific services (that is, as interpreters, astronomers to draw up the annual calendar, &c.), have been driven from the empire, the churches have been demolished or desecrated, and edicts put forth prohibiting the practice of Christianity under the most severe penalties. Such is the deplorable state of a mission which for nearly 200 years has been fostered with sweat and blood." Thus the prosperity which was due to the protection of one emperor, had disappeared at the first breath of persecution from his successor.

There were, of course, great and glorious examples of constancy in the faith—many heroic martyrdoms; but the desertions were so numerous and lamentable, as to prove that Christianity had not struck deeper root than in former ages. The Chinese, otherwise so tenacious of ancient usages, have no firmness or energy when religion is concerned.

Then came another gleam of sunshine. When Young-Ching died, he was succeeded by Kien-Long, during whose extended reign the Christians were on the whole left unmolested. Their numbers insensibly increased, and all was going on well, when the suppression of the Jesuits in Europe put a stop to the propagation of the faith. The old missionaries died out, no new ones came forward to succeed them, and the flocks, abandoned by their pastors, showed the greatest weakness when the persecution under Kia-King, the successor of Kien-Long, broke out. Whole Christendoms disappeared. Churches exist to this day where not a Christian is to be found. The very poor alone remained faithful: possessing nothing to excite the cupidity of informers, or to draw off their affections from the world to come, they were left unmolested, and they preserved their faith.

Then we arrive at the present century. The propagation of the faith in China is carried on at this moment under far other circumstances than in former times. The missionaries are no longer admitted at court, enjoying the favour of the great, and going to and fro with the state of mandarins. They are proscribed throughout the empire; they enter it in disguise, with all the precautions which prudence can suggest; and they are compelled to live in hiding-places, if they would be safe from the vigilance of the magistrates. It is with the greatest danger that they can show themselves at all to the pagans, lest by any misfortune they should jeopardise, not their own lives only, but the whole well-being of the mission. Thus it is impossible for the missionary to act directly on the population, and give free course to his zeal; not only can he not preach the Word of God publicly, but it is an act of great temerity, even in private, to speak to a pagan of whose goodwill he is not satisfied beforehand. His ministry is thus confined within very narrow limits. To go from one Christendom to another, to instruct and exhort neophytes, to administer the Sacraments to the faithful, to celebrate in secret the festivals of the Church, to visit the schools and encourage the master and his pupils,—this is the circle within which his labours are restricted.

And yet, notwithstanding all his precautions, a cruel death frequently puts a stop to his labours. In the following pages will be found the details of several glorious martyrdoms; of which, if we had space, a great number might be presented to the reader. Results are, indeed, gradually appearing—the number of Christians is increasing, but very slowly. The present state of Christianity in China is little consoling, considering how many centuries have been spent in preaching the Gospel—how many labourers have bathed the soil with their sweat—how many martyrs have shed their blood for the conversion of the country.

The cause of this opposition in the government, and inconstancy in the people, is certainly not devotion to any other religion. The authorities do not prohibit Christianity out of jealousy for Confucius, nor do the converts abandon it through any lingering affection for the worship of Buddha. As a nation, China is utterly sceptical. Infidelity is openly inculcated and practised. The Emperor Tao Kaoung, some time before he came to the throne, issued a proclamation, in which he passed in review all the different religions known in the empire, including Christianity; and he ended with the conclusion that all were equally false, and that all ought to be despised alike.

There are three great religious systems in operation in China, all admitted by government to be equally good, harmless, and absurd. The first is that which

claims Confucius for its founder, a philosopher who
flourished about six hundred years before the Christian
era.   His descendants, as founder's kin, fill the chief
posts of honour in the state; his name is revered by
more than 300,000,000 of men; temples are reared to
his honour in every town; he is the saint *par excellence.*   His religion consists in the simple philosophy
of making the most of life.   In this it is the exact
opposite to Christianity, which sacrifices this world to
the next.   Whether Confucius at all admitted the existence of an Almighty, who should judge men according
to their works, is not certain; but certainly no such doctrine is now taught by his followers, or enters practi-
cally into his system.   Virtues are simply recommended,
and vice forbidden, as bearing on the present happiness
and social usefulness of man.

   To his moral precepts were added a number of
superstitious observances, which survive to this day.
The state has preserved his worship of the heavens and
earth, the stars, the mountains and rivers, and the souls
of Anastris, as a civil institution; and in this sense
the system of Confucius may be said to be the established religion.   It is the religion of the aristocracy
and the men of letters   Each magistrate is a priest,
and the emperor himself is patriarch.   But the rites
which they perform are mere ceremonies of state or
social observances; and as such, were, with certain limit-
ations, allowed by Father Ricci and the Jesuits.   Other
missionaries had scruples as to the lawfulness of this
concession; and this difference of opinion was certainly
prejudicial to the propagation of faith.

   The second religion is that of Lao-tze, a contempo-
rary of Confucius, whose philosophy is of a very exalted character indeed.   He taught that before the
chaos which preceded the birth of heaven and earth
there existed one sole Being, vast, silent, unchangeable,
always in action; and not knowing the real name of
this Being, he called it Reason.   Man was made from
the earth, earth from the sky; the sky from Reason,

Reason from herself. His morality was equal to his dogma. Perfection consisted in being without passions, the better to contemplate the harmony of the universe. " There is no greater sin," said Lao-tze, " than unregulated desires ; no greater misfortune than the sufferings which are their just punishment."   The disciples of this elevated teaching are not worthy of their descent. They call themselves Rahmals, but they are guilty of the most irrational superstitions.   They profess to be possessed of the elixir of immortality, on which they also call themselves the Immortals.   But in this absurd claim lies their destruction, and they are of no repute except with the lowest of the people.

The third religion is the religion of Buddha, that vast religion which numbers more followers than any other system in the world, and extends more or less over the whole of Asia. Buddha, who by all accounts lived about 960 B.C., is regarded by his followers as a divine incarnation, a man-God, sent into the world to enlighten mankind and show them the way of salvation.   The idea of a human redemption by a divine incarnation is common to Buddhism in Ceylon, in Thibet, in ˙ndia, and in China, along with many other parts of the Christian faith. Some of the articles of the Buddhist creed — if creed there be where there is no faith — are so distinctly relics of revelation, that they may be briefly noticed here.

The mother of Buddha conceived by a divine influence while yet a virgin, and brought forth a son, who immediately gave evidence of his origin and his destiny by the wonderful miracles which he performed. After a retreat spent in the wilderness, during which the incarnate god prepared himself for his apostolic labours by fasting and mortification, he went through the world preaching the true faith. When he had completed his course, he was received up into heaven, and transformed into the god Zo, a being in substance one, but in person threefold. In the Buddhist temples these three forms of the one god; whose functions are seve

rally assigned to the present, the past, and the future,
occupy a prominent place behind the altar.   Again, a
conspicuous image in the temples is that of a lady holding an infant in her arms, of whom the following legend
is told by the Bonzes.   A virgin going to bathe in the
sea, left her garments on the shore, and upon her return
found a beautiful lotus lying upon them.   The lotus she
ate, and by it she conceived and bore a son; and after his
birth she was elevated to receive divine honours under
the name of Tien-how, which signifies Queen of Heaven.   She is also styled Shing-Moo, which means Holy
Mother; Kuan-Yin, that is, Goddess of Mercy.   She
is supposed to exercise a beneficial influence over the
affairs of men, and is invoked by charms of all classes.
Temples are dedicated to her honour, and inscriptions
in her praise grace the doorways.   For example: "To
the Holy Mother, Queen of Heaven, the Goddess of
Peace and Power, descended from the island of Moni-
tas, who stills the waves of the sea, allays storms, pro-
tects the empire."   And again: "The ancient temple
of the Goddess of the Golden Flower, through whose
influence fields are green and fertile like a grove of
trees, and benefits are diffused as the frothy waves of
the sea that shine like splendid pearls."   Over the altars
are placed pictures, which, if any confidence may be
placed in engraved representations of them, appear like
Chinese versions of the Madonnas of Christian masters.

These facts have not been lost sight of by Protestant
travellers in China, who do not hesitate to attribute
the worship of Shing-Moo to the Jesuits, and are never
tired of proclaiming the identity of the Chinese reverence for their goddesses with the devotion of Catholics
to our Blessed Lady.   But the legend of the lotus-
flowers, and the consequent adoration of Shing-Moo,
date back from the most remote antiquity; and in any
case, the undoubted similarity is worthless as an argument against Catholics, unless Buddhism generally be
of force against Christianity.   For the parallel between
the true and the false religions holds in a thousand other

particulars; and if our invocation of the Star of the Sea be proved to be pagan from its likeness to the worship of the celestial Queen of the Ocean, in the same way the Incarnation and the Divinity of our Lord, and the mystery of the Trinity in Unity, must be surrendered; for they may be traced in the virgin birth and deification of Buddha, and his transformation into the triune Fo. The more probable hypothesis is, that the Gospel was preached in China at a very early period, and again lost,—a theory quite in accordance with the subsequent history of Christianity in that empire; and that the converts endeavoured to amalgamate the doctrines of the Church with the tenets of paganism, as Judaisers, Platonists, and others, attempting a compromise between their new faith and their old. This theory will account for all the phenomena; and thus, so far from the similarity of the Buddhist worship of Shing-Moo being an argument against the *cultus Virginis*, it is a proof of its primitive antiquity. Whence could the Chinese derive it but from the Christian, whose successful labours are recorded in the monument of Si-gan-Fou? It is a coincidence not unworthy of note, that the Chinese books trace the introduction of Buddhism into China to the first century of the Christian era.

These are the three great systems in China; and in remote times were all living and energetic principles. The three sects were intolerant of each other, and constant bloodshed and disturbances were the consequence of their mutual rivalry. But they dispute no longer; their dissensions have not resulted in the supremacy of either sect, but in the destruction of all. They are dead bodies, with form indeed, but without life. Controversy has begotten scepticism, and the disciples of Confucius, Lao-tze, and Buddha, believe neither in their own nor in any other teaching; while the government, in thus representing the popular opinion, and dreading the consequences of religious bigotry, maintains a strict religious equality of creeds, supports and despises all.

The intolerance of the state towards the Christian

religion is due not to any hatred of the religion itself, but to dread of European influence. All sects are tolerated in China as sects; but those which seem to be organised for the subversion of the reigning dynasty are put down without mercy. Since the fifth century, there have been more than fifteen revolutions in China, all ending in changes of dynasty. This frequent overthrow of government has rendered the Chinese court exceedingly sensitive of any influence not under its own control. When, therefore, Europeans are seen to propagate a particular religion, it is at once assumed that they act with a view to the eventual invasion of the empire; and the more zealous they show themselves for the conversion of the Chinese, the more the government are convinced that their fears are well-founded. Sceptical themselves, they have not faith in the religion of others; and that men should brave hardship and death to propagate their faith, they rashly discredit. The thing is too ridiculous in their eyes; not even a European could be guilty of such folly. They regard religion as a mere pretext; as the cloak beneath which the barbarians conceal their designs upon the Celestial throne.

The profession of Christianity is regarded, therefore, as treason; the martyrs for the faith are punished as rebels. And this idea is shared by all classes alike. The name of the Christian religion is Tien-tchou-kiao, that is, the religion of the Lord of Heaven,—the idea of God being expressed by Tien-Tchou. If you ask a mandarin whom the Christians adore, he will answer Tien-Tchou; and if you inquire further who this Tien-Tchou is, you will be told, Oh, that is well known,— Tien-Tchou is Emperor of the French. And this feeling is further strengthened by the popular notion entertained of their own emperor. China is the Celestial empire; the emperor is king of heaven and God. What more natural than that the Chinese, having this opinion of their own emperor, should imagine that the Europeans have the same of theirs? Thus every Catholic

priest is supposed to be the emissary of a foreign
power.   Are the Chinese alone herein; and is there no
other empire in which the Catholic faith is hindered by
the like groundless suspicions?

Still, an explanation is required of the popular inconstancy in retaining the faith.   The true cause lies
in the profound indifference of the Chinese mind to the
things of another life.   The Chinaman is wholly en-
grossed in his temporal concerns; money is the end to
which every energy is devoted; a burning thirst to
make a profit, never mind how small, absorbs every
faculty.   Spiritual things, things relating to the soul, to
God, to a future life,—these he has not even the wish
to be occupied with.   If by chance he should read a
moral or religious book, it is only by way of relaxation,
to pass away the time, and as a matter of less consequence than smoking a pipe, or drinking a cup of tea.
He will listen to an argument on the vanity of this
world, and the truths of eternity, with the gravest ac-
quiescence, and assent to every proposition.   He will
lament with the missionary the blindness of mankind in
attaching themselves to a perishing world, and even
break out himself into a glowing disquisition on the
happiness of knowing the true God; and straightway
he will rise up and go his way, as if he had been speaking a part in a comedy.   He is as little interested in
the subject as if he were specially excluded from its
application.   The Chinese carry this indifference so far,
the religious sense is so dead within them, that they
care not whether a doctrine be true or false, good or
bad, a religion is simply a fashion, which they can
follow when they have a taste for it.   It is their natural hereditary indifference to all religion which makes
the Chinese so slow to embrace Christianity, and so
ready to give it up.

The women are by far the most devoted, and, indeed, form the mainstay of Christianity in China.   By
the usages of their country, they are doomed from their
birth to a life of degradation and suffering.   The birth

of a female child is regarded in the family as a male-
diction from heaven; and if she is not at once smo-
thered or exposed, she is at any rate brought up in the
most abject misery. She is treated by every one, and
especially by her own brothers, as of no use but to perform the lowest and most laborious offices. She has no
pleasures or amusements; she receives no education,
except in needle-work; she is condemned to vegetate in
an ignorance the most absolute, and a loneliness the
most complete, till her parents think of marrying her.
But she is not consulted in this important event. She
is a mere object of traffic, an article of merchandise;
and the highest bidder has her. In her married life
she is yet more miserable; her state of slavery is not
improved, and she is at the mercy of a stranger. According to a Chinese expression, the bride must be in
her house a mere shadow, a simple echo. She cannot
sit down to meat with her husband, nor even with her
sons; it is hers to wait at the table standing; to hold
her tongue; to fill his cup and light his pipe. He has
an entire right over her person and her life; he can
beat her; he can starve her to death; he can sell her as
he bought her; or he can give her away, or lend her
for a time. And she, poor wretch, has no redress, and
can find no one to pity her.

Is it strange, then, that the women of China, when
once converted, should cleave, with all the warmth of
their nature, to the faith which even in this life ennobles their condition? Christianity, discountenancing
slavery by its doctrine of the confraternity of mankind
by creation and redemption, especially forbids the en-
slaving of woman by its belief in the divine maternity
of Mary. Even in childhood the Christian Chinese
girl is regarded by her parents as created in the image
of God, and heir, like themselves, of immortality, and,
looking up to the Queen of Angels as her patron, is
raised far above the pagan children of the same village.
She is taught to pray; she is instructed; she is treated
as one having a soul. But when she comes to marry

then it is that the Christian wife chiefly appreciates the immeasurable distance there is between her and her pagan sisters. She has no rival, as they have, to contest her husband's love; she is the wife of his bosom, not the slave of his passions; she enjoys a liberty such as none of them possess. She is loved and respected by her own sons; and her daughters have no reason to lament their sex. And, in truth, the Christian women are profoundly impressed with what they owe to a religion which has drawn them out of the vile slavery under which they groaned, and which, besides conducting them to eternal life, has obtained for them even in this world joys and consolations that seemed beyond their reach. And grateful they are, full of fervour and zeal. They it is who maintain regularity and exactitude in prayer in the several Christendoms. They are to be seen braving the prejudice of public opinion, and performing works of Christian charity even towards pagans; tending the sick, receiving and adopting infants abandoned by their unnatural mothers. In the time of persecution, it is they who confess the faith before the face of the mandarins with the greatest courage and perseverance. And it would not be too much to say, that it is to them that is principally due the progress of the propagation of the faith in the Celestial empire.

China has often disappointed the hopes of the Church; yet the Church has never been discouraged. As soon as the storm has in the least subsided, labourers have appeared to preach the Gospel, not less devoted than those who went before. They have crossed the seas, and spread themselves over the country which has been ravaged by so many persecutions; hunting up anxiously the germs of the faith yet alive, cultivating them with eagerness, and every where sowing fresh seed. Their first care has always been to assemble the scattered Christians, and bring them to their duties; and to reconcile to God those families which have had the weakness to relapse during the persecution. During the last

twenty years the number of the missionaries has been
increasing, and the greater part of the old Christendoms have been revived. New ones have also been
formed by little and little, and in silence. The Holy
See has erected in the eighteen provinces of China
eighteen sees governed by vicars-apostolic, where the
priests of foreign missions, Jesuits, Dominicans, Fran-
ciscans, and Lazarists, labour night and day for the
extension of the kingdom of God. Each vicariate pos-
sesses, besides a great number of schools for both boys
and girls, a college for the education of native priests.
There are also houses for religious women; and out
of a horrible practice, fearfully prevalent in China, has
arisen an institution from which the very best results
are likely to arise. Infanticide is one of the crying ini-
quities of the Celestial empire. It is said that 3000
infants are annually exposed or murdered in the streets
of Pekin alone. These children are mostly females;
but even boys are sacrificed by their unnatural parents,
under the influence of poverty, vice, and superstition.
The Christian missionaries have established asylums for
the nurture and instruction of foundlings; and were
their funds larger, there is scarcely a limit which could
be set to the profitable fruits of these inestimable
schools. The Chinese government has strictly forbidden the practice of infanticide; but a Christian institution, founded in France a few years ago, and lately
introduced into China, called the Association of the
Holy Infancy, has saved a vast number of children;
and done more to check the exposure of others than
the emperor with all his treasures and his legions of
mandarins.

Protestants hardly exist in China, except in the five
ports open to European commerce. In the island of
Hong Kong, which was ceded to the British in 1842,
the English government has founded a bishopric; but
no Protestant missionaries have made any impression
in the interior, and no Protestant martyr has been
found to shed his blood for his faith. The operations

of the various English societies have been till lately
confined to the distribution of Bibles—thousands and
even millions of which have been showered upon the
natives; but with so little success, that it has been
thought necessary to vary the dissemination of the
Scriptures with scientific works, as on the electric tele-
graph, and the like.   The Evangelical missionaries
must be strangely ignorant of the Chinese character
and of Chinese civilisation, to suppose that any influence
is to be obtained over the natives by the diffusion of
works of which not a single Chinese understands one
syllable.   The only mode of converting the worldly,
sceptical, conceited, pusillanimous inhabitants of China,
is that pursued by the Catholic missionaries, and by
them alone.   Without wife or child, in utter contempt
of this world's good, in indifference to danger; in readiness even to die, if need be, for the faith; in unity as to
teaching,—for it is the ancient controversies between
the followers of Confucius, Buddha, and Lao-tze which
produced the national scepticism that now hinders the
Gospel; in painfulness and self-denial and fasting;—this
is the method by which for so many hundred years the
light has been diffused throughout this benighted empire.   And not a year passes but some glorious martyrdom ennobles the religion and advances the faith it
was intended to destroy.

The persecution is nowhere more severe throughout
the East than in the province of Cochin China.   The
Emperor Minh-Minh has shown himself a bitter enemy
of Christianity.   On his accession to the throne he
avowed his intention of extirpating Christianity in his
dominions, and pronounced a eulogy on the conduct of
the King of Japan, who had placed the cross on all the
crossings, that the passengers might insult it as they
passed.   Then followed a terrible period of distress and
persecution for the sixty thousand Catholics scattered
over that vast territory.   Of the missionaries many
were martyred, both European and native.   We have
selected the narratives of their deaths, those of three

P

French priests and one Anamite; we have also given the martyrdom of a priest in China Proper. What results may not be expected from such heroism as these noble confessors of the faith displayed!

I. MARTYRDOM OF M. MARCHAND IN COCHIN CHINA.

Nov. 30, 1835.

M. Marchand, whose death occurred under circumstances of peculiar atrocity, was a native of France, and early showed a desire to earn the crown of martyrdom. He left Europe in 1827, to join the mission in Cochin China. When the persecution under Minh-Minh broke out, he was the only European in that part of the country, and was the object therefore of the closer search. He had abundant opportunities of flight; but he disdained to quit his post, and chose rather to be concealed with some generous Christians of his flock till better times should come. It is possible that he might altogether have escaped, but that a cruel war broke out in the country. Two disaffected officers, Nghiêm and Khôi, excited a revolt, and possessed themselves of Gia Dinh, an ancient royal city. Nghiêm returned to his allegiance, and Khôi continued the insurrection alone, fortifying himself in Gia Dinh, and defending himself obstinately against the king's troops. M. Marchand fell into his hands, and was treated with great kindness by the rebel chief; not certainly from any affection for the Christian religion, but in order to attract to his own side the numerous Christians of the province. Of the missionary's life during the two years and a half that he was in Khôi's power, it is only known that he was permitted to execute the duties of his ministry freely. Khôi, however, died of sickness during the siege, and in September 1835 Minh-Minh carried the place by assault. Twelve hundred men were put to the sword;

but the Christian missionary, along with four of the leaders in the revolt, were reserved for more signal vengeance. Enclosed in cages, they were all sent to Hué, the capital, where they arrived on 15th October following.

M. Marchand was examined immediately on his arrival. The trial was ushered in by the ostentatious display of divers instruments of torture, scourges, rods, pincers, and tongs, for the intimidation of the prisoners. But the Christian priest was unshaken by any thing he saw, and answered the questions which were put to him in perfect calmness.

" Are you Phû-Koai-Uhou?" (the name given by the king to the Bishop of Isanropolis in 1827).

" No, I am not."

" Where is he, then?"

" I do not know."

" But you know him?"

" Yes; but I have not seen him for a long time."

" How many years have you been in this king-dom?"

" Two years."

" Have you assisted Khôi to make war?"

" Khôi took me prisoner by force, and watched me strictly. I did nothing but pray and celebrate the holy Mass. I know nothing of the art of war."

" Did you not send letters to Siam, to rouse the Christians there in behalf of the rebels?"

" Khôi commanded me to do so; but I refused, be-cause my religion forbad it. I said I would rather die than obey his orders. After that I was more closely watched than ever."

The rebel chiefs were then examined. They sought to inculpate the European missionary, in revenge for this refusal of his to throw the weight of his influence with the Christians into their scale. On his second examina-tion he was informed of the charges laid against him; and as he persisted in asserting his innocence, he was put to the torture, which was of the most horrible kind,

—pieces of flesh were pulled from his thighs with red hot pincers. Father Marchand invariably replied at each interrogation during his torture, that he was accused falsely, and was no rebel. But he was not believed. In his agony he raised his eyes to heaven; and sighs and groans, but no confession, forced their way from his breast.

He underwent a third examination without torture, after which he was placed in a cage only two-and-a-half feet high, three feet long and two feet broad, so that he could neither sit nor lie at ease. The other prisoners were put in similar cages hard by in the same prison. A small sum daily was allowed them for food by the king, but very little of it reached the sufferers. Charitable persons were, however, permitted to approach the cages and give them alms.

For nearly six weeks he lived cramped-up in the most painful posture; but at length St. Andrew's day was fixed for the execution. At sun-rise seven guns were fired, for the assembling of the mandarins who were to execute the sentence of death. Father Marchand and the rebel chiefs were taken out of their cages and brought to the place of execution, naked from the waist upwards. They were first led before the king, and compelled to make five obeisances with their foreheads to the ground; after which the tyrant gave orders that the executions should proceed. Their other garments were then removed, except a belt round the middle, and a label containing the name round the neck. Thus naked, they were laid upon their backs on stretchers, and covered with a cloth; each stretcher was borne by four men; and so they were conducted to the place of execution.

But on their way the *cortège* stopped. The hatred which Minh-Minh bore to the Christian religion was not to be appeased by the infliction of a punishment which every rebel not guilty of Christianity had to endure. For the missionary were reserved special torments, and the prisoners were accordingly conducted to the torture-chamber, that the martyr for the faith might undergo the question. This act of cruelty, designed by Minh-Minh to gratify his personal spite against M. Marchand, redounded to the greater glory of God; for had the confessor suffered simply as a rebel, though not the less a martyr on that account, his martyrdom had at least been obscured by the equal sufferings of undoubted criminals; whereas, by making a distinction between the confessor and the rebels, the people perceived that the European suffered those burnings for the faith of Jesus Christ, and not for rebellion.

At the door of the torture-chamber, the martyr started at the sight of the fire in which the irons were heating; for his old wounds were not yet healed, and the remembrance of his former agony produced an involuntary shudder in his whole frame. By this movement the cloth that covered his body was deranged, and the crowd set up a shout of derisive laughter at the sight of his white shoulders. He is then seized by the legs. At a signal from the mandarin inside the house, five executioners take five large pairs of tongs from the fire, red-hot, each a foot-and-a-half long, and catch up the flesh of his thighs in five different places. He cried out in his agony, and a fetid smoke arose from the burning flesh; but the glowing irons were kept there till they grew cold, and then put into the fire to heat again. Lest the executioners, out of pity, should spare their victim, soldiers with rods were placed behind each, ready to strike him if he showed any signs of humanity. The crowd of spectators were divided; some of them bewailed and and joined the "Father of the religion of Jesus," others mingled their cries with his.

Immediately after the torture the criminal mandarin put the following question: "Why do Christians tear out the eyes of the dying?" The missionary collected his strength to say, "It is not the case; I know of nothing of the kind." The tyrant Minh-Minh had revived this old heathen calumny, founded on the anointing the eyes in extreme unction.

He was then condemned to a second torture, which was an exact repetition of the first. When the irons were again cold, he was asked: "Why do persons about to be married come before the priest at the altar?" "They come," said the martyr, "to make known their alliance to the priest in the presence of the congregation, and obtain the benedictions of Heaven."

Upon that they passed to the third torture, when five more wounds were burned in his quivering flesh; making in all fifteen, besides those he had received six weeks before. He was then asked, "What is that enchanted bread, given to those who have confessed, that makes them so strong in their religion?" "It is not bread at all," said the martyr; "it is the Body and Blood of our Lord Jesus Christ, incarnate for our sakes, given to be the nourishment of the soul."

Then ceased the torture. It is not to be supposed, that in putting these questions to our holy martyr, the tyrant had any desire to know more of the mysteries of the faith, for he was in possession of all the books used by the missionaries in the instruction of their converts. He desired rather to hold up the Christian religion to ridicule in the person of its priest. After the torture, food was given, according to the custom of the country, to the criminals about to die. The mandarin told the slaves to ask the brave European what he would have to eat. M. Marchand refused to eat any thing; but the other persons took their last repast. Absorbed with the thought of death, and prostrate with pain, he remained outside with the multitude of spectators.

When the feast was over, the mandarin delivered the five prisoners to the executioner. They were all stripped of their cloth, a gag was put in their mouths, either to stop their cries or to prevent them from addressing the multitude, and they were then carried off on their stretchers to Tho-duc, a Christian settlement, about a league from Hué, where he was to die, for the terror of the inhabitants.

Five gibbets, formed in the shape of a cross, had

been erected in a line, ready for the execution. The stretchers were brought close up, a prisoner to each gibbet, M. Marchand occupying the second place to the left. Cans containing the heads of two of the chief re-bels who had been killed in battle, were also placed in the same line, in token that they had deserved the same fate. An immense crowd surrounded the gibbets, at a distance of thirty paces. The executioners then untied the victims from their stretchers, took off the labels round their necks, and without giving them time to make the least movement, seized them by the arms, placed their bodies up against the uprights, and tied them round the middle. They then stretched out their arms along the cross-pieces, leaving the legs and feet free. Two executioners then, armed with cutlasses, placed themselves on the two sides of each victim, ready to begin the work of butchery as soon as the appointed signal should be given. Then came a roll on the drums ; when it ceased, the savages flung themselves upon their victims. Those by M. Marchand began at his chest, and with one slice cut off a large lump of flesh six inches long. The heroic martyr endured it without a struggle. They approach him again, and two more slices fall to the ground. Convulsed with pain, the suf-ferer raised his eyes to Heaven, to pray for pardon upon his torturers, and offer up the sacrifice of his life. They seize him again, and the knives descend to the legs, and again two pieces of flesh are sliced from his body ; then nature gave way, the martyr's head fell forwards, and the soul of the confessor fled away to heaven. "Strike again, butcher! but the corpse cannot feel, thou hast already given the martyr his crown." With his left hand the executioner then seized his hair and adjusted the head, and with his right cut it off at a single blow, and hurled it into a tub of lime. As if all this was not enough, the mutilated trunk was detached from the gibbet and cut into four pieces. All these details are given from the mouth of a Cabchut, who was an eye-witness of the whole dreadful spectacle.

Lest the portions of the martyr's body should be honoured by the Christians, they were carefully collected and sent to the nearest port, with orders to the commanding mandarin to send them out in a vessel, and sink them in the deep sea. The head was then enclosed in a chest, and sent from province to province as a warning to all Christians. It was then brayed in a mortar and flung into the sea.

II. M. Cornay.

Martyred in Hong-Kong, Sept. 20, 1837.

Jean Charles Cornay landed at Macao in March 1832; he went there only a deacon, not having been more than twenty-two years of age when he left Europe. But he was soon afterwards ordained priest by Mgr. Havard, Vicar-Apostolic. Disguised as a Chinese, he penetrated as far as the royal city of Tong-king, where for a considerable time no European had been seen, and applied himself in the neighbouring mountains to the study of the language. There he remained three years and a half, suffering greatly from a disease in the eyes, and from general debility, produced by the unhealthiness of the climate; but still engaged in the constant discharge of his arduous duties. At the close of that period an edict was issued against all European missionaries, upon occasion of the martyrdom of M. Marchand; and Father Cornay was seriously advised to retire from a mission, the difficulties of which his physical weakness, under this fresh persecution, rendered it impossible for him to encounter. With great grief he had almost determined on returning to Europe, when, in June 1837, he was seized in a Christian village called Bau-No, where he had considered himself in perfect security. A bandit chief, who owed a grudge to that village because he had been refused an asylum there, was the unintentional cause of his arrest.

On Thursday, 20th January, 1837, at day-break, a labourer of Bau-No observed the place surrounded with soldiers. He gave the alarm, but escape was impossible; the military had taken possession of every avenue. Father Cornay was just about to say Mass; but as not a moment was to be lost, he was hurried away by one of his flock and concealed in a thick bush in the very centre of the soldiers' quarters. He was so close to them that he heard every word that passed; but he would probably have escaped, if the colonel of the regiment had not put the mayor to the torture, and so ascertained the existence of a European in the village. The thickets were all closely searched; but it was not till four o'clock in the evening that his hiding-place was discovered. When they came to his bush, they pushed in a long iron-shod lance; and the missionary, choosing rather to testify openly for the faith than perish for it in hiding, walked from his place of concealment. However, he did not surrender himself till he saw that discovery was inevitable, and he thus describes the search: "They set about examining all the bushes in the village, and as the danger was imminent, I said my chaplet. You may imagine to which of the mysteries I applied the decades; you may imagine also what sacrifice I offered in place of the Holy Mass; and what meditation supplied the meditation of the day." When he was seen, they tied his hands behind his back, and led him away. They had already discovered his chasuble, on which were embroidered the forms of Jesus crucified and of the Holy Virgin. This chasuble was now worn on the back of the mandarin; and as the prisoner was led away, his eyes fastened upon this image while he offered to Jesus and Mary the homage of his soul. When they observed this, they made him explain the meaning of those representations. Making the sign of the cross very distinctly, he unfolded to them the great mystery of his faith, and thus on several occasions he took advantage of questions of curiosity to speak of Jesus Christ. But his words fell on the hard highway; and though he was always listened to attentively, it does not appear that he ever made any converts on these occasions.

They then fastened the canque about his neck, that instrument of torture which has been to so many martyrs in China the aureole of glory. However, in Tongking the canque is not so large and ponderous as in China, where, by its size, all communication is cut off between the arms and the head. It is simply formed of two pieces of wood tied by four sticks, of which two unite the extremities, and the other two clip the neck. The wearer is left quite free in all his motions; but it is, nevertheless, a very painful and wearisome infliction, and Father Cornay was unable to sleep the first night that he wore it. The next morning a search was made for all his objects of devotion. The Christians had taken them away and hid them in different houses, but they were most of them discovered by means of the torture. One old woman feigned to be in her agony, and the searchers forbore to disturb her, and thus she saved many objects of religion. His papers were burned, as useless, being written in European characters. If they had fallen into the hands of the government interpreter, serious injury to the Church would have been the result, as they contained catalogues of priests, catechists, and communicants, besides other important information. They allowed him to retain the use of six of his books, and were much delighted to hear that he said his prayers out of them. The colonel gave him a crucifix also. The other objects, sacred vessels, books, &c., they examined with great curiosity, but not, as may be imagined, with all the reverence of a sacristan. This seizure was, however, a terrible loss to the mission; for the other priests were left without wine, wheat for the hosts, and the instrument for making the altar-breads.

To enhance the value of his prize, the colonel determined to treat the missionary as a rebel and a prisoner of state. The canque was accordingly taken off, and he was fastened into a cage. The change was a great relief to him, as the canque had begun to chafe his shoulders; and in this cage he was carried off to the seat of government to receive his sentence. It had no covering, and yet it was left in the open air when the *cortège* stopped for the night. However, the colonel allowed him to have an altar-cloth for protection from the cold. On the road he learned that the soldiers had been in search of a rebel when they came to Bau-No, and not finding him, had laid their hands on the missionary. He spent his time, to the great astonishment of every one, in reading, praying, singing, and talking, by turn. He had a beautiful voice, and the chants of the Psalms and tones of the hymns which he sang were so different from the music of the country, that his fame as a singer preceded him; and when they came to the prefecture, and he was brought before a mandarin, that functionary required him to sing for his amusement. He excused himself on the ground that he was fasting; but the mandarin refused to give him any thing to eat till he had heard his voice, and the missionary accordingly sang such old songs of Mont Morillon as he could recollect. The soldiers and people crowded round his cage, and from that moment he had to play the part of a bird that is kept to please its master by its beautiful warbling. After he had sung, the *cortège* proceeded till they came to the governor-general's.

They entered the town in quite a grand procession: first came a hundred and fifty soldiers; then the cage, carried by eight bearers, and crowned with the crimson altar-cloth; then as many more soldiers, and the mandarins under a canopy. In the rear, two unhappy Christians were dragged along, tied together by their canques. Perhaps the entry would have been more imposing to a European eye if the dress of the soldiers had been less grotesque: with red turbans, shaped like the cover of a stew-pan; black legs and feet, bare to the knee; loose and very ragged pantaloons, and particoloured sleeves. Such was the *cortège*, in the middle of which the confessor of the faith entered the chief place of government of the western province. It is no slight token of his great cheerfulness that he should have noticed such things as these. This place, called Doai, is the very place where, five years before, he had lived disguised as a Chinese. It consists of a single fortress, which at once answers the purpose of palace, courts, prisons, barracks, and granaries. In front of the governor-general's apartments the procession stopped, and the governor-general came out and regarded the European with a long stare, and then went in again. But he intimated that in a few days the prisoner would be sent to the court of Minh-Minh, to be dealt with at his discretion. As soon as the governor had retired, a crowd of children and idlers gathered round the cage, and asked Father Cornay a number of questions. All he would say, however, was, "I am not afraid."

"No, be not afraid," they said; "we are not going to hurt you; but we have never seen a European before."

To please them, he was made to purchase his dinner with a song, and he sang a couplet to the Holy Virgin.

The cage he had hitherto occupied was only a temporary construction hastily put together at Bau-No; but now he was put into another, that was to be his permanent abode. He was also chained by a chain of a singular construction : one large ring is passed round the neck, the chain then descends to the middle, and divides into two, one part of which is fastened by a similar ring to one leg, and the other by another ring to the other leg, and these rings are fastened by rivets ; so that they are never moved till death or bribery sets the prisoner free. The weight of it is about eight pounds, and the prisoners are sometimes made to bear the expense of their own chains. The chain having been put upon him, he was placed in the cage, and tied to it by the arms as before. It was the same size as the other, high and broad enough to move easily about, but not long enough to lie down at night in. It was about four feet every way, and rested on four legs six inches high. There were four handles, by which it was transported from place to place. It was boarded at the top and bottom, and the sides all round were ornamented with bars of wood, crossed, after the usual Chinese fashion, about six inches apart.

As access to Father Cornay was now easy enough, a Christian woman, a religious, contrived to see him and exchange a few words. He desired her to obtain a calendar from M. Marette, a missionary in the neighbourhood. M. Marette sent the calendar, and at the same time wrote a few words of encouragement. The success of this first attempt emboldened him to proceed, and thus a regular correspondence became established M. Marette had simply the precaution to send his note concealed in the food which was carried to the holy confessor. Father Cornay, on his side, had obtained paper from the colonel to write out the history of his confinement to send to his family, and so contrived to write many other things : *for every thing he wrote was supposed to have relation to his diary. The Chinese were never tired of seeing him write, their own mode being clumsy and complicated to the last degree. In his letter to M. Marette, he relates every thing that occurred to him, and it is through this channel that we are acquainted with the details of his captivity. He also forwarded, through him, several letters to his parents in France. His writings are full of the most holy sentiments, and lit up with an air of cheerfulness very remarkable in one so enfeebled with sickness.

On the 24th June, the festival of his patron saint, six months after his capture, he was informed that, for the sum of 10,000 francs, the governor-general would pardon him and the village of Bau-No, and forward him to Macao. This was a more honest proposition than had been made by the commander of the soldiers, who had asked 100,000 francs. The authorities, unable to realise the exalted motive which leads missionaries from their own homes to encounter danger and death in a foreign country,-are under the conviction that they come over to make money, which they remit to Europe, that when they have amassed enough, they may return and spend it. So renowned a preacher as M. Cornay must needs be very rich, and the governor-general was determined to demand a high ransom. The missionary assured him, that so far from making money in China, he could only support his mission by the alms he received from Europe. He promised, however, to acquaint the people at Bau-No with his proposal; and so he did. But the wretched cottagers could scarcely support their own lives, far less obtain so large a sum as the general's avarice demanded, and nothing came of the application.

In about three weeks arrived the king's order to the mandarins to decide the matter according to their judgment. The missionary began to think that he should escape, on account of their general kind treatment of him; but he soon discovered his mistake. The mandarins were determined to advance their favour with the king by accomplishing his death. He was confessedly a Christian; they would also make him out to be a rebel; and they endeavoured to make him criminate himself. As he refused to confess a crime of which he was not guilty, they suborned witnesses to prove him in league with the rebels. The holy missionary bore all with patience, only complaining that he was going to be a victim of malice and treachery, instead of a martyr for the faith. But as the certainty of death increased, so also did his courage; and when the colonel one day taunting him, said, "Can you sing now?" he answered with the French hymn:

"La religion nous appele,
Sachons vaincre, sachons mourir," &c.

When they took him back to his cage on one occasion, after a most cruel scourging, he sang the *Salve Regina*. Now they put upon him a canque, and tied him to the cage by a cord to his foot, which caused him intolerable agony. They were not content with once or twice endeavouring to extort a confession from our holy martyr; he was for nearly two months subjected to constant examinations, and he was thrice scourged. They employed a very cruel mode of torture. Instead of using the simple rod, flexible twigs were employed, loaded at the end with lead, and about three feet long. The reader may imagine the force which a powerful executioner may put into the blow, by comparing his instrument with a weapon in common use with us for the preservation of life. But he bore all with heroic constancy. In writing home to his father and mother, he says: "My blood has flowed in my torments, and must yet flow twice or thrice before I have my limbs and my head cut off. I have wept to think of the pain you will feel in learning these details; but let the thought that when you read these lines I shall be in heaven to intercede for you, console you, as well on your own account as on mine. Do not bewail the day of my death, for it will be the happiest of my life; it will be the close of sorrow and the beginning of bliss. After all, my torments are not so cruel as they might have been; they let my old wounds heal before they inflict new ones. I shall not be pinched with red-hot tongs like M. Marchand; and if they cut off my four limbs and my head, five executioners will strike me at once, so that I shall not have very much to suffer. Console yourselves, therefore; in a short time all will be over, and I shall be waiting for you in heaven."

On the 29th of August he was brought up for his third and last torture. They tried first to make him trample on the cross; but he threw himself down and kissed it, and pressed it to his heart. If they had shown him but little mercy on former occasions, now he was beaten with greater cruelty than ever. He was not suffered to return to his cage till he had received sixty four blows with a new rod. When he was shut up in t after his torture, they told him to stretch forth his foot. Expecting that they were going to pinch it with tongs, he obeyed, offering it to Jesus Christ; but they had no intention then of torture, but of insult. The cross that he would not himself trample on they placed under the sole of his foot, that after his death they might pervert the action to the scandal of the Church of Christ. M. Cornay took care that M. Marette should know he had not consented.

At length the day of his martyrdom was fixed. M. Marette had told him he would keep All Saints in heaven; and so it was. It is remarkable that he had inquired of his friend the exact date of the Ember-days, that he might fast; and it was on Ember-Wednesday that he received his crown.

It was the 20th of September, 1837. About one in the afternoon a courier was seen approaching the town bearing a flag. A Christian soldier instantly divined the object of his arrival, and informed the good woman whom we have already mentioned. She having hastily given orders to her old servant to provide two mats for the approaching execution, to stretch under the holy martyr, ran to his prison to announce the tidings to the prisoner himself. In another hour he was on his way to death.

About two o'clock appeared the fatal escort. It issued by the western gate of the fortress, and passed along the south side to the high-street. M. Cornay was alone in his cage without any of his companions. Four hundred soldiers head the procession; around the prisoner are the executioners with swords drawn and hatchets raised. In front is carried a board, on which the sentence is inscribed. Behind come cymbals, giving from time to time their mournful notes. Last of all, on horse-back, follows the presiding officer of the execution. No Europeans had ever been executed in that place before, and the novelty of the spectacle drew a great crowd of spectators, among them many Christians from the neighbourhood; but these abstained from all external marks of sorrow. During the circuit of the fortress the martyr sang songs of joy; while they were passing the high-street, and all the remainder of the way, he was in prayer. The idolaters were astonished at his tranquillity, and could not conceive its source. The escort having at length passed clear of the street, leaves the high road, and turns into a neighbouring field which had been selected for the place of execution. The march had occupied twenty minutes. On their arrival at the appointed spot, the cage with the martyr in it is set down in its place; the soldiers form a ring round it, to keep off the crowd who are pressing from behind. The presiding officer, with a cymbal and speaking-trumpet, takes his station outside the ring, and in a conspicuous place hard by is set up the board inscribed with the sentence. It ran as follows:

"The man called Tan, whose true name is Cao-Lang-Ne (the nearest approximation to Cornay of which the Chinese alphabet is susceptible), of the kingdom of Phu-Lang-Sa (of France), and of the town of Loudun, is found guilty of heading a rebellion. The supreme edict ordains that he be cut in pieces, and that his head be cast into the sea after it has been exposed for three days. Let this just sentence leave a universal impression. Given this 21st day of the eighth moon of the eighteenth year of the reign of Minh-Mihn."

This is the greatest of all punishments, and reserved for criminals of state. It consists in having the arms and legs *first* cut off, and then the head, after which the trunk is quartered. Although the limbs are usually chopped off by four different executioners, and as nearly as possible at the same moment, still one can conceive what intolerable agony the poor wretch has to endure before decapitation relieves him from his sufferings. As a missionary, and indeed merely for being a European, M. Cornay must have died; but unless judged to be inculpated in a revolt, he would never have been condemned to be cut in pieces. And now the cage is opened at the top, and inclined, to let the prisoner out. The martyr is then made to sit down on the ground while the chain is taken off. This operation is often performed with great brutality; but in this case the smith is a Chris-

tian, and he has the credit of having so skilfully opened
the three rings, that the father was not aware of its
execution.   The man asked for a remembrance of him,
and the missionary plucked out some of his hair and
gave it to him.   Then the executioners plant four stakes
in the ground, each about a foot long, to which to
attach the arms and feet of their victim.   The old servant offers the two mats she had brought; but being
forbidden to enter the ring, she sends them by the
executioners.   They lay them down on the ground, side
by side; upon them they place the mat out of the cage,
and over all the altar-cloth, folded in four, which the
mandarin had given him for a covering.   Such is the
altar on which the sacrifice is to be offered up.

Then the martyr is stripped of some of his clothes,
and laid face downwards upon the altar-cloth.   The
executioners fasten his hands and feet to the stakes, and
drive in two other stakes, one on each side of the neck,
to hold his head firm.   Natives only require one stake,
to which the head is attached by means of thin long
hair.   The arms are stretched out in the form of a cross,
but the feet are kept close together.

These preparations occupied twenty minutes; and
now the voice of the officer is heard through the speaking-trumpet, inquiring if all is ready.   A hundred voices
answer "Yes!" upon which he gives the following
orders to the executioners: That after the first stroke
of his cymbal they should first cut off the *head* of the
prisoner; then the limbs, and then quarter 'he trunk.
This order excited universal astonishment, as in direct
opposition to custom and the royal sentence; but it was
attributed to the mandarin's humanity.   Probably the
officer felt that the man was not a rebel, and should not
suffer the whole of a rebel's punishment.   In any case
he is worthy of all praise; for if his act of pity had
reached the ears of the king, he must have been seriously compromised.   However, the executioners prepare to obey the mandarin's orders.   With uplifted
swords they stand by their victim, and wait for the

appointed signal. The most powerful of them is placed at his head.

In painful suspense, and with eyes fixed upon the victim, the crowd wait for the stroke of the cymbal. Scarcely is it heard, when, with a single blow, the head is struck off, and the martyrdom is consummated. It was about three o'clock in the afternoon. The executioner takes the head by the ear, lifts it up, and throws it to some distance; then, like a wild beast, he licks his sword. The rest of the sentence is then performed: the arms are cut off at the elbows, and the legs at the knees, and the several parts are thrown aside, while the trunk which remains is cut into four parts. Horrible to relate, the executioners cut off morsels of the liver and devour them. The Chinese executioners have a superstition that the liver of great criminals is hard, and communicates to the eater the courage of the criminal in life. In this case the men remarked that the martyr could not have been a rebel, for his liver was soft. One of them tore off the nails, and kept them; with what object is not known.

After the execution, the cage, irons, and sentence of the martyr were taken away. But no one touched the clothes. The head was caught up by a boy, who ran with it through the town, terrifying all whom he met; it was soon taken from him by the soldiers. At the moment of his execution, it is said that the martyr gave one of his habits to an executioner, and that it was redeemed for twenty sous. The crowd remained on the spot, curious to see what the Christians would do. A physician and a sub-officer, both Christians, the religious and her old servant, came and gathered up the bits of flesh which were scattered here and there. As another religious, who ought to have arrived with linens prepared for the purpose, had not come, they began to soak up the blood with whatever they could find -- the martyr's clothes, paper, handkerchiefs. Instantly the whole crowd, Christians and pagans, rush to possess themselves of some drops of that precious blood. This act on the part of the Chinese idolaters is the more strange, since they have the greatest horror of the corpses of criminals; and it is forbidden throughout the province to collect the blood of any who have died a violent death. These relics were avowedly collected as charms against evil spirits. The execution became a general subject of conversation, and the collection of his blood, especially, was talked of as a very singular event. The remains of the martyr were religiously interred. The several parts of his body were collected and put into a coffin, and buried in the place of execution. Such was the sepulchre of the martyr; in life counted a rebel, and his grave with the graves of murderers. But Jesus, too, was numbered with the malefactors.

In July 1838 M. Marette succeeded in obtaining possession of his coffin. It was then enclosed in another coffin of great splendour, presented by a rich Christian family, and a solemn funeral service was held. Father Trien said a Mass of thanksgiving, and M. Marette the usual Requiem, and the holy relics were laid up in the most retired chamber of the convent.

III. Pierre Dumoulin Borie.

MARTYRED IN TONG-KING, DEC. 2, 1838.

Pierre Dumoulin Borie arrived at Tong-king in the year 1832, being then twenty-four years of age. He had left France with a burning desire to be a martyr, and a certain conviction that he should never see his home again. "Farewell till the day of the resurrection," were his words on taking leave of his dearest friends. For six years he laboured amid the greatest dangers and privations, living in the very fire of persecution; till at length he obtained the crown he so ardently desired. At the moment of his capture he had just been nominated Bishop of Acanthus; but he died without other consecration than of his own blood.

The mandarins had long been on his track; and at length, through treachery, he fell into their hands. A disciple called Peter Tu was also taken; but he would have been set at liberty on account of his youth, if he had not passionately begged to be allowed to share his master's captivity. Canques were put upon their necks, and they were led away to prison together. They found there already two native priests, Father Diem and Father Khoa, and a catechist of the name of Antoine Nam, besides other confessors.

Mgr. Borie was taken before the mandarin, who sought to make him compromise others. As he would reveal nothing, the judge asked him whether he would maintain the same reserve under the torture. He answered, "I dare not flatter myself till I try." He was then cast into prison again, and loaded with irons. Here he passed his days in chanting the Psalms, singing hymns with his fellow-prisoners for the faith, and answering the questions of his jailors. A great number of visitors came to see him, and he was allowed to speak to them freely of Jesus Christ. They were so struck with his holy joy, notwithstanding the weight of the canque upon his shoulders, that many of them expressed their intention to embrace the faith. The Christians from that time began to be left unmolested; the arrest of this shepherd was the safety of his flock.

When he was brought before the prefect, he was asked how old he was, what vessel he had come over in, how long he had lived in the country, and what place he had lived in. To all of these questions, except the last, he answered plainly.

"Well," said the court, "we take a great interest in you, for you are no highway robber. Your faith is your only crime, and we wish we could spare you. But the king's orders are very strict, and we must put you to the question."

"I know it," said the martyr calmly.

Preparations were immediately made for the torture Four stakes were driven into the ground, and his hands and feet were tied to them. Under his stomach and under his chin were placed tiles; and in this position they gave him thirty blows with a bamboo upon his back. For the first twenty blows he uttered not a sound, although his flesh was in strips and streaming with blood. At the ten last he was heard to groan; but he gave no sign of submission. They noticed that he had his handkerchief in his mouth all the time.

"That will do," said the mandarin to the exccutioners; "it is waste of time to beat this man." Then to the missionary, "Are you in pain?"

"I am flesh and blood like other people," was his answer; "but I am just as happy after being tortured as before."

"Ah, the courage of a European is unconquerable. Now try the disciple Tu. We shall succeed with him."

The brave young Christian received no less than a hundred-and-ten blows in four questions: thirty the first time; on the third day, before the wounds had cicatrised, as many more; after which not a particle of his natural skin remained. In eleven days he received again thirty blows, and shortly afterwards a final bastinado. Yet his courage never for an instant failed. The mandarins could not conceal their astonishment. "The young man, no doubt, is ambitious of being one day at the head of his religion; and fully equal he is to the post." Under God, he owed his constancy to the example and the lessons of his master. Before they were taken to the prefecture, Mgr. Borie had torn his handkerchief in two, and given him one half, and kept the other half himself. "If you wish to follow me," he said, "arm yourself with courage. Take care you make no revelation which will compromise any one else." That handkerchief was like the mantle of Elias; it conveyed to the disciple his master's spirit. Mgr. Borie was also several times put to the question, but always without success.

"Why are you so obstinate?" said the mandarin one day.

"Because you beat me like a brute. In my country a man is tried, and if guilty, punished; but he is not tortured till he makes a confession."

"But what if the king calls you to the capital? There you will find a huge fire and red-hot pincers, and your flesh will be torn away in bits. How will you stand that?"

"When the king calls me I shall see. I dare not presume upon my strength beforehand."

At last the sentence was passed; he was condemned to be beheaded. The two native priests were to be strangled, and the other confessors were to remain in custody till the tyrant had fixed a day for their execution. As soon as the warrant arrived, the jailor ordered a fowl to be dressed for the three fathers, according to the invariable custom of the country, to regale those who are going to be put to death. It happened to be Saturday, on which day they always fasted. Mgr. Borie intimated to the jailor that they could eat no meat that day. However, to please the Mandarin Bo, they consented to take a little wine. Then all the other prisoners rose to salute the three martyrs for the last time. Mgr. Borie did not forget the heroic Tu. Before leaving the catechist he gave him to Wam, and said, "This young lad is as my own son. If you have any affection for myself, transfer it to him when I am gone." They all parted with mingled sobs and smiles, and the kind jailor expressed his sorrow that the execution could not be deferred for another day, to let them enjoy the death-feast. The three martyrs thanked him for his kindness and attention to them during their imprisonment, and marched forth to their glory with faces radiant with joy.

On their way Mgr. Borie saluted all whom he knew. The Mandarin Bo met the procession, and commanded it to halt.

"Are you not afraid of death now?" he asked of the holy missionary.

"Am I a rebel or a criminal, that I should fear? I fear only God. To-day I am to die, to-morrow it will be another's turn."

"What insolence!" said the mandarin, with an oath; "let them be beaten."

The soldiers did not obey this order; but the martyr sent to the mandarin, to beg his pardon if his answer had given him offence.

When they came to the place of execution, the three martyrs knelt down and prayed towards Europe. After their prayer, the irons which connected the two parts of their canques were broken. Father Diem and Father Khoa were stretched out face downwards to be strangled; Mgr. Borie was put into a sitting posture to be beheaded. The cymbals then sounded, and at the third blow the executioners began to do their duty. The two native priests were soon despatched; but the agony of the European missionary was frightfully prolonged. The executioner was in a state of partial intoxication, and scarcely knew what he was doing. His first gash fell upon the martyr's ear, and went down to his jaw-bone; the second stroke hit on his shoulder, and glanced up on to his neck; the third was better directed, but still the head was only half-separated from the trunk. Even the cruel Mandarin Bo shrunk back in horror at the sight. The executioner took seven strokes to finish the work, and all the time the holy martyr gave not one cry of impatience or pain. The man received fifty blows for his unskilful performance. The martyrdom took place on the 2d Dec 1838.

After the execution, Christians and pagans altogether made a rush to obtain the relics of the martyrs, and disputed for the possession of the holy treasures. Strange to say, all attempts at exhuming the bodies were for a long time rendered fruitless by the exceeding reverence paid to them by the pagans themselves, who regarded the confessors as tutelary divinities, and were accustomed to burn paper in their honour, and render them other marks of respect, according to the rites of their superstitious worship. But at length, after more than a year, M. Masson, Missionary-Apostolic, obtained permission to take away the holy remains. They were found perfectly sweet and uncorrupted, notwithstanding the damp and unfavourable condition of the tombs. They were received by a number of native and European clergy, and a solemn funeral service was said for their souls.

IV. JEAN-BAPTISTE VACHAL.

MARTYRED IN CHINA, APRIL 12, 1851.

After four years' labour in the sacred ministry in France, M. Jean-Baptiste Vachal left his native country to embrace the yet more arduous life of a missionary in China. In Siam, where he was first established, he contracted a disease, from which he never fully recovered, known in the country as the wood fever. To save his life, he was compelled to seek change of air. With a shattered constitution he reached the north-east of Yan-nan in 1846, and in 1849 he took up his residence in the suburbs of the capital of that province.

He had long desired to penetrate farther into the interior—into those vast countries which border on Tong-king; and in September of that year, with the authority of Mgr. the Bishop of Philomelia, he set off on that expedition. At Mong-tse-kien he found some old neophytes who had almost lost all idea of their religion. At a large town called Kay-howa-fou M. Vachal, not wishing to lodge at an inn, took up his abode in a pagoda, where he found and made acquaintance with a painter of idols, and converted him. The new convert deserted his idols, and took the European missionary and his catechist, Sen-san-te, to his own village, the name of which was Chhe-Nghai-Io. Here the catechist preached morning and evening to great crowds, who flocked from all the country round: the people listened with the most intense interest, and received the truths of our most holy religion with wonderful facility. So great was the success that attended their efforts, that in a short time the missionary and his catechist erected a small chapel for the infant Christendom.

But the day of trial was at hand. Two of the chief people of the village informed against the new teachers. They were described as endowed with such wonderful powers, that they could disappear under the earth when they chose. A mandarin visited the village to inquire into the matter. M. Vachal, the catechist, and four of the converts, went forth to meet him. He received them graciously, to disarm their suspicions and induce them to follow him quietly to the neighbouring town, where the missionary had first met the painter. The priest and the catechist did so, and were immediately brought before a tribunal. M. Vachal was ordered to kneel, and he refused, alleging the contrary customs of his own country; he was then bastinadoed, and received forty-eight blows.

The tyrant then turned to Sen-san-te, the catechist, and asked him if he, being a Chinese, was not ashamed to be seen following a European?

"And how is it," he replied, "that you, who are a Chinese yourself, have become a mandarin to a Tartar emperor?"

The retort was more powerful than judicious; and as it contained too much truth to admit of argument, the unfortunate catechist received the severer beating. From that time forward the prisoners never appeared together at the tribunal, and occupied different cells. This examination took place on the 17th January, 1851.

On the 8th, the mandarin put up the following placard in the town:

"A man, who calls himself falsely a European, has come into this country to preach the detestable religion of the 'Master of Heaven.' I, your mandarin, and a native of Canton, am perfectly acquainted with this foreign religion. It is an abominable doctrine; the people of this sect do not believe in any spirit, and they snatch out the eyes of the dying, and commit many other crimes. Therefore I most severely prohibit that religion. I will punish with the utmost rigour whoever shall be detected practising it, and I will set my officers to spy out every where those who are guilty of doing so. Every one who follows the religion of the Master of Heaven shall be punished without mercy."

On the 14th, this mandarin departed for the capital to learn the emperor's pleasure. In his absence, the prisoner had not much to suffer from the Chinese; but his old complaint returned, and a Christian, who obtained access to his cell in disguise, found him in a very feeble state. In about three weeks the mandarin returned, and immediately gave orders that no food whatever should be given to the European prisoner, and that he should be put in irons. For three days M. Vachal remained without taking the slightest nourishment; at the end of that time, a man about the court, moved with compassion, procured for the poor captive enough to serve for three meals. By some means or other the mandarin obtained information of this relief, and in consequence took such measures for the future as rendered it morally certain that from that time forward no food of any kind was given to M. Vachal. The exact day when this privation became total and complete is not known; but this is certain, that on the tenth day of the third moon, in the night, the blessed martyr gave up his soul to God; that is to say, on the Feast of the Compassion of the Blessed Virgin, Wednesday, 11th April, 1851. The next night the catechist also died; but his was a less painful death, as it was hastened by opium.

The holy martyr is said by some persons not to have perished wholly from want of nourishment; but

to have been subjected to a species of torture very com
mon in that country. The poor wretch is supposed to
go without food for several days, when a glass or two
glasses of the very best Chinese wine is given him to
drink. Scarcely has he drunk it, before, either by force
or of his own accord, he is laid upon his back; and then
a piece of paper, dipped in the same kind of wine, is
placed over the mouth and nose of the victim. It appears that death is then instantaneous. Whether M.
Vachal was subjected to this process after some days'
starvation or not is not certainly known. It is said
that, in his last moments, he was seen sitting up on the
ground against his prison-wall with his hands joined,
and from time to time raising his eyes towards heaven,
but speechless from exhaustion. But of what occurred
in that cell during the days of his torture nothing has
positively transpired. Nothing is certain except that
he died on the 11th April of starvation, and that on
the 12th he was buried.

The report of the death of this noble athlete of
Jesus Christ was spread abroad even before the catechist had breathed his last. A Christian in the town, to
test the truth of the rumour, set himself early in the
morning at the gate of the prison, to watch whether
any corpses were brought out. Towards nine o'clock,
he saw issue two coffins of a disproportionate length.
The first, which contained the body of M. Vachal, was
far the longest, as he had been in life extraordinarily
tall. The second coffin, in which had been placed the
body of the catechist, was partially open. Towards
the head the boards were loose, and the Christian distinctly recognised Sen-san-te, frightfully emaciated.
The mandarin, to destroy every vestige of his crime,
had all the effects of M. Vachal burned on the very
spot of his interment, with the exception of his chalice
and a little money which he had.

V. Philip Mink.

Martyred in Cochin China, July 3, 1853.

The previous martyrdoms which we have related have been those of European missionaries; but there are not wanting glorious examples of the courage and devotion with which the Christian faith inspires even native priests and catechists. We have already seen how bravely two Anamite priests suffered with Mgr Borie, and the catechist Sen-san-te with M. Vachal. It is a greater miracle of grace when a Chinese continues firm in the faith in the face of a bloody death, on account of his natural pusillanimity. We shall conclude this sketch of the Chinese missions and martyrs in China with the following account of the death of Philip Mink, a native priest of great eminence and sanctity, who suffered so lately as July 1853.

Philip Mink was a native of Cochin China, born of Christian parents, and early instructed in the faith. He was first brought up in the diocesan seminary, but afterwards transferred to the general college at Penang. Here he completed his theological studies with distinction. In 1846 he was ordained priest; and the duties of his vocation he discharged so laboriously, and with so much zeal and ability, that the superior of the mission was induced to confer upon him the power of administering the Sacrament of Confirmation. By this privilege he was exposed to the greater danger from his greater celebrity, on account of the additional publicity given to his name, and the necessity of travelling about from place to place.

In Jan. 1853 he was called to Mâe Bâe to administer Confirmation to a large number of candidates, and on his arrival he was denounced to the authorities as an apostle of the Christian religion. On Saturday, the 5th Feb., a detachment of soldiers arrived about six in the evening, and invested the house where he had been lodged.   Escape being impossible, he made his host open the doors, and he was immediately seized and carried off by the soldiers.   The house was pillaged of every thing, and the plunder divided among the robbers; except the ornaments of the altar and the images, which were saved to be produced as evidence at the trial. The troops then proceeded to arrest the notables of the village, who were also the chief men in the Christendom; and having secured their prisoners, they proceeded to the court-house.

Father Philip was soon brought up before the mandarin, who offered to release him upon condition of his trampling under foot the Cross, which was placed for that purpose below his feet.   On seeing the easy terms on which he could escape a horrible death, the holy priest says he felt a sensation of fear lest he should be induced, in a moment of weakness, to deny his Saviour. He therefore invoked the assistance of God, and replied to the judge: " I cannot obey you; my religion forbids it.   This image I have hitherto reverenced, and can I now trample it under my feet? God forbid!"   Upon this the judge ordered the officers to compel him by force to tread upon the sacred symbol.   But the courageous confessor resisted: and surely he had other strength than his own infused into his limbs; for the executioners were unable to force him upon the crucifix, and at length they desisted from their attempt. The court then pronounced the sentence.   By an edict, promulgated at the commencement of the reign of Tu-Duc, the native priest could only be condemned to perpetual exile.   Father Mink was accordingly sentenced to be banished under irons to the province of Tongking.   The six Christians who were arrested with him, were beaten with the rattan, and then released.   The sentence upon Father Mink was forwarded to the emperor for his sanction, and the prisoner was meanwhile kept in confinement.   It was not till July that the answer arrived.   The sentence of banishment was changed into a death-warrant.   A later edict had been put forth, although never enforced, that native and European priests were to be punished alike; upon the strength of this proclamation, Philip Mink was condemned to be beheaded.

When the holy martyr heard that his life was required of him by the Saviour he had served, he fell upon his knees to implore the Divine grace, and offer himself as a sacrifice to God.   On being asked where he would be interred, he replied that he had a more important subject to occupy his attention; and he continued his prayer.   When the soldiers entered his cell, he rose with his rosary in his hand, and invoking the aid and intercession of Mary, walked to the place of execution with a firm step and a courageous heart. Several times on his way he threw himself on his knees in prayer; and when he arrived at the appointed spot he again asked permission of the executioners to pray. With an unwonted charity they allowed him a few minutes, and he knelt down by himself.   At length he gave a sign to the executioners that he was ready, and his head was immediately severed from his body. Scarcely was the sacrifice accomplished than the pagans themselves, moved by some irresistible impulse, exclaimed, "The holy priest has ascended to heaven."

This martyrdom, be it remembered, took place no longer ago than the 3d July, 1853.   And even while we are writing there may be others awaiting in prison the day of suffering, or actually undergoing the pagan's sentence.   For the arrest of Philip Mink was the signal for renewed hostilities against the Christians; the emperor awarded to each of the informers against him a large gift of money, and this has stimulated the ardour of the heathen.   There was, moreover, an apostate Christian acquainted with all the priests of the mission, and from his treachery every evil was to be anticipated.   Surely the day is coming when this blood, so freely shed, shall produce its fruit; surely all the centuries of labour, all the miracles of Divine love that have been performed in the midst of a pagan world, all the graces which have been showered so abundantly on the East,—must at length result in the conversion of the people and the exaltation of the Cross; surely the Church will one day reap the harvest she has sown. May God hasten the time!

XII

FATHER THOMAS OF JESUS.

HERE is scarcely a more melancholy or a more romantic page of history, than that which records the tale of King Sebastian's expedition into Africa in the year 1578. Had the enterprise been successful, it would perhaps have placed its leader among the foremost ranks of Christian heroes; and the poetry of Portugal might have immortalised him as the founder of his country's glory, instead of, as now, connecting his name with the story of her ruin and disgrace. And surely, when the brilliant armament set sail that was intended to attack the Moors on their own soil, each vessel crowded with the flower of a young and chivalrous nobility, who were led by a king whose boyish ardour (for he was but twenty-three) urged him to this daring undertaking " that he might do somewhat for God and Portugal," the doubting hearts of his sage councillors, who were unanimous in dissuading him from the attempt, might well have been roused to something of his own high enthusiasm, as they saw the martial preparations of the Christian leaders, mingled with something of that religious character which betokened that the war was undertaken in defence of the Cross. Sebastian himself was not unworthy, in many ways, to be the chief of such an expedition. He was a warm, perhaps an extravagant admirer of those days of chivalrous glory, which he rashly attempted to bring back when their time was past in Europe; his personal character, rash and headstrong as it was, had yet a generosity and frankness in it which endeared him to all who knew him. Even such men as Bartholomew of the Martyrs were forced to acknowledge the charm of the young king

R

over their affections; and it was probably the very power
and success of his influence, winning the hearts of men
against their judgment, that proved his ruin, by enabling
him to overcome the opposition of his advisers to the war
which was to cost him his kingdom and his life.

We are not, however, about to enter into the details
of the campaign, terminated as it was by a single battle, so bloody and terrible, that it is said but fifty Portuguese survived the disastrous day; whilst the fate of
Sebastian himself was sunk in an obscurity which long
kept alive among his subjects the hope that they should
see him return, and gave rise to similar legends concerning him as have been associated with the names of
Roderic of the Goths and our own Arthur. Our present
interest with the gallant and unfortunate crews of those
gay vessels, so proudly riding over the Atlantic in all
the pomp and glitter of warlike display in the sixteenth
century, is confined to one man, perhaps the least
thought of among them all. Yet, if so, it was for no
want of noble birth; for the Counts of Andrada belonged
to one of the most illustrious houses of Portugal. But
the knightly renown which had formed the most distinguished inheritance of his ancestors was little regarded
by him of whom we speak, and who had joined the
company of the army from a very different motive from
any which stirred in the hearts of the hot-blooded com-
batants. Mixing with the gay nobles and soldiery, in
the coarse habit of the Austin Hermits, Father Thomas
of Jesus thought but little of the worldly honours he
had renounced, when fifteen years of age, to embrace his
present life; his business among them was, as he said,
to nurse the sick and tend the wounded. But this did
but conceal another design, which lay at the bottom
of his heart, and which some may think to have rivalled
that of the king in romance and Quixotism. The Christian slaves who were groaning out their lives in the
Moorish dungeons were often subjected to such hard
and terrible sufferings, that many were induced to renounce their faith, and purchase an easier life at the

price of conformity to Mahometan unbelief. Father Thomas had formed the resolution to join them, since he could not release them; that, sharing in their sufferings, he might strengthen them in the faith, and preserve them from the terrible danger of apostasy. He was therefore in the army of Sebastian, to whom he was singularly dear, with the fixed determination in his soul to be taken captive, and voluntarily to embrace that life whose terrors were best attested by the long succession of military orders founded for the express purpose of its relief. Nevertheless, during the time of his presence with the army, he was not idle; but devoted himself, and successfully, to the prevention of disorders, whilst his daily occupation was found among the sick. In the fatal engagement which destroyed all the hopes of the unhappy monarch, Father Thomas might be seen exposed to the hottest of the fire, assisting the fallen, and encouraging the soldiers to valour in the cause of the Cross. While doing so, an arrow struck him in the shoulder; and being seized by the enemy, he was carried away with a crowd of other prisoners, and soon after sold to a marabout, or what we might call a Mahometan monk or religious. This man was a fanatic in his own religion, and at first treated his prisoner with indulgence, in the hopes to win him by gentle means to the abjuration of his faith; but the scorn with which Father Thomas treated all such overtures so enraged him, that he condemned him to the treatment bestowed on the lowest slaves, and threw him into a horrible dungeon, where he daily received most cruel beatings, was almost starved, and was dragged during the hottest of the day to labour in the mines. In this miserable manner he continued to live, consoling himself in his sufferings by continual contemplation of those of his Lord.

It may perhaps have occurred to some of our readers to feel at times that curiosity concerning what we may call the romance of literature, which prompts one to wish one could, as it were, see the composition of some of those great works that are destined for immortality,

How were such books written? and what were the outward accidents that perhaps inspired some of the happiest strokes of genius? There was surely some sylvan solitude that inspired Spenser with the idea of that forest hermitage he has painted more like an artist than a poet; some night of special loveliness, that put the sleeping moonlight into Shakspeare's head; and the knowledge of deep sorrowfulness, that taught another poet how to tell us of those sad eyes "whose lids were filled with unshed tears." Chance has given us some pictures of the thought-maker at his work,—such as that of Dante on his stone-seat at Sienna, lost in profound contemplation of the unseen world from the hour of noon to vesper — sitting there so rapt and riveted in thought, that a gay wedding-procession swept by him unheeded and unperceived; or the blind Milton dictating to his daughter; or, again—how different from either!—the angel of the schools, at the foot of the crucifix, writing of the nature of God and of the angels, yet so mindful of the obligations of his religious state all the while, that you might see him committing those sublime speculations to the backs of letters and torn scraps of paper, that he might not offend the law of poverty.

Another of these pictures we have in the case of Father Thomas. If we look into his dungeon, we may see the making of a book, which, though it has no claim to rank its author among those whom we have named, has at least a world-wide reputation in its own way, and has found a home in almost every language. Chained to his damp cold floor, with the walls and roof of his prison so low and narrow that he can neither stand upright nor lie at full length, the prisoner of Christ writes by the light of a single ray of sunshine that finds its way through the breathing-hole in the wall above his head. And what is his subject? If he were a poet, he would be writing of his own sufferings, thinly veiled, it may be, under the imaginary sufferings of another; but he is nothing but a friar and a Christian, and his words are of the "Sufferings of Christ." It is a remarkable feature of this well-known work, that, from the first page to the last, there is not a word of the author himself. He never tells you that he is suffering; one knows it only by the intensity of that sympathy which has taught him the depths of the sorrows of His Lord. He had learnt in religion the sublime lesson of self-forgetfulness while absorbed in the contemplation of God; and it is only when reading the chapter wherein he so touchingly describes the awful night when the world's Redeemer was lying in the Jewish dungeon, watching for the first dawn of that day which should announce to Him that the hour of His last victory was at hand, and where he paints with so lifelike a tenderness the bitterness that filled that Heart which man had abandoned, and from which even God had, as it were, hidden His face, that we remember that the writer was himself stricken of God, and forsaken of all men,—a prisoner, and in chains, suffering stripes, and spitting, and reproach,—and that he had but to draw from the shame and the suffering that made up his daily life when he wanted the materials for the sublime picture with which he has presented us. And yet none of these things did he seem to count as sufferings. For days they left him without food; and when nature was sinking under exhaustion, his brutal persecutors would order him to the mines; and yielding them as gentle and willing an obedience as though in his beloved Convent of "Our Lady of Grace," he would drag his manacled limbs to his weary work, and answer their blows and reproaches with a sweet and happy smile. But if the torture of the body had no power to disturb the peace and tranquillity of his soul, the apostasies and sufferings of his fellow-captives often moved his heart to anguish, whilst he had little or no opportunity of encouraging them by his presence and support. At length the arrival in Morocco of Don Francesco d'Acosta, the ambassador whom the king had sent to negotiate the ransom of some of the Portuguese captives, effected some change in his position. He was removed to Morocco, and placed with a

Christian merchant,—nay, he might even have remained with some of the Portuguese nobility who were awaiting their ransom, and who were treated with a certain indulgence and respect; but nothing was further from the thoughts of Father Thomas than a life of ease, or the hopes of liberty.

"Your excellency," he said to Don Francesco, "has, I know, a kind intention; but so long as I am here, my health will never mend."

"You are thinking of the orange-groves and gardens of our own Portugal," replied the ambassador. "Take courage, good father: in a few weeks, if God will, the ransoms will arrive, and you shall get back health and strength in the cloisters of our Lady of Grace."

Thomas smiled gently. "I believe it will not be there God will restore my strength," he said; "my resting-place and hospital is nearer at hand; and if your excellency's influence is powerful enough to obtain me that favour, I might remove there even now."

"And where is that?" asked D'Acosta. "I know of no house where you have a better chance of rest and kind nursing than that where you now are: there are not many hospitals for Christian slaves in the town of Morocco."

"But there are prisons," replied Thomas; "and it is the Sagena that I am thinking of, and where, I pray you, if you wish me kindly, to have me speedily conveyed."

"The Sagena!" exclaimed the ambassador, with amazement; "why, it is the worst of all the wretched holes which these dogs of infidels have invented for our unhappy brethren. Its very air is pestilence; and it must surely be as a quick road to heaven that your reverence can think of such a resting-place; or, perhaps, it was indeed the grave you spoke of as your hospital-bed."

"Not so, my lord," answered Thomas; "for it would ill beseem one of my habit either to fear death or to court it, apart from the will of God. A religious man, indeed, can never be in love with life, or afraid of dying; but still he lives or dies of obedience, and not of self-will. I spoke but what I meant when I said that in the Sagena only shall I be restored to health. Your easy homes and gentle treatment will but quicken my disease; for I am not sent for this, but for a work which abides no delay."

In vain did D'Acosta try every argument to dissuade him from the design on which he had set his heart. Nothing availed to turn him from his purpose; and in a short time he was removed to the Sagena, where, wholly employed in the service of his unfortunate companions, he did indeed, as he had foretold, rapidly recover strength, in the midst of privations and sufferings hardly to be described.

When we remember the horrible state in which even the Christian prisons of Europe were to be found only at the early part of the last century, and then remind ourselves that the dungeons of the Sagena were expressly arranged for the torment and prolonged agony of the unhappy victims of Moorish cruelty and superstition, we may picture to ourselves something of that suffering, voluntarily and cheerfully embraced by this heroic man, only that he might bring comfort and encouragement to his companions. He had no small difficulties to encounter in his efforts to be of any use to them; for, taken from all classes, the Christian slaves were for the most part men of rude and licentious habits, and the Sagena too often presented scenes of a worse character than simple suffering.

Abandoned to despair, some took refuge in the miserable pleasure which was to be found in petty gambling, or the forgetfulness of intoxication. Others were sunk in a gloomy lethargy, from which it was hard to rouse them; and many, unable to endure the burden of this life, had openly apostatised from the faith, and were living in ease and comfort under the turban of the renegade. It was not in the Sagena, where they were watched by a thousand jealous eyes,

that Thomas was able to find an opportunity of addressing them. To do this he had to seize the inter-
vals of their work, either in the mines or in the fields;
and little by little he so far gained their confidence,
as to induce them to assemble every day during the
scanty moments allowed for rest in the middle of the
day, when the burning rays of the African sun rendered work impossible even for a slave. He summoned them to him by the ringing of a little bell, and
they never failed to come. At first he spoke to them
only of their suffering; but gradually winning them by
the expression of a sympathy to which they had long
been strangers, he was able to get them to listen to him
whilst he exhorted them to resignation and a firm faith,
and called on them, if they were indeed willing to suffer
for the Cross of Christ, to come and kiss the sacred
symbol, which he displayed before their eyes. What a
sight was that! Ten or twenty years had passed over
the heads of many since last their eyes had rested on
the crucifix: what recollections of their Christian homes,
and the churches and cities, the olive hills and convent-
bells of Spain; what thoughts of a lost innocence, and
of the days when, with the sinless hearts of children,
they learnt the name of Jesus from a mother's lips!
Thomas had gained his first victory over their hearts,
when he found and opened within them the source of
tears; and he no longer hesitated to use his power for
their reform as well as for their consolation. Before
long the horrible dungeons of the Sagena presented a
totally different character; the time was regularly divided for different exercises, marked by the sound of the
little bell, which called the inmates to prayers, instruction,
or various employments with which he induced them to
supply the place of the low amusements that had formerly been their only occupation and resource. The
prison assumed the air of a religious house; and
Father Thomas, presiding over every department, pre-
venting every disorder, and reconciling every difference,
became the father of all; and was accustomed to beg

about among those who were a little better provided than the others, in order that, with the trifling alms he was able to collect, he might relieve the sufferings of the sick or more indigent among them. In short, he had found his vocation, and the Sagena had found its apostle: the desolate wilderness of that shocking prison began to blossom like the rose; and as the flowers of faith and hope revived among its inmates, the fruits also of charity ripened in their time. Four years thus passed away, the Sagena was becoming evangelised, and many among the Christian renegades had been recalled from their apostasy, and even suffered martyrdom for the faith; but meanwhile, the captivity of Father Thomas was bitterly felt by his relations and his order. Their efforts on his behalf were unceasing; and while his sister, the Countess of Linares, strained her utmost efforts to collect the sum necessary for his ransom, King Philip II. of Spain, by means of his ambassador at Morocco, constantly treated with the authorities for his release.

One day, on returning from his daily labours among the slaves employed in the mines, he was not a little surprised to find the marabout, to whose service he was attached, waiting to receive him with a certain air of respect and consideration. "You are free," were his first words, "and may go where you list; your ransom has been offered and accepted, and so the hospitality of the Sagena need no longer be forced on you."

Father Thomas received the intelligence with a bewildered air: "Free!" he exclaimed at length; "and where am I to go?"

"By the prophet, that is a strange question for a captive," said the marabout: "I doubt not it would find a ready enough answer with others of these Christian dogs who defile our land, and who babble to us so often of their country and their homes. And if you," he added, "have forgotten yours, this letter may chance to remind you of it;" and so saying, he placed a letter in his hands. Father Thomas took it, and glanced over

its contents: it was from his sister, and written with all
the warmth of an affectionate disposition; welcoming
him back to his recovered freedom, and dwelling on
the thought of their meeting, and the happy days once
more before him.   It touched on every string that
could rouse his hopes and aspirations for a glorious
future.   There was his order, wherein he still held so
distinguished a name; the favour of the king, and the
celebrity won by his late labours and sufferings for the
faith,—fame and friendship alike were waiting for him;
and if he had, perhaps, thought himself, during the last
four years, a stranded and forgotten man, the full tide
of the world's fortunes was once more rolling to his feet.
Yet Father Thomas turned from it with a heavy heart.
"And my captive brethren," he murmured to himself;
"what is to become of them! What claim has Portugal or the world on one who left his home to become
a slave, and has found the thing he came for?   The
world does well enough without me, and I better still
without the world; but in the Sagena I have children,
and they have none but me."

"If you desire to answer the letter," interrupted
the marabout, as Father Thomas pursued these reflec-
tions, and seemed so lost in thought as scarcely to be
aware of his presence, "there is an opportunity of presently despatching a reply.   An envoy departs for
Europe this evening; and you may either write, or, if
it suit you better, I doubt not you could accompany
him; for, as I guess, your luggage is not great."

"I will write," replied Father Thomas, rousing
himself from his reverie; "and I will only pray you to
tell me one thing: This ransom of which you speak is
certain to be paid; but it is no great matter to you
what captives it redeems."

"The ransom is a large one," answered the marabout; "but the followers of Islam act not from caprice
in these matters: and for such a sum as the thousand
gold crowns promised by the king's ambassador they
are bound to release one of your dignity, or two of

inferior rank; for the Christians, we are told, value
their priests at double the price of their citizens.   The
thousand crowns is a priest's ransom, and you are the
only priest in the Sagena: the wrath of Allah hath
long since fallen on the others; the last of whom
watered the sands of Morocco with his blood some
seven weeks ago, giving glory to the prophet by his
death, as he had blasphemed him during his life."

"I am the only priest, but not the only captive,"
said Father Thomas eagerly; "and what I would ask of
you is this: the thousand crowns are yours; but leave it to
me to send back to Europe the Christian blood purchased
in exchange.   You shall have the bargain whole and
entire, according to your own estimate. Is it agreed?"

"As you will," said the Moor, "though I scarcely
guess your meaning. We take the money, and we agree
to send its worth; and there is no room for fraud or
trickery, for the captives ransomed are delivered to
your envoy by our own officers. Have it as you will,
however; the crowns will be paid this evening into the
sheriff's hands, and he will come here immediately
afterwards to receive from the captain of the Sagena
the slave who is to be released: you see there is no
possibility of evasion, if the thought of such a thing
has suggested itself."

"I have no such thought," replied Father Thomas;
"let the sheriff come, and he shall find me ready. Meanwhile I will busy myself with the letter."

The marabout was gone, and the Christian captive
sat down to write. If there had been a moment's
struggle in his heart, there was no evidence of it on his
cheek or brow; and almost without pause or hesitation
he wrote the following lines:

"A thousand thanks, my sister, for your goodness in
thinking of me, and for the sacrifice you have made to
enable me to return to you; but that return is impossible. I am not half so desolate and badly off as
you may think. I have the happiness of being the only
priest in this country, and so my presence here is well-

nigh necessary for the salvation of these poor people, whom I am able to support amid the sufferings of their wretched life. I cannot therefore leave them, and shall not return to Europe. Why should I? Have I not long since renounced the ties of family and society? Were I necessary to you, I should be with you; but you know well I can be of little use to you. Remember me in your prayers, and do not cease to love me; for indeed I love and pray for you. I will, however, accept your offer of the ransom, not for myself, but for two poor Christian slaves, who are in a far more miserable position than I am, and about to abandon their faith in despair of regaining their liberty. You shall be the means of procuring it for them, and they shall owe to you the happiness of returning to their families and their God."

On the following Saturday a little group stood on the quay outside the town, apparently engaged in watching the movements of a Spanish merchantman in the harbour, busily preparing to weigh her anchor and hoist sail for the European coast. Father Thomas was in the midst, and gathered about him were several of the captives of the Sagena: a little boat lay waiting at the foot of the pier to receive the released prisoner; but it was not Father Thomas who descended into it.

"Farewell, my children," he said to two of those who stood by his side. "God has sent you liberty, to use for Him and for His glory. Carry back to Spain the memory of His mercies; and when you hear the welcome of your home-voices, forget not the brethren you have left behind."

A minute after, and the little boat was making its way to the vessel, bearing on board the two ransomed captives: whilst their deliverer stood where he had left them, and watched them with a beating heart. Nature made itself felt, that he might have the merit of its conquest; and when, as the sail of the merchantman grew less and less as it sunk away into the sunny horizon, beyond which lay the coast of Spain, he felt his sight dim with tears, and his heart overflowing with a yearning to follow in its homeward track; but rousing himself with a powerful effort, he turned back to the Sagena, to give comfort to those who needed it even more than himself.

The fourth year of his captivity, as it drew to its close, found his sufferings greatly increased. Not only were his own labours severer under a new master to whom he was consigned, but he had the additional affliction of seeing many ready to fall away from their faith, unable to endure the hardships of their condition; and his own more rigorous imprisonment prevented his doing all he desired in protecting and encouraging them in their danger. These combined sufferings of mind and body were too much for his strength, which rapidly gave way; and the austerities which he practised during the Lent of that year had their share in increasing the malady which devoured him. Still, not a day passed without his preaching to those whom he could collect around him; and it was during the closing scenes of his life that we are told he completed those chapters on the last sufferings of Christ which perhaps owe their sublimity to the sorrow in which they were composed.

Holy Week was at hand, and, as it seemed, the servant was to follow his Master even to the very time of his decease; for none thought he could live over Good Friday, on which day Don Francis of Acosta, the Portuguese ambassador, succeeded in gaining admittance to him. Believing him to be dying, he determined to stay with him to the last; but Father Thomas would not hear of his doing so.

"You are mistaken," he whispered, as the ambassador bent over his miserable bed; "for I shall live to see another Easter sun, and to finish the work which God has given me to do."

And indeed, contrary to all probability, he continued to survive until the Monday of the following week, when a momentary restoration of strength and energy seemed given to him. He felt it, and knew its purpose.

"Those miserable men who were about to take the

turban," he said to one of his fellow-captives who attended him,—"is it too late? call them, wherever they are; for I must see them before I die."

"Do you speak of the Spanish renegades, father?" said his companion. "Alas, it is too late. They have not yet publicly renounced their faith, but their design is to do so this very day: all men cannot suffer as you have done."

"They have not yet renounced their faith?" repeated Thomas; "then, I charge you, bring them here; for I have a message for them ere I go. And tarry not too long, for the time is very short."

A few moments sufficed to bring the slaves he spoke of to his presence; and as the news spread through the Sagena that Father Thomas was dying, all the inmates hurried to his little cell, that they too might catch his last words, and receive his blessing. There he was, lying on his heap of straw; the Easter sun, of which he spoke, struggling through the narrow hole above his head on a face pale and emaciated by sickness, but beautiful with the peace that passeth knowledge, and the faith that saw far over the grave that was waiting for him. He caused them to raise him in his bed, and his eyes grew bright, and his voice firm and clear, as he spoke to the trembling renegades who stood before him.

"You will leave Jesus Christ, my children," he said, "because you are tired of your slavery; well, listen to my words, and think if I have ever deceived you. In eight days your ransom will arrive, and you will be free; persevere till then, and cast not your souls into a worse bondage than the chain of the Moslems. And for you," he added, turning to the others, "there is nothing but my blessing, and that is little worth the giving. Be of good heart; there is a better home than Spain waiting for us, and the ransom has long since been paid."

They crowded round him, kneeling as he blessed them, and sobbing like children over his outstretched hands. Dark and miserable as was the dying cell, it was filled with a wonderful and solemn beauty at that moment; and there was one looking on to whom its teaching was a revelation of faith. Leaning against the open doorway, concealed from view, the Maho-metan marabout was watching the death-scene of his slave. He saw the Christian faith creating strength out of weakness, and illuminating a dungeon with the radiance of its glorious hope. As the feeble daylight gleamed over the features of Father Thomas, he could mark his upturned gaze, as though he met the wel-coming look of One whose greeting was more than the greeting of a home. He saw those also who knelt around, their lips moving in prayer, their hands tracing that mystic sign which seemed to give so strange a courage and endurance to these suffering men; and the grace of God came down to give the last glory to His servant by the conversion of a soul. In another minute the marabout was kneeling with the others; and as he kissed the feet of his dying slave, he exclaimed: "My father, I too am a Christian; I can believe in no God but yours: and before the sun sets I wish to receive the baptism of faith."

The saint raised his hand and murmured a blessing —"My God, I thank Thee," were the last words he ut-tered, and with them he expired. It was even by his death-bed that his master received the rite of baptism; and in later years a Carmelite convent was raised over the scene of his long and glorious martyrdom of cha-rity. His death took place on the 7th of April, 1582; and eight days after, his last prophecy was completed, and the ransom of the Spanish captives arrived as he had foretold.

The influence of Father Thomas was felt in his own order even after his death. Previous to his departure from Portugal he had laboured ineffectually to bring about a reform in the Augustinian monasteries of his own country, similar to that already attempted in Italy. His zeal for a more severe observance had resulted, how-ever, only in exciting violent opposition, and much per-sonal suffering to himself; and he was forced to abandon the undertaking even by the advice of those most disposed to favour and encourage it. Nevertheless, when, some time after his death, the plan was again started, and the reform of the Discalced Hermits of St. Austin was finally and successfully carried out, those charged with its execution could find no fitter groundwork for their design than the regulations which had been before suggested by Father Thomas, and these were accordingly adopted. To him, therefore, may in some sort be attributed, in addition to his other merits, that of being the reformer of his order.

The End.

LIST OF BOOKS

PUBLISHED BY

D. & J. Sadlier & Co.,

31 Barclay Street,

NEW YORK.

☞ *Any book on this list will be sent by mail, postage paid, on receipt of the published price.*

A Sure Way to find out the True Religion. 16mo. cloth,	$0 25
Abbey of Ross. 16mo, 50 cts. ; cloth gilt,	0 75
Adventures of a Protestant in Search of a Religion. $1 50 ; cloth gilt,	2 00
Agnes of Braunsberg. 16mo, 50 cts. ; cl. gt.	0 75
Alice Harmon ; and other Tales. By an Exile of Erin, $1 25 ; cloth gilt,	1 75
Alice Sherwin : an Historical Tale. 12mo,	1 25
cloth gilt,	1 50
Anecdotes of Napoleon. 32mo, cloth,	0 60
Art Maguire ; or, The Broken Pledge,	0 75
cloth gilt,	1 00
Art of Suffering, The. 16mo, 50 cts. ; cl. gilt,	0 75
Augustine the Mysterious Beggar. 16mo,	0 50
cloth gilt,	0 75
Aunt Honor's Keepsake. By Mrs. J. Sadlier. 16mo, $1 ; cloth gilt,	1 25
A Stormy Life. By Lady Fullerton. 8vo, cloth,	1 50
cloth gilt,	2 00
Babbler, The : a Drama, in One Act, for Boys,	0 25
Balmes's Fundamental Philosophy. Translated by Brownson. 2 vols., $4 ; half mor.,	6 00
Banim's Works Complete. 10 vols. 12mo, cl.,	15 00
half morocco, $20 ; half calf,	25 00
Benjamin ; or, The Pupil of the Christian Brothers, 50 cts. ; cloth gilt,	0 75
Bessy Conway ; or, The Irish Girl in America. 75 cts. ; cloth full gilt,	1 00

Sent by mail, postage paid, on receipt of the price.

BIBLES :
Sadlier's Pocket Edition, from $1 50 to   . $7 50
"   Post Quarto Edition, from $4 to .   8 00
"   Small Quarto Edition, from $4 to   13 00
"   Roy. Quarto Edition, from $11 to   20 00
"   Imp. Quarto Edition, from $17 to   32 00
"   Folio Edition, from $18 to   .   38 00
"   Canvassing Editions, from $16 to   18 00
Bible History. By Rev. James O'Leary, D.D.
   Half bound, ...   1 50
   cloth, $2 ; cloth gilt,   .   .   .   2 50
Bit o' Writin', and other Tales. By Banim, .   1 50
Black Baronet, The. By Carleton,   .   .   1 50
Black Prophet : a Tale of the Famine. By
   Carleton. 1 50
Blakes and the Flanagans. By Mrs. J. Sad-
   lier. $1 25 ; cloth gilt,   .   .   .   1 50
Blanche Leslie, ...   0 60
Blighted Flower, The. 16mo,   .   .   .   0 50
   cloth gilt, ...   0 75
Bohemians in the 15th Century,   .   .   0 60
   cloth gilt, ...   0 90
Bossuet's History of the Variations of the
   Protestant Churches. 2 vols. 12mo,   .   3 00
   Do.   do., half mor.,   .   .   .   5 00
Boyhood of Great Painters. 2 vols.,   .   .   1 20
   cloth gilt, ...   1 80
Boyne Water, The. By Banim. 12mo, .   .   1 50
Bridge's Algebra, with Additions by the
   Christian Brothers. Half bound,   .   .   0 45
Bridge's Ancient History. 12mo,   .   .   1 25
Bridge's Modern History. 12mo,   .   .   1 50
Brownson. Conversations on Liberalism,   .   1 00
Brownson's Essays. Cloth, $2 ; half mor.,   .   3 00
   half calf. 3 50
Burke's Primary Arithmetic,   .   .   .   0 25
   "   Practical Arithmetic,   .   .   .   0 60
   "   Practical Key to Arithmetic,   .   .   1 25
Bits of Blarney. By Dr. R. Shelton Mac-
   kenzie, 12mo, ...   1 50

Cæcilia : a Roman Drama in 3 Acts,   .   .   0 40
Calista : a Sketch of the Third Century. By
   Rev. John H. Newman,   .   .   .   1 25
   cloth gilt, ...   1 50
Card-Drawing. The Half-Sir. and Suil Dhur.   1 50
Carleton's Works. 10 vols. 12mo, cloth,   .   15 00
   half morocco, $20 ; half calf,   .   .   25 00
Carpenter's Speller, ...   0 20
Castle of Rousillon. 75 cents ; cloth gilt,   .   1 00

CATECHISMS :
Butler's Catechisms, with Scriptural Cate-
   chism for U. S. Per 100, net,   .   .   4 50
   Do. do. with Prayers at Mass, cloth,   .   0 15
   Do. do. for Diocese of Quebec. Per 100, net   4 50
   Do. do. for Diocese of Toronto. Per 100, net   4 50
   Do. do. for Diocese of St. John's. Per 100, net   4 50

*Sent by mail, postage paid, on receipt of the
   price.*

Small New York Short Abridgment Christian Doctrine. Per 100, net,	$2 75
Boston—an abridgment of Do. for Diocese of Boston. Per 100, net,	2 75
Do. do., with Prayers at Mass. Per 100, net,	4 50
Do. do. do., flex. cloth. Per 100, net,	8 00
General Catechism Christian Doctrine. By order National Council. Per 100, net,	2 75
A General Catechism prepared by order of National Council. Illustrated with 50 Engravings and Descriptive Text,	0 25
Catechism Sacred History. By Mrs. Sadlier,	0 25
Catholic Youth's Library. 1st series, 12 vols.	6 00
cloth gilt,	9 00
Do. Do. 2d series, 12 vols.,	6 00
cloth gilt,	9 00
Do. Do. 3d series, 6 vols.,	3 00
Catholic Youth's Library. 3d series, 6 vols., cloth gilt,	4 50
Do. Do. 4th series. 6 vols.	3 00
cloth gilt,	4 50
Catholicity and Pantheism. By Rev. J. De Concilio,	2 00
Catholic Choir-Book. By Garbett,	2 50
Catholic Harp. By Kirk,	0 50
Catholic's Rule of Life.	0 25
Catholic Legends. 12mo, cloth,	1 00
Catholic Anecdotes.—Vol. 1,	0 75
Do. Do. Vol. 2,	1 00
Do. Do. Vol. 3,	1 00
Do. Do. 3 vols. in one,	2 50
cloth gilt,	3 00
Catholic Crusoe, $1 25 ; cloth gilt,	1 75
Catholic Christian Instructed. Paper,	0 25
cloth,	0 40
Celt's Paradise. By Banim. Cloth gilt,	1 00
Children of the Abbey. 12mo,	1 50
Christian Armed against the Seductions of the World,	0 50
Christian Brothers' First Reader. Per doz.,	1 50
Do. Do. Second Reader,	0 25
Do. Do. Third Reader,	0 63
Do. Do. Table Book. Per 100,	5 00
Christian Instructed. Quadrapanni,	0 40
Christian Missions. By Marshall. 2 vols.,	4 00
half morocco, $6 ; half calf,	7 50
Church Architecture.—Ten Working Designs for Catholic Churches. By Chas. Sholl. Large folio, $15 ; half morocco,	20 00
Circles of the Living Rosary. Per 100 sheets, net,	2 50
Clare Maitland. 50 cents ; cloth gilt,	0 75
Clock of the Passion. By St. Liguori,	0 45
Cloister Legends. $1 ; cloth gilt,	1 50
Cobbett's History Reformation,	1 25
" Legacies to Parsons,	0 60
Collegians : a Tale of Garryowen,	1 50
Collott's Doctrinal and Scriptural Catechism,	0 63
Con O'Regan. $1 ; cloth gilt,	1 25
Confederate Chieftains : a Tale of 1641,	2 00
cloth gilt,	2 50

Sent by mail, postage paid, on receipt of the price.

Confessions of St. Augustine, ... $0 75
   cloth, red edges, ... 1 00
Confessions of an Apostate. 75 cts. ; cl. gt., 1 00
Consolation for the Afflicted and those who
   Mourn. 32mo, paper, 25 cents ; cloth, 50
   cents ; cloth, red edges, 75 cents ; roan,
   red edges, $1 ; morocco, $2 ; calf, . . 2 00
Cottage and Parlor Library. 12 vols., . . 10 75
   cloth gilt, ... 13 75
     Do.   Do.   2d series, 10 vols., 10 75
   cloth gilt, ... 13 25
Croppy. By Banim. Cloth, ... 1 50

Daily Steps to Heaven. By Nun of Kenmare, 1 50
   cloth gilt, ... 2 00
Daughter of Tyrconnell. 50 cts. ; cloth gilt, 0 75
Davis, Thomas. Poems and Essays, . . 1 50
De Smet's New Indian Sketches, . . . 0 60
   cloth gilt, ... 0 90
Denounced, The. By Banim, . . . 1 50
Devil, The. Does he Exist ? . . . 1 00
Devotion to St. Joseph. $1 ; cl., red edges, . 1 25
Disappointed Ambition. 75 cts. ; cloth gilt, 1 00
Duke of Monmouth. By Griffin, . . 1 50
Dumb Boy of Fribourg. 50 cents ; cloth gilt, 0 75
Duties of Young Men. 75 cents ; cloth gilt, . 1 00
Duty of a Christian towards God. . . 0 63
Dyrbington Court. $1 25 ; cloth gilt, . . 1 75

Easter in Heaven. By Rev. F. X. Weninger,
   S.J., ... 1 00
   cloth gilt, ... 1 25
Elder Brother : a Drama in 2 Acts for Boys, 0 25
Elinor Preston. 75 cts. ; cloth gilt, . 1 00
Ellie Laura : a Drama. By Rev. Jas. O'Leary, 0 40
Emigrants of the Adharrah. By Carleton, . 1 50
End of Controversy. By Milner, . . 1 00
   paper, ... 0 50
Epistles and Gospels. Cloth, . . . 0 80
Evil Eye. By Carleton, ... 1 50
Exile of Tadmore. Cloth, 50 cts. ; cloth gilt, 0 75

Fabiola. By Cardinal Wiseman, . . . 1 50
   cloth gilt, ... 2 00
Faculties of the Soul : A Drama, . . . 0 25
Fardorougha, the Miser, ... 1 50
Fate and Fortunes of O'Neils and O'Donnells, 2 00
Father Connell. By Banim, . . . 1 50
Father Jerome's Library. 12 vols., cloth, . 3 60
   paper, ... 2 40
Father Mathew. Maguire, . . . 2 00
Father Mathew. Nun of Kenmare, . . 1 00

Sent by mail, postage paid, on receipt of the
price.

Father Sheehy. 50 cts. ; cloth gilt,   . $0 75
Father De Lisle. 60 cts. ; cloth gilt,   .   0 90
Fetches and Peter of Castle. By Banim,   .   1 50
Fireside Library, Sadlier's. 12 vols., cloth,
   extra, $9 25 ; cloth gilt,   .   .   12 25
Florence McCarthy. By Lady Morgan,   .   1 50
   cloth gilt, ...   2 00
Flowers of Christian Wisdom,   .   .
Following of Christ. 24mo, cloth, 60 cts. ; red
   edges, 75 cts. ; emb. gilt, $1 13 ; morocco,
   extra, $2 50 ; 18mo, emb. gilt, $1 50 ; full
   gilt, $1 75 ; morocco, extra,   .   3 00
For Husks, Food. By author of "Lascine,"   1 50
Family, The. By Mrs. James Sadlier. Paper,   0 25
   cloth. 0 60

Garland of Flowers,   .   .   2 50
Gerald Marsdale. $1 25 ; cloth gilt,   .   1 75
Germaine Cousin. By Lady Fullerton,   0 25
Ghost Hunter, The. By Banim,   .   1 50
Giles's Lectures. $2 ; hf. mor., $2 50 ; hf. cf.   3 00
Golden Primer. Per dozen,   .   0 75
Goldsmith's Poems and Vicar of Wakefield.
   16mo, $1 ; cloth gilt,   .   1 25
Gospel of St. John, in Latin. Per 100,   .   0 75
Graces of Mary. 60 cents ; red edges,   .   0 75
Great Day, The. 50 cents ; cloth gilt,   .   0 75
Gahan's Sermons.   .   .   .

Handy Andy. By Lover. Cloth, $1 50 ; paper,   0 75
Heiress of Kilorgan. $1 25 ; cloth gilt,   .   1 50
Hermit of the Rock. $1 25 ; cloth gilt,   .   1 50
Heroines of Charity. $1 ; cloth gilt,   .   1 25
Hidden Saints. 12mo,   .   .   1 25
History, Manual of Ancient,   .   .   1 25
History, Manual of Modern,   .   .   1 50
History of Captivity of Pius IX.,   .   0 40
History of Ireland. By McGeoghegan,   .   3 50
   half mor., $4 50 ; half calf,   .   5 00
History of Ireland. By John Mitchel,   .   3 50
   half morocco, $4 50 ; half calf,   .   5 00
History of Ireland. By McGee. 2 vols., cloth,   3 00
   half mor., $4 ; half calf,   .   5 00
History of Ireland. By Nun of Kenmare.   4 00
   half mor., $5 ; half calf, $6 ; mor., extra,   8 00
History of Irish Saints. $2 50 ; cloth gilt,   .   3 00
History of Irish Martyrs. $2 ; cloth gilt,   .   2 50
History of War in La Vendée. $1 25 ; cl. gt.,   1 50
Holland Tyde. By Grimm,   1 50
Holy Way of the Cross. Paper, 10 cts. ; cloth,   0 15
Hornehurst Rectory. By Nun of Kenmare,   2 50
   cloth gilt,   .   .   .   3 00
Huc's Christianity in China and Japan. 2
   vols., $3 ; half mor., $4 50 ; half calf,   .   5 00

Idleness ; or, The Double Lesson,   .   .   0 50
   cloth gilt, ...   0 75
Ierne of Armorica : a Tale of the Time of
   Chlovis, ...   1 50

Sent by mail, postage paid, on receipt of the
price.

Immaculate Conception. By Lambruschini, $1 00
Invasion : a Tale of Conquest. By Griffin, . 1 50
Invisible Hand : a Drama, . . 0 25
Ireland—Mitchel and McGeoghegan. 1 vol.
    4to, half morocco, $15 ; mor., extra, $17 :
    panelled, $20 ; blocked, $22 ; imitation
    blocked, $16 ; 2 vols. half mor., gilt, $20 ;
    cheap edition, 8vo, cloth, 2 vols., $7 ; half
    mor., $9 ; half calf, $10.
Irish in America. By Maguire, . 2 00
Irish on the Prairies, and other Poems, . 1 50
    cloth gilt, ... 2 00
Ivan, the Leper's Son, 50 cts. ; cloth gilt, . 0 75

Jane Sinclair. By Carleton, . . . 1 50
Jim Fagan. 50 cents ; cloth gilt, . . 0 75
Julia ; or, The Gold Thimble : a Drama, 0 25

Keighley Hall and the Maltese Cross, . . 0 50
    cloth gilt, ... 0 75
King and Cloister ; or, Legends of the Disso-
    lution. $1 ; cloth gilt, . . . 1 50

Langalerie, Month of St. Joseph. Translated
    by a Sister of St. Joseph. Cloth, . . 0 75
Lady Amabel. 50 cents ; cloth gilt, . 0 75
Legends and Stories of Ireland. By Lover,
    $1 50 ; do., paper, . . 0 75
Letter-Writer, The Practical. Half bound, . 0 31
Legends of St. Joseph. $1 ; cloth gilt, . . 1 50
Life of Blessed Margaret Mary Alacoque. By
    Rev. Geo. Tickell, S.J. $1 25 ; cloth gilt, 1 75
Life of Blessed Virgin. 8vo, cloth, $4 ; half
    mor., $5 ; half mor., gilt, . . 6 00
Life of Blessed Christ. Cloth, $4 ; half mor.,
    $5 ; half mor., gilt, . . 6 00
Life of Blessed Virgin. 32mo, . . . 0 40
    cloth gilt, ... 0 60
Life of St. Bernard. $1 50 ; cloth gilt, . 2 00
Life of St. Elizabeth. $1 50 ; cloth gilt, . 2 00
Life of St. Francis of Assisium, . .
Life of St. Francis of Rome. $1 ; cloth gilt, . 1 25
Life of St. Francis Sales. $1 ; cloth gilt, . 1 25
Life of Vincent de Paul. $1 ; cloth gilt, . 1 25
Life of St. Joseph. 75 cents ; cloth gilt, . 1 00
Life of St. Patrick. $1 ; cloth gilt, . . 1 25
Life of Father Mathew. Maguire, . . 2 00
Life of Father Mathew. Clare, . . 1 00
Life of St. Paul of the Cross. $1 50 ; cl. gilt, 2 00
Life of Empress Josephine. $1 50 ; cloth gilt, 2 00
Life of Gerald Griffin. $1 50 ; cloth gilt, . 2 00
Life of John Banim. $1 50 ; cloth gilt, . 2 00
Life of Mary, Queen of Scots. $1 50 ; cl. gt., 2 00
Life of Curran, ... 1 75

Sent by mail, postage paid, on receipt of the price.

Life of Catharine McAuley. $2 50 ; cloth gilt, $3 00
Life of Brig.-Gen. Thos. F. Meagher, . . 2 00
   cloth gilt, ... 2 50
Life of Sœur Marie, ... 1 25
Life of Dr. Doyle. 75 cents ; cloth gilt, . 1 00
Life of Fathers of the Deserts, . . 1 25
   cloth gilt, ... 1 75
Lives of Irish Saints and Martyrs. 35 plates.
   4to, cloth gilt, $10 ; half morocco, $15 ;
   morocco, extra, $17 ; panelled, $20 ;
   blocked, ... 22 00
Life of Blessed Virgin Mary. 34 plates. 4to,
   half mor., $15 ; imitation mor., $14 50 ;
   mor., extra, $17 ; bevelled, $18 ; panelled, $19 ; blocked, ... 20 00
Life of Our Saviour, Jesus Christ. 34 plates.
   Half mor., $15 ; imitation mor., $14 ; mor.,
   extra, $17 ; bevelled, $18 ; panelled, $19 ;
   blocked, ... 20 00
Life Duties. By E. E. Marcy. $1 50 ; cl. gilt, 2 00
Lily of Israel. 75 cents ; cloth gilt, . 1 00
Little Testaments, Jesus, Mary, and Joseph, 0 25
Lives of Fathers and Martyrs, and other Principal Saints. By Rev. Alban Butler. 4 vols.,
   cloth, $8 ; arabesque gilt, $12 ; half
   mor. $15 ; mor., extra, $20 ; imit. mor., 16 00
Do 12 vols. half roan, $15 ; half mor., 25 00
Do. Quarto Edition. 2 vols., with 57
   plates, imit. gilt, $25 ; mor., extra, $28 ;
   bevelled, $30 ; panelled, $35 ; blocked, . 38 00
Lives and Times of Roman Pontiffs. 2 vols.
   8vo, cloth, $14 ; imit. gilt, $18 ; half mor.,
   $16 ; mor., $20 ; mor. bevelled, $22 50 ;
   panelled, ... 25 00
Lives of the Early Martyrs. 12mo, . . 1 25
   cloth gilt. 1 50
Lost Genoveffa. 60 cts. ; cloth gilt, . 0 90
Lost Son. 75 cents ; cloth gilt, . . 1 00
Love. By Lady Herbert. 75 cts. ; cloth gilt, 1 00
Lucille, the Young Flower-maker, . . 0 50
   cloth gilt, ... 0 75

Maguire's, John Francis, Works. 3 vols., . 6 00
Mangan's, Jas. Clarence, Poems, . . 2 00
   cloth gilt, ... 2 50
Manning, Archbishop, Vatican Council, . 1 25
  "   "   Sin and its Consequences, 1 00
Manual Devotion Sacred Heart, . .
Marion Elwood, ... 1 25
Martyrs of the Coliseum. By Rev. A. J.
   O'Reilly. Cloth, $1 50 ; cloth gilt, . 2 00
Martyrs, The. By Chateaubriand, . 1 50
   cloth gilt, $2 ; half mor., . . 2 50
Mass, Prayers and Ceremonies of, . . 1 50
Maureen Dhu. $1 25 ; cloth gilt, . . 1 50
Mayor of Windgap. By Banim, . . 1 50
McCarthy More. $1 ; cloth gilt, . . 1 25
McGee's, Thos. D'Arcy, Poems, . . 2 50
   cloth gilt, $3 ; half mor., $3 50 ; mor., ex., 4 50

*Sent by mail, postage paid, on receipt of the
price.*

McGee's Ireland. 2 vols. cloth, . . .	$3 00
McGeoghegan's History of Ireland. (See History.)	
Meditations on St. Joseph, ...	1 50
cloth, red edges, ...	2 00
Meditations on the Eucharist and Sacred Heart. By Brother Philip, . . .	2 50
Metropolitan Old First Reader, . . .	0 25
" " Second " . . .	0 45
" New First Reader, . . .	0 25
" " Second " . . .	0 45
" " Third " . . .	0 60
" " Fourth " . . .	0 75
" " Fifth " . . .	1 13
" " Sixth " . . .	1 50
" Spelling-Book, . . .	0 25
" Ill. Speller and Definer, . .	0 45
Miner's Daughter. 60 cts. ; cloth, gilt, . .	0 90
Mission of Death. By Walworth, . .	0 75
cloth gilt, ...	1 00
Missions in Japan and Paraguay, . . .	1 00
cloth gilt, ...	1 25
Mitchel's History of Ireland. (See History.)	
Month of May. 60 cents ; cloth, red edges,	0 75
Murray's Grammar, abridged. By Putman,	0 20
" Introduction to the English Reader,	0 31
Mysterious Hermit. Cloth, 50 cts. ; clo. gilt,	0 75
Month of St. Joseph ; or, Exercises for each Day of the Month of March. Cloth, .	0 75
Mrs. Gerald's Niece. By Lady Fullerton. 8vo, cloth, $1 50 ; cloth gilt, ...	2 00
Napier's History of the Peninsular War. 8vo, cloth, $4 ; half-mor., $5 50 ; half-calf,	6 00
New Indian Sketches. By De Smet, . .	0 60
cloth gilt, ...	0 90
New Lights ; or, Life in Galway, . . .	1 00
cloth gilt, ...	1 25
New Testament. Cloth, ...	0 63
" Fine edition, 18mo, emb. gilt,	1 00
full gilt, $1 25 ; morocco, $2 50 ; calf,	3 00
Old Chest, The. Translated from the French by Anna T. Sadlier, $1 50 ; cloth gilt, .	2 00
Olive's Rescue, and other Tales, 16mo, cloth .	0 50
cloth gilt, ...	0 75
O'Connell, Life of Daniel. By the Nun of Kenmare. Cloth gilt, $10 ; half mor., $15 ; mor., $17 ; mor. bev., 18 ; mor. panelled,	20 00
Oddities of Humanity, 60 cents ; cloth gilt, .	0 90
O'Donnells of Glen Cottage. By D. P. Conyngham. 12mo, $1 50 ; cloth, gilt, .	2 00
Office of the Blessed Virgin, in Latin and English, ...	0 40
Old and New, $1 25 ; cloth gilt, . .	1 50
Old House by the Boyne, $1 25 ; cloth gilt, .	1 50
O'Leary's Bible History. Cloth, $2 ; cl. gilt,	2 50
" School Edition, hf. bound,	1 50
One Hundred Tales. By Schmidt, . .	0 60
cloth gilt, ...	0 90
Oram's Table Book, ...	0 20
Orphan of Moscow, 75 cts. ; cloth gilt, . .	1 00
Our Lady of Lourdes, $2 ; cloth gilt, . .	2 50

Sent by mail, postage paid, on receipt of the price.

Pastorini's History of the Church, . . . $1 25
Peep o' Day. By Banim, ... 1 50
People's Martyr, The. St. Thos. à Becket, . 1 00
  cloth gilt, ... 1 50
Perrin's French and English Conversations, 0 38
  half bound, ...
Perrin's French Fables, half bound, . . 0 38
Perry's Instructions, ... 1 00
Pictures of Christian Heroism, cloth, $1 ; cl. gt. 1 25
Poachers, The, 50 cts. ; cloth gilt, . . 0 75
Poems. By Griffin, ... 1 50
  "   By McGee, ... 2 50
  "   By Mangan, ... 2 00
  "   By Lover, ... 1 50
  "   By Rev. T. A. Butler, . . 1 50
  "   By Goldsmith, . . . 1 00
Points of Controversy. By Smarius, . . 1 50
Pope and Maguire's Discussion, . . 1 25
Pope's Niece, 50 cts. ; cloth gilt, . . 0 75
Poor Man's Catechism. Paper, 25 cts. : cloth, 0 40
Poor Scholar. By Carleton, 75 cts. ; cloth gilt, 1 00
Pope Pius the Ninth and Temporal Rights of
  the Holy See, ... 0 40
Prayer-Books :
  Altar Manual. 24mo edition. 50 cts. to . 5 00
    Do.   18mo edition. $1 to . . 10 00
  Daily Prayers. 18mo, with Epistles and
    Gospels, $1 to 12 00
    Do.   18mo, fine ed. 75 cts. to . 10 00
  Golden Manual. $1 25 to . . . 30 00
  Gems of Paradise. Red line ed. $1 50 to 30 00
    Do.   48mo. 31 cts. to . . 15 00
    Do.   64mo. 25 cts. to . . 10 00
  Gate of Heaven. 32mo. 38 cts. to . 20 00
  Garden of the Soul. 18mo. $1 to . . 16 00
  Help of Christians. 18mo. $1 25 to . 20 00
  Manual of the Passion. 18mo. $1 to . 13 00
  Mission-Book. 18mo. 75 cts. to . . 20 00
    Do.   24mo. 60 cts. to . . 15 00
  Garland of Prayer. 32mo. $2 50 to . 20 00
  Mass-Book. 50 cts. to . . . 5 00
  Path to Paradise. 32mo, new ed. 38 cts. to 15 00
    Do.   48mo. 31 cts. to . . 10 00
  Key of Heaven. 24mo, old ed. 38 cts. to . 5 00
    Do.   24mo, new ed. 50 cts. to 25 00
    Do.   18mo, new ed. 75 cts. to 30 00
  Little Key to Heaven. 64mo. 20 cts. to . 5 00
  Way to Heaven. 18mo. 75 cts. to . 30 00
  St. Dominic's Manual. 24mo. $1 to . 12 00
  St. Patrick's Manual. 18mo. $1 to . 40 00
  Pocket Manual. 48mo. 25 cts. to . 8 00
  Raccolta, The. 24mo. 63 cts. to . . 6 00
  Journée du Chretien. 50 cts. to . . 15 00
  Paroissen des Petits. 25 cts. to . . 10 00
Preston's Sermons, ... 2 50
  "   Lectures on Christian Unity, . 1 50
Pretty Plate. By Huntington. 50 cts. ; cl. gilt, 0 75
Priest's Sister. 16mo, 50 cts. ; cloth gilt, 0 75
Prophecies of St. Columbkille, . . 0 60
Public School Education. By Muller, . . 1 50

Sent by mail, postage paid, on receipt of the price.

Ravellings from Web of Life. By C. J. Cannon. Cloth	$1 50
Recluse of Rambouillet. 50 cts. ; cloth gilt,	0 75
Reeve's Bible History,	0 90
Religion in Society,	1 50
Resume of Meditations. By Bro. Philippe,	2 00
Revelations of St. Bridget,	0 60
Rise and Fall of Irish Nation. Barrington,	1 50
Rivals, The. By Griffin,	1 50
Robert May. 50 cents ; cloth gilt,	0 75
Rome and the Abbey. Cloth, $1 25 ; cl. gilt,	1 75
Rome and its Ruler. By Maguire,	2 00
Roothan's Meditations,	0 50
Rory O'More. By Lover, $1 50 ; do., paper,	0 75
Rosary Sheets. Per 100, net,	2 50
Rosemary. By Huntington, $2 ; cloth gilt,	2 50
Rule of Life,	0 25
Redmond Count O'Hanlon. By Carleton.	0 60
Rose Le Blanc. By Lady Fullerton. 16mo, cloth, $1 ; cloth gilt,	1 50
Sadlier, Mrs. J., Original Works of :	
Alice Riordan,	0 60
Blakes and Flanagans,	1 25
Red Hand of Ulster,	0 60
Willy Burke,	0 60
New Lights ; or, Life in Galway,	1 00
The Confederate Chieftains,	2 00
Elinor Preston,	0 75
Bessy Conway,	0 75
Confessions of an Apostate,	0 75
Con O'Regan,	1 00
Father Sheehy, and Other Tales,	0 50
The Old House by the Boyne,	1 25
Aunt Honor's Keepsake,	1 00
Daughter of Tyrconnell,	0 50
MacCarthy More,	1 00
The Heiress of Kilorgan,	1 25
Old and New,	1 25
The Hermit of the Rock,	1 25
Catechism of Sacred History,	0 25
Maureen Dhu,	1 25
The Secret : a Drama,	0 25
The Talisman : a Drama,	0 25
The Babbler : a Drama,	0 25
Julia ; or, The Gold Thimble : a Drama,	0 25
The Elder Brother,	0 25
The Invisible Hand,	0 25
Sadlier's, Mrs. J., Translations from the French :	
Orphan of Moscow,	0 75
Castle of Rousillon,	0 75
Consolation for the Sick and Afflicted,	0 50
Benjamin,	0 50
The Pope's Niece, and Other Tales,	0 50
Idleness ; or, The Double Lesson,	0 50
The Knout : a Tale of Poland,	1 00
The Blighted Flower,	0 50
Ten Stories,	0 50
Valeria ; or, The First Christians,	0 50
The Exile of Tadmor,	0 50
Tales and Stories,	0 50

Sent by mail, postage paid, on receipt of the price.

The Vendetta, and Other Tales, . . $0 50
Wilhelm and Agnes of Braunsberg, . . 0 50
The Lost Son, ... 0 75
Catholic Anecdotes. Part I., . . . 0 75
The same. Part II., . . . 1 00
The same. Part III., . . . 1 00
The same. 3 vols. in 1, . . . 2 50
The Mysterious Hermit, . . . 0 50
The Poachers, ... 0 50
The Bohemians, ... 0 60
The Spanish Cavaliers, . . . 0 75
The Devil, Does He Exist? . . . 1 00
The Priest's Sister, and the Inheritance, . 0 50
Legends of St. Joseph, . . . 1 00
Faculties of the Soul. A Dialogue for
  Young Ladies. In one Act and three
  Scenes, ... 0 25
The Year of Mary; or, The True Servant
  of the Blessed Virgin, . . . 1 50
Selim; or, The Pacha of Salonica, . . 0 50
The Great Day, ... 0 50
Life of Christ. 8vo, cloth, . . . 4 00
Life of Virgin. 8vo, cloth, . . . 4 00
Life of Christ, for youth, . . . 0 75
Wonders of Lourdes, . . . 0 60
Sanctuary, The. Sunday-School Vocal Class-
  Book. Net per dozen, . . . 2 75
School of Jesus Crucified. Cloth, . . 0 75
  cloth, red edges, . . . 1 00
Scottish Chiefs. By Miss Porter, . . 1 25
Sebastian, the Roman Martyr, . . 0 40
Secret, The: a Drama for Girls, . . 0 25
Selim; or, The Pasha of Salonica, . . 0 50
  cloth gilt, ... 0 75
Sermons on Moral Subjects. By Wiseman, . 2 00
  " Our Lord and his B. M. " . 2 00
  " Preston, . . . 2 50
  " By Gahan,
Sick Calls, 75 cts.; cloth gilt, . . 1 00
Sin and its Consequences. By Manning, . 1 50
Snatches of Song. By Una, . . . 1 50
Song Books:
  Harp of Erin Songster. Paper, 20 cts.; cl., 0 40
  Forget me Not. Paper, 20 cts.; cloth, . 0 40
  Emerald; or, Wearing of the Green Song-
    ster. Paper, 20 cts.; cloth, . . 0 40
  Shamrock Songster. Paper, 25 cts.; cloth, 0 50
Songs for Catholic Schools, . . 0 50
Songs of Ireland and Other Lands, . . 1 00
Spanish Cavaliers. 75 cts.; cloth gilt, . 1 00
Spirit of the Nation, . . . 0 50
Stations of the Cross. Paper, 10 cts.; cloth, 0 15
Stepping Stones to Grammar, . . 0 20
Stepping Stones to Geography. . . 0 20
Stories of the Beatitudes. 50 cts.; cloth gilt, 0 75
St. Augustine's Confessions, . . 0 75
  cloth, red edges, . . . 1 00
Sullivan's Spelling-Book Superseded, . 0 31
Sure Way to find out True Religion, . 0 25
Straw Cutter's Daughter, and The Portrait in
  My Uncle's Dining-Room. By Lady Ful-
  lerton, $1; cloth gilt, . . . 1 50

Sent by mail, postage paid, on receipt of the price.

Tales and Legends from History. $1 ; cl. gt., $1 25
Tales and Stories. 50 cts. ; cloth gilt,   0 75
Tales and Stories Irish Peasantry. Carleton,   1 25
   cloth gilt,   1 75
Tales of the Jury-Room. Griffin,   1 50
Tales Five Senses and Night at Sea. Griffin,   1 50
Tales from the Diary of a Missionary Priest,   0 75
   cloth gilt,   1 00
Tales of the Five Senses, 75 cts.; cloth gilt,   1 0C
Talisman : a Drama for Girls,   0 25
Ten Stories. 50 cts.; cloth gilt,   0 75
Ten Working Designs for Catholic Churches,
   containing all Details and Specifications,
   etc. Folio, $15 ; half mor.,   20 0C
The Family. Translated from the French by
   Mrs. James Sadlier, paper,   0 25
The Two Brothers. 50 cts. ; cloth gilt,   0 75
Think Well On't. By Dr. Challoner,   0 31
Tithe Proctor. By Carleton,   1 50
Travels in the East and Holy Land. By Ve-
   tromille. 8vo, cloth, · 3 ; cloth gilt,   4 00
Treasure Trove. By Lever. $1 50 ; paper,   0 75
True Spiritual Conferences. St. Francis De
   Sales,   1 50
Truth and Error. By Dr. Brann,   1 00
Tuber Derg. By Carleton, 75 cts. ; cloth gilt,   1 00
Too Strange not to be True. By Lady Ful-
   lerton. 8vo, cloth, $1 50 ; cloth gilt,   2 00
True to the End, and Cardan the Galley-Slave
   18mo, cloth, $0 50 ; gilt.   0 75
Two Victories, The. A Catholic Tale. By
   Rev. T. J. Potter, 16mo, cloth, $1 ; gilt,   1 50

Victims of the Mamertine Prison. By Author
   of Martyrs of the Coliseum. 12mo, cloth,
   $2; cloth gilt,   2 50
Valentine McClutchy, the Irish Agent,   1 50
Valeria. 16mo, cloth, 50 cts. ; cloth gilt,   0 75
Vatican Council and its Definition. By
   · Manning,   1 25
Vendetta. 16mo, cloth, 50 cts. ; cloth gilt,   0 75
Vessels of the Sanctuary. 16mo, cloth,   0 50
   cloth gilt,   0 75
Vetromille's Travels in East and Holy Land.
   8vo, $3 ; cloth gilt,   4 00
Virtues and Defects of a Young Girl,   0 75
   cloth gilt,   1 00
Walsh's History of the Irish Church. 8vo,
   half mor., marble, $4 50 ; half mor., gilt,   3 50 / 5 00
Ward's Cantos. England's Reformation,   1 00
Ward's Errata of the Protestant Bible,   1 00
Well ! Well ! By Wallace. $1 25 ; cloth gilt,   1 50
Which is Which : a Drama for Girls,   0 25
Wilhelm and Agnes of Braunsberg,   0 50
   cloth gilt,   0 75
Willie Reilly and his Dear Colleen Bawn,   1 50
Winefred Jones. 16mo, cloth,   0 50
   cloth gilt,   0 75
Winefried, Countess of Nithsdale,   1 00
   cloth gilt,   1 25
Wiseman, Cardinal, Sermons. 2 vols.,   4 00
Witch of Melton Hill. $1 ; cloth gilt,   1 25

Young's Complete Sodality Manual,   1 00
Young Savoyard. 60 cents ; cloth gilt,   0 90

Lightning Source UK Ltd.
Milton Keynes UK
UKHW020706251021
392801UK00004B/169